LILIAN PIZZICHINI

KT-444-623

DEAD MEN'S WAGES

PICADOR

First published 2002 by Picador

This edition published 2003 by Picador
an imprint of Pan Macmillan Ltd
Pan Macmillan, 20 New Wharf Road, London N1 9RR
Basingstoke and Oxford
Associated companies throughout the world
www.panmacmillan.com

ISBN 0 330 48446 X

3 5 7 9 8 6 4 2

A CIP catalogue record for this book is available from
the British Library.

Typeset by Intype London Ltd
Printed and bound in Great Britain by
Mackays of Chatham plc, Chatham, Kent

DEAD MEN'S WAGES

'A beguiling performance: nostalgic, dead-pan, humorous, authoritative . . . Pizzichini's story is as chilling as fog, as banal as a Biba feather boa, as casual as a razor slashed across a cheek . . . the protagonists are sharply and unsentimentally observed; the supporting cast, and the period London settings, are Ackroydian (which is as good as saying Dickensian) and the narrator herself is always unflinchingly engaged'
The Times

'Lilian Pizzichini hasn't just written a terrific real-life thriller, she's written a book about what happens to a family when overwhelming personal greed replaces love and compassion'
Mirror

'Breathless and compelling'
Evening Standard

'A riveting biography'
Books Magazine

'Pizzichini is excellent at conveying the changing ecology, as it were, of London crime'
New Statesman

Lilian Pizzichini was born in London in 1965.
This is her first book.

For Dolly

FAMILY TREE OF THE TAYLORS

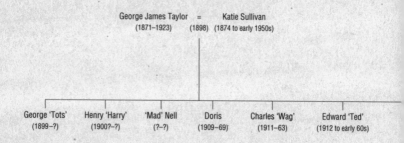

George James Taylor = Katie Sullivan
(1871–1923) (1898) (1874 to early 1950s)

George 'Tots'	Henry 'Harry'	'Mad' Nell	Doris	Charles 'Wag'	Edward 'Ted'
(1899–?)	(1900?–?)	(?–?)	(1909–69)	(1911–63)	(1912 to early 60s)

FAMILY TREE OF THE KINGHAMS

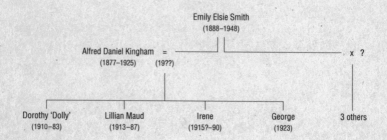

Emily Elsie Smith
(1888–1948)

Alfred Daniel Kingham = ⎯⎯⎯⎯⎯⎯⎯⎯⎯⎯⎯ x ?
(1877–1925) (19??)

Dorothy 'Dolly'	Lillian Maud	Irene	George	3 others
(1910–83)	(1913–87)	(1915?–90)	(1923)	

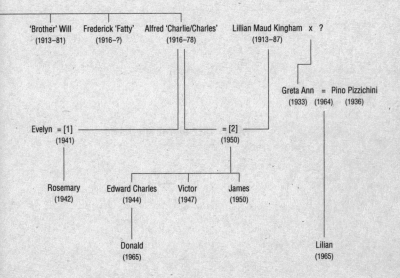

'Brother' Will   Frederick 'Fatty'   Alfred 'Charlie/Charles'   Lillian Maud Kingham   x   ?
(1913–81)   (1916–?)   (1916–78)   (1913–87)

Greta Ann   =   Pino Pizzichini
(1933)   (1964)   (1936)

Evelyn   = [1]   = [2]
(1941)   (1950)

Rosemary   Edward Charles   Victor   James
(1942)   (1944)   (1947)   (1950)

Donald
(1965)

Lilian
(1965)

Contents

Foreword

For years I have had the same dream every night. It is a grey winter's afternoon, and I am walking up Kensington Church Street. The shops are lit for Christmas. Art Deco lamps glitter in the antiques arcade, a boutique displays ostrich feathers and floppy hats. The windows of the French patisserie are lined with immaculate glazed tarts. I am overwhelmed by the show of prosperity as I eagerly approach my grandfather's house. But first, looming ahead of me, are the black and silver steamliner curves of Winchester Court, from the great portals of which, as a child, I would imagine elegant ladies emerging, adjusting their gloves, on their way to take tea at Derry & Tom's. The old-money refinement of Kensington's residents lends a semblance of orderliness to my journey home.

I reach the red post-box that stands guard outside Number 1 Inverness Gardens. My grandfather's vintage Rolls-Royce is parked alongside it. I remember that he used to drive his sons around London on a tour of his old haunts. One day, he stopped outside Pentonville Prison. 'I did time in there,' he told them.

'I wouldn't boast about it, if I were you,' his wife advised.

To me she was Nana, and the source of all things warm and merry. I can't wait to see her and I run up the tiled steps of the majestic white house that was bought for a song in the Sixties. Carriage-lamps are lit either side of the door, and

I enter a dingy corridor. I experience the same feeling of excited anticipation I had as a child every time I visited this house. The fug of intrigue still lingers in the passage, so heavily that it instantly belies the grandeur of the exterior. My grandmother is sitting in her bedroom by the bay window. Music is coming from a record-player somewhere in the deep recesses of her house. Packing-cases are stacked around her. She opens a jewellery box, and shows me rings, bracelets, and the lost toys from my childhood.

There is a photograph of my grandparents' house in Kensington Public Library. It was taken in 1971, and shows the plum-coloured Rolls parked outside. I instantly recognized it as my grandfather's, and felt a pang of nostalgia for Christmases I had spent in Kensington. When I look back on those times, though, all I recall is a sense of bewilderment that has grown as I have uncovered layer upon layer of secrecy. Scratch the surface of any family and you will find stories of intrigue, abuse and illegitimacy. It is just that, because of the nature of my grandfather's business, our secrets are more sinister.

My grandfather was a long-firm conman and fraudster. According to gangland historian James Morton, 'Charles Taylor was a face.' He was Charlie to his friends and family, and Number 1 Inverness Gardens was the showpiece of his criminal activities. But it was also the house his children considered their home. It was a grand town house to which few working-class men could aspire. I do not think anyone in my family ever got over the sense of unreality that they were actually living in such salubrious surroundings. I go back there sometimes, to sit on the wall overlooking the private gardens. They are filled with jasmine that curls around stone benches and iron rails. The scent is barely discernible though I can conjure it up at will.

The only indisputable facts that I have managed to

uncover concerning the house I shall always consider my true home come from volume XXXVII of *Survey of London: Northern Kensington.*

In it I read that the crescent of eight four-storey houses that make up Inverness Gardens was built in 1860 by William Lloyd Edwards, a builder from Paddington. Number 1 is a classic example of his work. He gave its decorative features, the pediments and niches framing the windows, and the Ionic columns that grace its doorway a Mannerist treatment. His stucco façade bestows an air of quiet dignity. It was, and remains, an eminently respectable address. The Vicar of Kensington, who commissioned Lloyd Edwards, saw to that, stipulating in his tenants' lease that no trade or business was to be conducted on these premises that would prove 'hazardous, noisy, noisome or offensive'.

I know, from the electoral register, that in 1963 my grandparents, Charles and Lillian Taylor, were living there. And I know that Charlie, who, even supposing he had read the lease, would have ignored its terms, had moved in with the aim of turning it into a private gaming club. I have heard how the dividing wall of the ground floor was knocked through, and two marble pillars that had been purloined from war-damaged hotels on Park Lane were installed in its place. Enormous chandeliers were hoisted to the ceiling, and a green baize baccarat table was installed. The idea was that the feckless rich would be brought here, to be cheated of their inheritances in the privacy of my grandfather's home.

But Charlie's life is so fogged with mystery it is hard to ascertain how a man with no bank account and a false identity managed to acquire the lease. Some say that he won it on the toss of a dice. My mother recalls Lily cooking breakfast for a young Scotsman of good family who had lost the deeds to his family's distillery the night before. Afterwards, Charlie, who felt sorry for the man whose fortune he had just decimated, gave him a lift to Paddington Station. She remembers the distinctive burr of the red-headed man's accent, and still has a gilt-framed landscape of haywains amongst rolling hills that once belonged to his family. It is now so surely a part of our past that we regard it as our rightful heirloom.

Perhaps it was just this picture that he lost to my grand-father in a game of cards, because the same electoral register states that, in 1962, a certain Wing-Commander Eaves was in residence at Number 1. And 'Wing-Co' Eaves, as Charlie came to know him, is a name I remember from my child-hood. He was a charming, cultivated man with moustaches of Daliesque proportions. Whether he really was a wing-commander was considered entirely beside the point. He bought and sold property on the black market, specializing in ridding landed families of their manorial homes. When his gambling debts became too much for him, he would offer as collateral the leaseholds of houses he had collected from his clients. Perhaps it was in a toss of the dice with Eaves that Charlie won the house. At any rate, Wing-Co didn't hang around for much longer; he vanished from London's demi-monde midway through the Sixties when he was charged with molesting a schoolboy with the tip of his umbrella.

Most of the characters from my family's past came to inauspicious ends. But the intrigue in which they manoeuvred has left a potent residue.

It all started so innocently. The vicar was Hugh Lorimer Octavius Rees, the church was St Mary Abbots, and the occasion was my baptism. It was 1965, London was swinging, but no one had thought to tell Lily. My parents bowed to her insistence that her one-month-old grandchild and namesake be received into the Church of England. For Lily, it was an act of absolution, and a break with the familial tradition of illegitimacy.

A question mark hangs over each child born to my great-grandparents. No one was sure of their father. Lily herself was in the unusual position of not possessing a birth certificate. So from the very start of her life, the questions are mounting. Perhaps her mother was unmarried when she was born and did not care to advertise it. The clues are tantalizing – the stuff of a Victorian melodrama in which my grandmother played the starring role. The lack of a father's name on her own daughter's birth certificate was another shameful act.

My mother holds on to her secret shame, guarding it as though it were treasure. The sadness and guilt are not hers alone. I have weathered them without knowing their cause, extent or nature. But the only way she and Lily could cope with her illegitimacy was by pretending it had never happened. The urge to be respectable overrode any other concern. So it was a triumph that my legitimacy should be confirmed within a venerable parish church.

There has been a place of worship on the site of St Mary Abbots for over a thousand years. And the building itself is constructed from the clay on which London rests. This gritty mud is burned and compressed into a yellow-brown brick called London Stock. The city's more prestigious buildings are given a coating of a finer substance to cover up their workaday mud.

On that particular day in June the procession, which included my parents, my grandmother, my godparents, and me swaddled in white, made its way down Kensington Church Street, past Kensington Palace, and into the graceful cloisters of the church. It was a perfect summer's day in a proud and lofty borough, and the blue Bath cladding of the walls was bathed in luxurious warmth.

My family assembled in the south baptistry. None of us believed in God – and we each had our reasons. You can take or leave the content when form is paramount. I was placed in the marble font decorated with the rivers of Paradise, and the ceremony began. Under the stained-glass depiction of Old Testament prophets, the devil and rebellion against God were rejected. Deceit and the corruption of evil were renounced and sins were repented. When all was said and done, my little band of sinners went home for tea and crumpets in the serene, civilized and seemly front room of their fabulous Kensington house.

My grandfather did not attend my christening. He was too busy attending to business. He had opened a hotel in far-away Streatham, south of the River Thames. Here he entertained his associates. Billy Hill, the self-proclaimed boss of Britain's underworld, was one of them.

Billy was born in Seven Dials, a thieves' rookery near Leicester Square, in 1911. He was one of twenty-one children and his family constituted a mini-crime wave in itself. His father picked fights with the police and his mother was a receiver. His brother was a pickpocket and his sister was an extremely effective shoplifter called 'Queen of the Forty Elephants'. Billy made his first killing at the age of fourteen. His victim had taken 'a liberty with [him]', so Billy drove a pair of scissors into his back. It came 'quite natural', he said.

Looking into Billy's eyes was like looking into black glass, people said. They were cold and remorseless. Not even my grandfather matched him in callous villainy. Everyone was frightened of Hill – except the Krays, of course.

Amongst the other guests to be found in the saloon bar of my grandfather's plush hotel were east London's favourite twins. Ronnie carried a .32 Beretta. He spent many a long night filing the tips of his bullets so that they would make a bigger hole in his enemies. He also carried with him a list of people who 'had to go'. He sipped his free drinks in the company of Charlie's friends from the Flying Squad.

When I try to summon memories of my grandfather, they trickle through in discrete episodes. He smoked forty Embassy a day, I remember him boasting, and I can still see him sitting in his shabby, upholstered armchair, an ashtray balanced on his knee. His swollen, stubby fingers curled around a cigarette, the scars on his knuckles facing out. He had a booming voice which he raised even louder to shout down resistance to his views. Once, the newscaster announced that the tradition of presenting débutantes to the Queen was to be abolished. Charlie took it as a personal affront; he liked these remnants of an old tradition, and had once had an affair with a deb.

His minder was always lurking around Number 1. He was a looming presence called Teddy Machin, 'a fucking mad fighting dog' as his enemies called him. Teddy was famous for his flair with a razor blade. True to type, he was large, silent and forbidding, and had deep hollows for eyes. He would be there when the men turned up after lunch. They would huddle in corners with Charlie, hatching the latest plot.

Charlie would raise his eyes despairingly as, upstairs in his bedroom, my uncle Victor turned up the volume on the record-player. Although Charlie didn't realize it, the drug-induced paranoia of the Doors and the Stones was the perfect soundtrack for his malevolent conspiracies. At this point, just as things were getting exciting, my grandmother would hurry my mother and me out of the house. It felt as though she was turning us on to the street. We were lost without the solid walls of that house.

But whatever was going on in the world outside, Charlie wanted a part of it; and whoever was pre-eminent, he wanted a piece of them as well. I cannot remember not knowing that my grandfather was a criminal, not that anyone told me. Families involved in crime are not so crass as to spell out the obvious. It comes out in dark hints and asides. I knew we were different and was proud to be a member of this glamorous tribe.

Everyone was expected to think that little bit faster than anyone else; to talk sharp, fill the spaces, dispense with useless protocol; to get to the point, go in for the kill. It is a fierce and exciting pulse that dictates your every thought and action. If you use your eyes and brain that little bit better than anyone else around you, you'll be on top. Be *anti-social*. Exploit the situation; let the people talk and store the information they give you for future use. Lean on people, raise the ante. Psychological weaknesses are the point of departure for a con man. Charlie could winkle out gaps of security, and opportunities to make a quick buck, because he was concerned with survival. The way he saw things, it was him against the rest.

My family went along with him because that was all they knew – Charlie had seen to that. It was easy for him to prevent someone as fragile as my grandmother breaking rank. To do so would have been to break herself in two. And to betray Charlie was to betray her, too. The Italian code of *omertá* is hard to crack because its secrets are compromising and insidious. Keeping mum and circumspection become as second nature in a family where fear is the first tie that binds. The second tie to have a stranglehold is the admission of fear; because to admit it is anything other than love is to acknowledge that all is not well within the family. And in the old days, once the family goes, there's nowhere to go but the workhouse, the madhouse, or prison.

My mother tried to be the moral centre of the family. She made her distaste for her stepfather obvious. She condemned his sons' mindless antics. Her manners were impeccable, her morals beyond reproach, but there was an unspeakable tension within her. I could only guess at it, since she was protected by a coat of stone cladding. It looked good, but there were cracks, and I could glimpse a mess of brickwork underneath. I sensed that the merest blow from a hammer would cause the entire edifice to crumble.

∎

When my grandfather died I had not seen him for three years. I did not know that he had been remanded on bail, and that his friends and acquaintances from the past twenty years had been hunted down and interrogated. My mother had sensed danger long before the raid and had removed us from the family circle. I felt entirely unmoved when she told me Charlie had died. She was overwhelmed with relief.

The official cause of death was a heart attack. But many years later, Uncle Victor sent me an article he had written for his local newspaper on the anniversary of Charlie's death. He wrote that he could not bear to see his father on the edge of despair, or witness his nights that were wracked with regrets. So he had given him some barbiturates.

'Take these, they'll make you feel better,' he'd said.

He lives with the suspicion that Charlie took them all at once.

But an old friend from Charlie's days as a criminal kingpin maintains, 'The word is he was murdered.'

When I asked him what he remembered about my grandfather, he said: 'Charles Taylor was a man of mystery. I doubt if even his wife knew his real name.' He is right, no one really knew Charlie, and that wasn't his real name. Secrecy was so integral to his way of life that he revealed nothing of himself to anyone. It is hard to recall anything about him except a continually blustering presence. He never seemed to show any genuine emotion or reveal any vulnerability. He protected himself, and instilled the code of secrecy into the rest of his family.

As a result, his story – especially the mired circumstances of his death – continues to haunt me. The fact that his love of intrigue has inspired conflicting, and apocryphal, anecdotes serves only to inflame my curiosity. The fact that he mixed with the leading lights of London's demi-monde adds a heady glamour to the enigma. Just like the policeman who eventually hunted him down and interrogated his past, I have added ballast, facts and dates to the shadowy figure of my grandfather. More than that, I have gleaned from the effect he had on those who survived him, and from piecing together the rubble of ruined lives he left in his wake.

■

By the time I had come on to the scene, the palatial front room, with its tall sash-windows looking on to an avenue of cherry trees, was where we gathered for Sunday lunch. Great-aunt Dolly would be confined to the kitchen, roasting a joint. She had come to live with her brother-in-law, as a kind of live-in servant, after a spell as a bag lady when she had slept on a bench in Holland Park. Dolly had become destitute, and lost her mind, after she had lost her house and life-savings to Charlie. She became my closest companion, and would take me for walks around Kensington's parks, where she felt most at home, trailing her shopping-trolley behind her. The rest of us, my parents, Uncles Edward, Vic and James, would join the head of our family around the table. There would be arguments – my mother valiantly opposed to every fiercely held principle Charlie espoused. The subject was always politics (his were far right), the Royal Family (he was a monarchist), the miners (he was vehemently anti-), and blacks. 'They've got it all sewn up in South Africa,' was his take. I laughed at them all, aided and abetted by my Uncle James, who refused to take anything seriously, even his ruinous drug intake.

When the shouting became too insistent I would beat a retreat into the parlour, where Dolly was eating her lunch surrounded by smelly old dogs. We would sit in front of the television and an imitation log fire, and Dolly would rain curses on Charlie. 'Effing potato-face,' she called him.

Since the front room was also where my grandfather wrung money from his marks, she only went in there to clean it. She did an excellent job. The leather sofas were always shiny, the coffee-tables free of clutter and dust. Guests invariably gasped with amazement at the richness of our ornaments, at the brazen chandeliers and massive windows. Charlie must have been very plausible in this impressive setting, although he didn't feel the need to exert his charm in front of us.

His mere presence was enough to instil resentment and fear. My own father, handsome, severe and exotically Italian, paled beside him. All the men of my family were dwarfed by Charlie's sense of his own power.

■

Whenever I crossed my grandfather, Dolly would tell me that I had better watch out; that his minder, Teddy Machin, had killed a man. My mother reinforced the sense of danger. She hated Charlie, and told me that when she was seventeen he had asked her to sell drugs on the street for him. 'There's nothing to worry about,' he had assured her. 'The police would never stop someone who looks as young and innocent as you.' He sent her to his friend Black Fred's house. She was so frightened that Black Fred did not even bother trying to seduce her. She told me that Charlie was a violent man, but that, unlike the Krays, he wasn't good to his mother, and he always hit women. This was just the bait I needed to provoke a confrontation. I wanted to explode the myths that were building up around me. I willed my grandfather time and again to explode, to show me what he was made of. But he just looked sad, and wearily ignored me. So all I could do was watch him.

There are three long-lost photographs of Charlie that I have seen just a few times. But such was his sense of theatre that I can visualize them quite clearly. The first was taken in the Thirties; it shows him, in stark black and white, as a burly young man wearing the black shirt of Oswald Mosley's British Union of Fascists. I can imagine Charlie being swept away by the rhetoric of radical action for working men. But perhaps I am romanticizing his need for action; perhaps he was just a thug in search of a fight.

Then, in softer, sepia tones, he is photographed as a guest at a wedding in the House of Lords. The occasion demanded top hat and tails, and I imagine he is standing proud. But this feeling of social triumph did not last long. When he was told that real gentlemen leave the last button of their waist-coat undone, he was devastated.

In the photo taken twenty years later, he is kitted out in panama hat and khaki shorts. He is in South Africa, having his photograph taken outside a segregated WC. Despite his rampant racism, I feel sorry for him. In my mind's eye, the sharpness of the colours has dimmed, and despite the effort he has put into his costume, I can still detect an unwholesome city pallor, and a heavy trunk weighing down his spindly legs.

Clothes were important to him, an essential factor in his *modus operandi*. He had to look the part in order to succeed at his game. So he went to Italian tailors in Soho for his suits, and to Jermyn Street for his hand-made shirts. He had his own cobbler, and all. In the Forties, when he was broke, he took his friend Black Fred into a gentleman's outfitters in St James's, claiming that Fred was a Nigerian prince (he was in fact a Ghanaian cabaret artist who sold marijuana on the side). They left the shop with armfuls of off-the-peg suits, acquired on the strength of Fred's regal bearing. These are the kinds of stories that have grown up around my grandfather; like the photos, they reveal only what he wanted people to see.

But I did see the strange men who came to see him, and whom my grandmother ushered into his presence. I saw them leave the house wordlessly, after pocketing brown envelopes. I noticed that adults would abruptly terminate their whispered conversations in my presence. I knew they were indulging in a covert pleasure in which I was not allowed to partake. I would press for answers. I would get dark looks, embarrassed silences and evasions for my troubles.

Charlie could be expansive. During lunch, he would reel off a list of high-ranking contacts: Major Stoop was the name that came up most often. He was a friend of Lord Lucan, so we all felt the privilege of being 'in the know' when we read that it was Stoopie's bloodstained Ford Corsair that was found in Newhaven after Lucan had vanished. My uncle Edward even remembered borrowing the car himself. Then there was Jock Wilson, head of the Flying Squad, who was, somewhat notoriously, photographed with my grandfather at a party; Lord Colwyn, whose wife had an affair with Charlie but who nevertheless bequeathed him thousands of pounds on his death; Omar Sharif, with whom he used to play backgammon; Maxwell Scott, John Aspinall's right-hand man; Prince Philip; Miss World; and the Krays. Charlie was dismayed when he was splashed all over the front page of a tabloid coming out of the 100 Club on Oxford Street. He had been photographed side by side with Reggie Kray. He even managed to have a hand in pop music, claiming he had kick-started Rod Stewart's career by giving him a gig at his hotel.

After lunch, my mother would take me to Kensington

Gardens. I do not think Charlie ever went there, so she must have found it the only place she knew not to be under his malign influence. We would take the great south walk leading to the palace, and sit for a while in the deckchairs by the Guards' bandstand to listen to military waltzes.

The park acted as an escape route from the unpredictable atmosphere at Inverness Gardens. But it was this volatility that made my grandparents' house so enticing. At times, the air would be heavy with a fraught tension – the frisson of not knowing who would come knocking at the door next was almost unbearable for the adults, irresistible for me. When the men came, they sat on the edge of my grandfather's four-poster bed as though he were an ailing king.

Once, though, it was me and my mother knocking. I remember my feeling of hurt and incomprehension when my grandmother shooed us away, saying that we couldn't come in, that we'd have to come back later. At times like this, when my grandparents' house was too 'hot', and the park too cold, my mother would take me to my favourite Italian restaurant, Dino's, on Kensington Church Street. Its basement seemed, to me, to exude the same mysterious air as Number 1. The plaster on the walls was painted a glistening muddy brown and moulded to resemble the interior of a grotto. Dimly lit statues of Neptune and mermaids languished on plinths. I would drain my bowl of minestrone, and the waiter would laugh. He knew my father was Italian, and he liked to tease me in a language I did not understand.

At other times, the occupants of Number 1 would be reeling with a visceral triumph. Music played from morning to night. My grandmother and I twisted and twirled to the Kinks. My uncle James bombed out to Cockney Rebel. At Christmas we sang along with John Lennon – war was over. We were addicted to the adrenalin of the latest sounds. We decoded the lyrics and swung with the rhythms that made sense of our disordered lives. The record player was stacked with 45s and my grandmother led the dancing. Elton John's guileless piano-bashing was best suited to her undiluted sense of joy. These moods, I suppose in retrospect, were dependent on the state of Charlie's various affairs, which were mercurial. And we gave full vent to them.

Charlie never forgot the deficits – both physical and emotional – of his childhood and was determined not to see them visited on his own brood. The excitement he generated was intense, and anything is possible when a collection of volatile, irresponsible people gather to indulge themselves without restraint.

When things were going well, and he came home with carrier-bags full of money, my grandmother would summon his gofer, Leonard Ash, to fetch the Rolls and drive us a few hundred yards to Biba on Kensington High Street. We would wander around the marble wastes of the shop-floor. 'To be Bibaesque was to be beautiful,' so she bought me a purple negligée trimmed with sequins, and a matching feather boa to swirl around my shoulders. I wore it at Christmas, when she asked my cousin and me to serenade our grandfather. The song was in the charts, and she'd bought the record. It went something along the lines of, 'I love you, Grand-dad'. He gave us ten pounds every time we sang it.

I revelled in the lavishness of it all. Great heart-shaped boxes of chocolates with painted lids were scattered around the house on occasional tables. Satin-fringed lampshades shed a funereal light, we lounged in cherry-red leather sofas, and the Christmas tree shed sharp needles at our feet. But every time I lifted the lid to take a chocolate, I would find that someone had taken a bite out of each one before putting them back in the box.

For New Year's Eve, Charlie took the whole family

(except Dolly, of course) to Newquay, in Cornwall. We stayed at the best hotel, and my parents drank champagne and danced in the ballroom every night. My uncle Victor and his girlfriend were there, though we did not see them once. They refused to leave their room, and subsisted for an entire week on room service and drugs. Charlie footed the bill. His magnanimity always came with grand gestures. You could not help but feel secure in the knowledge of his money-bags. This endless generosity quelled the paranoia that threatened to overwhelm. Naturally, Charlie's cheque bounced. But the hotel never caught up with him, because he always got away with it.

Not for long, though. Only a year later, and he had suffered a devastating dip in his fortunes. The atmosphere was increasingly tense, and he would hardly ever be at home. I would sit with my great-aunt in the parlour, eating tinned salmon sandwiches, our special treat. We tramped round Holland Park, walking the dogs. Dolly told me that Charlie was setting up a long-firm with Leonard Ash, who had wormed his way into Charlie's affections. The rest of the family was anxious. Charlie was starting to lose his edge, and was mixing with villains who were more ruthless and more professional than him. It was not good old Black Fred who was selling marijuana these days. It was syndicates of mob-heavy gangsters.

This was 1975, the point at which my mother stopped taking me to Kensington. She told me that the house had been sold, that Charlie was unwell. I never saw him again.

She had always been keen to stress to me that Charlie was not her real father. When I asked who, then, was her real father was, she muttered something about never having known him because he'd been killed during the war. When I asked Dolly, she improvised a variation on the theme; he was an air-warden during the Second World War, and died trying to rescue a family in the Blitz. Like the rest of my family, she was a compulsive story-teller. When I had finally read between the lines, I was compelled to know more.

Charlie's life ended in a flurry of accusations. I knew that much. That Leonard Ash had set him up. That Leonard's mistress, code-named 'Henry', was recording my grandfather's activities on behalf of MI5. I knew that Charlie had been charged with defrauding the Bank of England, and with counterfeiting gold sovereigns. Dolly read in the *News of the World* that if he had succeeded he would have disrupted the British economy. I rather liked what I heard. And felt a thrill of recognition when, eating dinner with my mother and Dolly on lap-trays in front of the television, my grandfather's face suddenly appeared on the screen.

∎

If, like Billy Hill's first murder victim, I have taken liberties in telling my grandfather's story, that is because I have been following in his footsteps. Down a dirty old river, that keeps me rolling, as it flows into the night. That was 'Waterloo Sunset' – a song by my grandmother's favourite band. There is a lot more that I have uncovered about her. No one's secrets are safe with me. Not even my own.

I had only seen Charlie through my mother's eyes, and so what I saw was the ogre. To see something different, I went back to the beginning: Willesden, north-west London, and the working-class Irish diaspora. Here, I found that he had been audacious as a child, and that he saw how easy it was to make a living depending solely on his wits. In essence, I found a more desperate and deprived version of myself. His delight in schemes and games was like mine; the pride in getting something for nothing was mine.

But as the years go by, you have less time to lose, less years to lose in prison. This is how Charlie felt. You begin to get a bit edgy. You become more unscrupulous, more fearful, more treacherous.

I followed Charlie's progress like a hawk. The journey I made describes an arc through west London before plummeting into the verdant south. Where I passed my childhood. Which itself passed me by in a blur of fog and dreams.

Sometimes I was not sure whether I was sleepwalking or wide awake. But I was in a state of high excitement, as I skipped down the road in my mother's anxious company. In the darkness, the Christmas lights beckoned. I let slip my mother's hand. As I surged forward a wall of mist fell between us. A large, horny hand took hold of mine; these were not the slim, maternal fingers that had been curled round mine. I looked up into the face of a pale man. He had black and white hair. His eyes were like flint. A suggestive smile played on his lips. My mother cried out my name, and I ran to her. But I could not resist turning back for one more look at the strange man. He was still smiling.

PART ONE · ALFRED

And the demon took in hand
Moleskin, leather, and clay,
Oaths embryonic and
A longing for Saturday,
A chest exceedingly stout,
A soul – (which is a question
Open to many a doubt),
And fashioned with pick and shovel,
And sharpened in mire and mud,
With life of the road and the hovel,
And death of the line or hod,
With fury and frenzy and fear,
That his strength might endure for a span,
From birth, through beer to bier,
The link twixt the ape and the man.

Patrick MacGill, 'The Navvy Chorus'

1 · Stonebridge Stew

Charlie's origins are as muddy as the earth he worked as a builder. He wanted it that way. The plain truth lacked the vigour of the folk songs he'd heard as a child. He was born Alfred Taylor, and he was the last in a line of labouring peasants. The names of the men who went before him – the Georges, Jameses and Henrys – do not matter: they can be condensed into a single type. Pick and shovel in hand, they were a fixture of the agricultural landscape. Their lives were short and brutishly confined to the physical necessities.

Slap, bang, in the middle of the First World War, he was born the eighteenth child of an aggrieved and careworn mother. His father, George James Taylor, was a labourer, the son of James, also a labourer, from the parish of Willesden, Middlesex. Like Charlie, Willesden was not created from scratch, but grew out of what came before. Unlike Charlie, its contours and boundaries remain clear to this day.

Around the time of the Domesday Book, the ancient parish of 'Wilsdon' comprised some 4,300 acres of pleasantly undulating land on the London clay belt. It lay five and a half miles north-west of London Bridge, and to the west of the old Roman road to Edgware. To the south it was bounded by 'Padynton' and to the west by Twyford Abbey. By the eighteenth century, Willesden had made a name for itself as a popular country resort for holiday-making Londoners. The traveller entered the parish at the Kilburn Toll

Gate, and paid his penny for the upkeep of roads. On crossing the River Brent, he exited some three miles farther on at Harp Bridge. A guide to the 'Beauties of England and Wales' published in 1816 gives this description: 'We are now in a neighbourhood more rural and tranquil than might be expected in the vicinity of London, the place would appear calculated for the retirement of the Citizen if contrast and repose be the objects which he seeks in a country residence.'

Apart from the long march of the Edgware Road, the earliest factor to influence Willesden was the Inclosures Act of 1815. This set in stone the boundaries of the meadows once marked by hedgerows and bridle-paths. The meadows are now housing estates fixed in their place by concrete thoroughfares and Victorian railway lines. George James Taylor had a hand in this.

Perhaps he was unlucky. Perhaps if George had been born in Willesden when its acres comprised lush pastureland and shady lanes, he would have passed on a gentler disposition to baby Alfred. But, since he was born in 1871, he was thirty years too late to amble through the low-lying fields of neighbouring Harlesden. And far too late to stalk the wild boar that crunched on acorns in the forests of Middlesex.

George was a new type of man, a modern town-dweller. The social observer C. F. G. Masterman describes the phenomenon in his 1901 study *The Heart of the Empire*. The 'characteristic physical type' that he outlines is 'stunted, narrow-chested, easily wearied; yet voluble, excitable, with little ballast, stamina, or endurance – seeking stimulus in drink, in betting, in any unaccustomed conflicts at home or abroad'.

He worked in a gang demarcating the fields of Willesden into navigation canals. These were London's 'navvies' – wild men marooned on swampy islands throughout the city. The sheer physicality of their labours kept them apart from the rest of society. Carts filled with beer and prostitutes arrived every pay day. They did not even have to leave the site to carouse. They were rowdy and lawless, and didn't give a damn who knew it. Their story comes laden with Victorian sentiment.

The exiled sons of Irish peasants, driven abroad by famine, they were the unconscious of England's body politic. The lyrics of an Edwardian parlour song describe the new Irish immigrants as caught between a tear and a smile. The Police Reports in the *Willesden Chronicle* found them caught dead drunk in the gutter.

Want drove them to undertake the back-breaking work of excavating London's stubborn earth. The lines they dug radiated outwards from the new station of Willesden Junction to the far east and west of the country, and north and south of the Thames. Willesden was losing its status as a rural country residence for city merchants. The first immigrants came from Paddington, then the provinces of western England. In 1885 there were 38,000 inhabitants. A thoroughfare here and an estate development there led to a sea of houses spreading in all directions. The merchants moved further out and speculative investors, builders and mortgage brokers took their place. By 1895 the Metropolitan Line Railway had arrived from Baker Street and the population had increased to 79,000. The streets were heaving with city clerks rushing to catch their connections, their throats clogged with steam and smut.

George James was not one of them. He was a powerful man with hands like shovels, said his sons. On 15 January 1898, after fifteen years of paving, blasting, cutting, tunnelling, drinking, fucking and fighting, George James married. He was a feckless twenty-seven. His bride was Miss Katie O'Sullivan, twenty-four, and fresh off the boat from Cork. On disembarking she dropped the 'O' from her surname. But George liked the irony of marrying a real Irish girl – the thoroughly anglicized Londoner had gone back to his bucolic roots. Katie was having none of it. She had watched her mother break her back tilling and ploughing the estates of an English Marchioness. She wanted a better life amongst the rootless ranks of Willesden.

Charlie's mother was a walking master-class in evasiveness. Each of her children and grandchildren has a different version to give of the tiny brown woman with her hair screwed tight in a bun. In her day, her inscrutability was called 'black Irish'. The shame was unspeakable if the Moorish influence of Spaniards showed in brown skin and hair. Charlie resented her for the lack of light she brought into her house, and loaded her image with all the racial slurs he could muster. His Katie was mired in bog-dirt and booze. He never called her mother, preferring 'rank-Irish'.

Ireland was the thorn in the British side. The imputation of Irishness was in itself an insult. Like the rest of his generation, Charlie scoffed at the jokes about Paddy who was sent by his foreman to buy elbow grease, or Mick who was told to buy a glass hammer and nails for the glass bricks of the glass house his mates told him they would be building. This did not stop Charlie longing to belong to the mythical race of rebels and wordsmiths. Katie didn't let him. She renounced her past and came up with an ingenious excuse for her looks. She may have been a Paddy but she looked like a squaw. The myth took flight and landed in the wild west of America, which was preferable to African blackness. Since she was born on 26 June 1876 she could safely say that she was born 'during Custer's Last Stand'.

George and Katie's wedding was in Harlesden Baptist Church because both sides had put popery behind them. The first live birth was in 1899, and the boy was named George, for his father. Katie would have called all her boys George because it was the Sullivan tradition to give every son his father's Christian name. That way, at least one of them would survive childhood to carry it on.

However, it was the Taylor tradition to name their sons after the kings of England. They need not have bothered. George and Katie's brood had no time for tradition. They changed names at the drop of a hat, and with every brush with the Law. Each baptism was a fresh act of vandalism. Within the strictures of George and Katie's family, the Taylor boys constructed their own version of society. Their new names gave them history and an identity. It was a way of reinforcing their otherness.

On the building sites where they laboured, the reasoning behind a new name was not so psychologically fraught. With the preponderance of Taylors and Smiths it was hard to differentiate between all these voluble and excitable men. A typical timekeeper on a building site had hundreds of kings of England to contend with; much easier to allocate a name more suited to their particular characteristics.

This is why my grandfather had so many names. It is really rather endearing how hard he tried, and how hard he laughed at himself and everyone else in their pantomime costumes. First there was Alfred the Reform-school Boy and Navvy. Then a brief foray as Henry the Master Builder, before finding his true role in life as Charlie the Spiv and Man about Town. His final resurgence as Charles the Hotelier and Fraudster is the one I knew. Each name carried its weight of associations. Each had a different outfit, and was a creature of his times. He learnt this quick-change act from his mother and elder brothers.

George, the eldest, was known as 'Tots'. He abandoned his humble lot as a stable lad to take up his true calling as a 'totter'. This was the name given to those who made their living by scavenging for scraps of cast iron. At night, George continued his totting in pubs where he cadged food, fags and drink.

Henry was second to Tots, and was called 'Piccolo Pete' because he had a wife and two girlfriends. Like Henry VIII, he had a way with women. Unlike the king he lost his head in a grotesque and bloody accident on the North Circular Road.

Edward, who was just a regular Borstal-boy, housepainter and thief, warranted Ted. The misshapen anomaly in the shape of Frederick was summarily dismissed as 'Fatty'. He was not a king of England, since there was a question mark over his paternity. Fatty had been conceived while George James was choking on mustard gas down a trench in France. But he was the honest cuckoo in the nest. His preaching earnestness so rankled with his family they called him 'Holy Joe'. It did not go down too well when he came back from Dunkirk in 1941 with nothing to show but a broken-down watch. 'It didn't even have hands on it,' Charlie sniffed.

Two girls, 'Mad' Nell, who could pack a punch as devastating as her brothers', and sensible, motherly Doris, preceded William. He was known simply as 'Brother' Will. I thought this was because he had been reduced to his fraternal connection to my grandfather. It would be entirely in keeping with the hold that Charlie had over his family. But it seems Brother Will had a life apart from his younger brother. In the Thirties, on account of the Depression, he had taken the radical step of joining the Communist Party. He was known as Brother Will henceforth.

Charles was my grandfather's immediate senior but was known from early childhood as 'Wag', an antique term for 'ruffian' or 'truant'. Like his brothers before him, and the one after him, he was sent to reform school in Hertfordshire. He was eight years old when he ran away in the middle of the night, dressed only in his nightshirt. He walked across two counties to get home to Katie, and she sent him straight back the next morning. Wag never held on to his real name. My grandfather saw to that.

By the time he was born Katie could only guess that he was her eighteenth baby. She had lost count of the number of births, live and dead. She had also lost interest in child-rearing. Luckily, Charlie was born cunning. It was this that helped him survive his infancy.

George and Katie's young family was known collectively as the 'funny Taylors' – funny as in peculiar – long before Charlie was born. They lived in a house built on what had once been a field lying fallow by Hill Farm. The old stone bridge that crossed a feeder of the Grand Union Canal had been demolished to make way for yet more urban labourers. They were needed to make more tracks and tunnels for the Metropolitan Railway and the increasing volume of commuters cast down into its underground system. As each child was born to George and Katie so was the great wen of London stifling the blood and bone of the rural outlands, complained the great and the good. As for the Taylors, they were contained in a flimsy brick dwelling with five rooms and a yard.

This was 130 Carlyle Avenue, Stonebridge. My grandfather, Alfred Taylor, was born on 9 May 1916 in a dingy upstairs bedroom. The conditions of penury and grime exist well into the twenty-first century in the concrete blocks of Stonebridge Park Estate. One night on the news sixty-year-old Charlie saw a report from the towering high-rise that had replaced the old two-up two-down. It was one of the most notorious housing developments in England, said the reporter, and a hotbed of drug-dealers and joy-riders. Charlie laughed in affectionate remembrance.

For little Alfred, though, Number 130 was a cauldron of despair and frustration. His parents kept a disorderly house.

The children's comings and goings went unremarked. They were too many to be accounted for. The rowdy lawlessness of the building site was brought into the domestic sphere. One thing is certain about Katie: motherhood did not suit her temper. She was fierce, and her bids to instil discipline were erratic. Even her husband was frightened of her.

For a supposedly devout Catholic, who at the end of her life was surrounded by pictures of the Virgin, she left no mark of devotion in her children. And when she withheld maternal affection from my grandfather she did so not at her own peril, but at my grandmother's, my mother's, and every other man, woman or child with whom he came into contact.

As soon as it was decently possible, Charlie was left in the care of eight-year-old Doris. Katie had hoped that he would go the way of babies who had come in the six years between him and Wag. But he didn't, and little Doris wheeled her baby brother along the narrow street. Their neighbours were the immigrant papists for whom no room could be found in Willesden. Some of them had the great luck to be working in one of the finest factories in Europe, Messrs H.J. Heinz & Company. The production lines started rolling around the same time Charlie was born. Alongside the factory, on the banks of the canal, was the Old Oak Wharf. Every day boats docked to unload cargoes of coal from Warwickshire collieries. The coal was then transported by cart to the furnaces of Park Royal's power station where George James was employed as a stoker.

This new and frenetic township was called Stonebridge. It had everything a working-class family could want: its own railway station, a tram depot, a Board of Education infants' school, a Baptist church, a Catholic church, and two public houses. There was even a workhouse-cum-infirmary at nearby Twyford Park where the poor of the parish were sent to die.

To see Stonebridge in 1746, when it was three farmhouses clustered around a bridge, is to see London in a pastoral mist. Even a hundred years later, it was still a pretty spot. A low-lying meadow fringed with open fields and crossed by a meandering feeder of the canal. It was not long before the idyll's links to Harlesden by Harrow Road and to Neasden by Dog Lane came to town planners' attentions. The London and Birmingham Railway in 1868 separated Stonebridge from the rest of Willesden. A police station and eight houses followed in hot pursuit. By the late 1860s there was a shop-keeper and beer retailer and in 1875 Stonebridge Park Station followed. The proximity of Edgware Road was irresistible to Willesden's property developers, and the following year some eighty 'smart new villas for city men', all detached, were erected.

By 1911, the year of Wag's birth, these houses were divided into smaller units to accommodate the increasing population. Stonebridge was rapidly being transformed into a factory town. Four years later the streets which once housed middle-class pretensions were housing working-class drudges.

Down the road from Carlyle Avenue was the Orange Tree public house – home from home for the Taylor family. Second-generation Irish immigrants, even if they had an English father, did not bother with the more salubrious Stonebridge Hotel up the road, or its licence to serve spirits. That was reserved for commercial travellers. Charlie soon came to know the popular 'wine and beer' establishment that doubled as a 'small and spit'.

By placing a raised platform in the saloon bar the Orange Tree was transformed into a miniature music-hall with spit-toons on the sawdust-covered floor. The baccy-chewing drinkers were treated to the exotic spectacle of sand-dancers. Their burlesque of the Sheik of Araby and his harem shuffling across the desert went down a storm. Izzy Boon, the Jewish Comedian, and Kevin O'Connor, the Wandering Irish Singer, took their turns in regaling and wooing the crowd now deep in their cups. The Orange Tree was all things to all Irishmen. It was handy for Katie and George when they needed a drink to accompany the card games they hosted in their grimy kitchen. Young Alfred would be sent to the Jug Room to fetch a pewter jug of ale from Stonebridge Peg, the landlady.

My grandfather's birthplace was the nexus of 'Poets' Corner'. Every district has such a corner. This one was so called because the developer, Mr Chas. Penny, a prominent man in local Wesleyan circles, had named these streets after his favourite literary giants. There were Shakespeare, Milton and Shelley, each with an avenue of his own. But neither they nor Thomas Carlyle, not even his Age of Machinery, meant much to the little boy. On the first of many attempts to run away from home, he was apprehended by a policeman who asked him where he lived.

'Carlyle,' said the four-year-old.

'What, you've come all the way from up north?' asked the incredulous rozzer.

'Nah, Carlyle, Wembley, yer silly bastard.'

Gus Elen, Cockney king of the music-halls, sang a song about just such a street as Carlyle Avenue. 'By climbing up the chimbley,' he maintained, 'You can see across to Wembley / If it wasn't for the 'ouses in between.' Stonebridge, Willesden and Wembley, and everything they contained within them, were more than enough for Charlie to be getting along with. Stonebridge was packed to the gills with two-ups, two-downs and great, sprawling families like the Taylors. Unlike the Taylors, though, most of these families found gainful employment in local light industry.

The showcase was 'The British Home of Heinz Famous 57 Varieties'. The spanking new factory was at the hub of an exciting innovation in technology. Its russet-red exterior with triumphantly flowering window-boxes signalled the industry that was taking place within. Heinz's factory was a paragon of 'spotless cleanliness, a polished hygienic world of white uniformed workers; a world of machinery'. All these machines needed humans to tend to them. So Mr Chas. Penny was making a fortune from the jerry-built housing on his favourite philosopher's street.

From his doorstep, Charlie watched men hustling a living and women rushing to the laundries of Willesden where they scrubbed, rinsed and mangled clothes dry. His father had just come back from the muddy death-traps of France. He was still useful enough to be enlisted, though, as a Private in the Civil Defence Regiment. He was not at home that much.

Charlie's older brothers served as his early role models. Their father had long given up on them. They seemed to have learnt all his bad habits without picking up on his industriousness. Drinking and gambling filled their days, street battles crowned their achievements in the evening. Tots achieved early fame as the 'King of Stonebridge's Gas Meters'. His astonishing ability to prise open his neighbours' meters and extract handfuls of coins earned him his title. By the age of seven, Charlie had seen enough of the world to be seen, in his turn, as 'Monkey', because he was always up to tricks.

The Fitzpatricks, who lived at Number 180, were notorious wine-drinkers and willing punters for the Taylors' Friday-night card games. Charlie recalled fights breaking out in the kitchen. But the Fitzpatricks' accusations of cheating did not stop them returning for their weekly bouts. The Taylors' grief was great when they woke one morning to find that their favourite source of income had done a moonlight flit. When the bailiffs came to clear out the Fitzpatricks' abandoned house, they found empty wine bottles behind the sink, in the cupboards, and in the yard. They had to bring them out in tin baths.

Charlie saw them come and go, as well as hundreds of anonymous others. When they weren't chasing the work they were fleeing the landlord. He watched the women – their men having gone to the Front – stagger home from the pub each night. Drink was Lloyd George's biggest enemy after the Germans, but to these women it was their only friend.

Outside the bus depot, Charlie and the other children would chase the tradesmen's vans as they careered along the highway. So action-packed were his days that when Stonebridge Primary School opened its doors Charlie did not deign to attend. Charlie preferred to trace the course of the stream that had evaded the navvies' paving. Perhaps it was just as well. Each winter found its pupils blighted with scabies, cholera or diphtheria. There was at least one death each term.

Opposite the school are the low-beamed roof and gabled windows of the Orange Tree. Charlie spent hours watching the types who stopped off for a jar. Tattooed sailors who boasted of far-off places, and gypsies with eyes as dark as his – some even wore earrings. Where the stream ended the Harrow Road led the small boy's eye towards the nether regions of Park Royal's industrial estates and the fabled Grand Union Canal.

He wanted to get away, and the long stretches of newly paved road offered a route out of the confusing and dangerous environs of home. 'Mad' Nell, Charlie's other sister, added to the clamour of voices bouncing off the walls of Number 130. She had muscles like pineapples, he said.

'Feel them!' she would command. When her youngest

brother reached up to squeeze she swiped him round the head with a left hook. This was the Taylors' rough-housing humour. Nell had her place on the bench under the window, from whence she screeched out obscene ditties. Even the coarsest of her neighbours were shocked. Her raucous singing pierced a swathe through the whirls of tobacco but failed to deter her suitor. 'Long' Harry Sears was a boxer, and the only man capable of keeping up with the sixteen-year-old girl and her talent for trouble. He swept her off westwards to Neasden.

The fights would start at around midnight when uniformed and plain-clothes policemen cheerfully joined in the smashing of heads and breaking of limbs. The 'Law' is no better than us, thought Tots. Just like the navvies, the busies were a step down from the gentry of Willesden. They addressed the professional classes as sir or madam, they doffed helmets and were humble in their presence. By day, coppers were jeered in the streets, and if one dared to walk the streets of Stonebridge alone he'd be mobbed. But at night, his brothers-in-arms would bestir themselves and avenge their wounded comrade's honour by hunting down the ringleader. George's head was pitted with scars from being beaten with truncheons. When, to Katie's great delight, the apple of her eye pushed Sergeant Elmo down the stairs, he broke the policeman's back.

Of the kind of street Charlie lived on, Basil Jellicoe, Vicar of St Mary's Somers Town, said: 'Overcrowding and poverty are here being used by the Devil in order to steal from the children of God the health and happiness which are their right.' Or as Charlie later exclaimed, when he became cigar-smoking, Tuinal-popping Charles: 'We didn't have a pot to piss in.'

Omnibuses, trams and horse-drawn carts contributed their sounds and smells, mishaps, grease and dung to the

stew of the streets and the stink of the Stonebridge sewer.
Even as far away as Willesden, the local gentry were complaining about the smell. They were appalled, on their forays
into this wilderness, to find unattended children playing cards
on street corners and splashing about in horses' water
troughs. Katie Taylor, minding her own business, wheeled
her latest baby and two screaming toddlers in a pram while
Doris and Will hung off the sides. A labourer stopped his
digging to ask the little woman:

'Blimey, is all them yours, love?'

'Oh no,' she protested, covered with shame at the proof
of her reckless fertility. 'I'm looking after 'em for a friend.'

She did not like to tell him she had more at home.

And what a handful they were. Tots, seventeen when
Charlie was born, was a hulking six-footer and beyond
anyone's control. He had got the best of his mother's milk,
and the others had guzzled what was left. The last and
definitely the least, Charlie was puny, and learned quickly
that he could not compete with his brothers. Even in the so-
called safety of his mother's womb, he had been in danger
from the ferocity of Tots's volcanic fits. Three months before
his birth, there had been a terrible scene at home.

That February morning, Katie had been hanging clothes
out to dry in what she liked to call her garden. George James
was patrolling areas vulnerable to air attack – docks, railway
bridges, power stations. He didn't care, as long as it wasn't
home.

From the yard, Katie heard her eldest come in from a
night on the tiles, tramp up the stairs and head out again.
She went upstairs to fetch her purse which she kept under
her pillow. She knew she had left seventeen shillings in it,
but she found only sixteen. When George came home that
night she taxed him with stealing a shilling.

'I only wish I'd taken the lot,' he roared, then proceeded

to wave a plank of wood that he always kept hanging from his belt around her head. When he brought out a knife from his pocket, she took flight. Pregnant Katie ran into the street, made a hue and cry, and the local constabulary, in the shape of Sergeant Elmo, answered her call. He took George away and a remand was ordered. In court a month later, where Katie gave evidence against her favourite, a Detective Farquhar gave the boy a bad character. 'He is thoroughly lazy and never does any work,' he told the magistrate. George was sentenced, not for the first time, to twenty-one days' hard labour.

Despite his brothers' form, it was baby Alfred who was considered the bad apple. Never mind that Wag thought that a fork was something with which you stabbed people if they tried to steal food from your plate. Katie just didn't take to her youngest. Perhaps it was because he was so underhand and cunning – she just could not read him like the others. Besides, she was worn out by all those pregnancies.

No wonder the neighbours called them the 'funny Taylors'; they weren't just odd, they could be frighteningly nasty. They could turn on you, snarling like a dog, at any time. For Charlie's part, all he remembered were the beatings and the smell of booze emanating from his mother. If she never took to him, well, he didn't take to her either.

The domestic scene plays out like this. Katie, feeling the full weight of her forty-eight years, is lying in bed recovering from last night's lock-in. Downstairs, twelve-year-old Doris is doing what she does every morning: sweeping out the grate, making the tea and keeping guard over Wag and Charlie. Unbeknownst to Katie, the Monkey has scattered tin tacks on the ground beside her bed.

On waking she lands her two feet in a pile of them. Verbal abuse swiftly degenerates into all-out attack, and she chases Charlie into the street. He keeps running.

The consequences were severe. The following morning he arrived back at Carlyle Avenue and was hungry and thirsty. He drank the pint of milk that sat on the doorstep. Katie beat him till he was unconscious for depriving her of the dash of milk for her morning cup of tea.

Charlie was determined to survive against the odds. The bigger boys, Tots and Harry, never needed an excuse to beat him. His mother had no time for his complaints. When the going got tough, he slept in sheds. There was enough excitement on the streets of Stonebridge for a young entrepreneur to keep his momentum going. He was in on all the action.

He was schooled by sharks, and knew he had to load the odds in his favour. On its vertical advance across north-west London, Harrow Road passed by the end of Carlyle Avenue. Charlie's favourite game was placing bets on the number of the first bus to appear around the corner. He planted his brother Will on the junction. They had agreed on a signal which involved folding a newspaper a certain way to indicate which bus was approaching. Apart from cheating, Charlie had learnt one other vital component to the cardsharp's art. He made sure not to 'guess' correctly every time. His friends were convinced he was on the level, and he could keep on fleecing them without fear of reprisal.

But Charlie was not so different from the other little boys growing up in the shadow of the brand-new Wembley Stadium. He could be excited by spectacle, too. In April 1923 he witnessed the first Cup Final to be played at Wembley. He was seven years old and managed to wangle his way in without a ticket. So did another 70,000 spectators. The stadium could not accommodate them, so some ended up on the pitch. For a while it appeared that the match would not go ahead. Charlie could not recall who was playing and did not care who had won (Bolton Wanderers beat West Ham

2–0), but he did remember PC George Scorey. Astride his magnificent white horse, he pushed the masses back to the sides of the pitch. At last, a memory he could share with thousands of others.

Four months later, George James Taylor died. He was fifty-five. He had been out of sorts for some weeks, with a high temperature and stiffness in the back of his neck. After a few days of being even more irascible than usual, the symptoms worsened, and George's head was bursting with pain. He dealt with this intense provocation in his usual fashion. Charlie hid in the doorway of his parents' bedroom and watched his father bashing his brains against the wall. All the while he was wailing like an angry cat. He screamed profanities and rained curses on his family. He would not allow anyone near him, and could not bear to be touched. Not that anyone wanted to – even on his deathbed they were wary of him. But, from the safety of the foot of the bed, Charlie could not stop watching as the symptoms of meningitis devastated his father's body. He watched as George James shivered convulsively under the bedclothes. When he finally reached the oblivion of a coma he was taken to die at Twyford Park.

2 · Gentleman Scholar

On the night of 24 August 1924 Charlie decided to run away from home for the last time. The police had been to Number 130, and Tots had been arrested for being drunk and disorderly. He did not go quietly. It took four policemen to hold him down and cost Katie 10s 6d for the doctor to patch him up again. The girl whose head he had smashed with a bottle could not be persuaded to press charges. Tots got away with a fine of twenty shillings for the drunk and disorderly charge and ten shillings for the use of obscene language.

A week earlier Harry had been charged with theft.

His friend William East, known throughout Willesden as 'Burglar Bill', had persuaded him to break into the tobacconist's stall at Wembley Stadium. They made off with cigarettes, a fountain pen, and a bottle of whisky.

On being arrested, Burglar Bill, who read penny dreadfuls, declared: 'You have made a mistake. This is not a Major Sheppard case, but I hold the trump card. Taylor knows nothing about it. I went round the back, put my arm through the window and did the job.'

The police were unimpressed. The defendant Taylor, 'of no fixed abode', was brought before the magistrates at Wealdstone Court. Harry had come out of Borstal three months previously and been unable to get a job. He confessed to taking the whisky in an attempt to appease his starvation. The fountain pen was for his girlfriend, Nora O'Brien.

Perhaps Harry had foreseen that it would not be long before another enforced absence meant more letter-writing. If so, Nora would have to find another pen. The magistrate warned her to be more careful when accepting presents. As for her lover, four previous convictions, including one for sacrilege, were taken into account and he was sentenced to six months' hard labour. This was the big time for Harry.

Charlie was still in little league, and determined not to end up like his elder brothers. He could see where they had gone wrong. Tots was a desperado; Harry was a dimwit. To better his lot he had no choice but to become sharper and more ruthless in his defence.

While Tots was being manhandled into the waiting Black Maria, he jumped out of the bedroom window, hopped over the wall and ran. The screams and shouting that reverberated in his head were blotted out. He needed to think of a story suitable for a respectable matron of Willesden.

The lady who took in the pouting child was kind. She gave him a slice of bread and jam, and left him to savour the treat in the kitchen.

'This is all right. I don't mind if I stay here,' he decided.

He was wrong to trust an adult. She had already alerted the police, and he was forced to give up his new berth. He never forgave her. She had instilled a false sense of security, then mercilessly thrown him to the wolves.

After careful deliberations, the Middlesex Board of Guardians concluded that Alfred Taylor's fate lay at Church Farm Boys' Home in East Barnet. Call it a reform school, a ragged school, an industrial school, or a haven, the stigma remained the same. The appendage of 'Home' was a give-away. The common-entrants' examination Charlie had to pass was before a magistrate under the 1858 Industrial Schools Act. This decreed that children aged between seven and fifteen be committed to such an establishment if they 'appeared to be neglected or in danger of turning to crime'. My eight-year-old grandfather was just one of eighty-four 'difficult cases' sent to Church Farm that year.

Charlie often spoke fondly of his schooldays. He would talk, sleepy with Sunday lunch, of endless games of cricket in the summer, and Saturday morning football in the winter. Of sitting round blazing camp-fires with the Scouts, and dreaming up gung-ho antics for the following day. He could recite Rudyard Kipling by the yard. The Empire, barrel-chested men in uniforms, gleaming brass buttons and the White Man's Burden stirred the pride of the patriot never far from his heart.

Those hazy, far-off days were spent in the village of East Barnet in rural Hertfordshire. Even now its gentle hillocks and discreet valleys are replete with emerald greenery. At the top of Hill Rise, next to the ancient stone church of St Mary the Virgin, is a quiet courtyard that leads into Church Farm. The boys' home is now a school for children with learning difficulties. The terminology changes, but the children are always the same.

Church Farm is a small and soothing establishment that rises like St Mary herself in a graceful nave flagged by two wings. The Mansard roof and copper clock tower, which Charlie took his sons to see when they were little, are the hallmarks of Late Victorian domestic harmony.

Within this nest of neat shrubbery, the rascally Alfred, 'not convicted of any crime' but on familiar terms with Willesden's constabulary, was received into the care of the authorities. After passing through the arched Gothic doorway, and into the Matron's study, she checked him for lice. She gave him a rigorous going-over to ensure that he was fit to be trained for labour, and after a beef dinner in the refectory, sent him to bed in the dormitory. Five ounces of cooked meat four nights a week was not a gargantuan allowance but it was better than the bread and dripping Katie dished out.

The dorm was as cold as charity, so he did what he knew best and began his descent from the window. As he did so, his eye was caught by the clock tower. The copper cladding glinted in the moonlight, the valleys spread peacefully before him. Boiled salt beef was on the menu the following day.

The happiest days of my grandfather's life were not to start just yet, however. On his first full day at Church Farm, he got up, brushed and washed himself, and prepared himself for anything they could throw at him. He was put to work, none too happy about it, in the hayloft. A prefect called Budge was told to supervise him as he baled straw. He soon grew impatient with Charlie's malingering – this just wasn't his idea of time well spent. When Charlie had the nerve to cheek him, Budge stabbed him in the thigh with a pitchfork.

Rugby was the model for Charlie's new home, and Thomas Hughes was its very first patron. The school was divided into four houses. Rivalry in sports, cleanliness, and good behaviour was encouraged, and success was rewarded by marks and a Cup. Charlie flourished in the race for rewards. There was a shortage of overcoats, but the lads were 'appropriately clad' for all weathers. Charlie, on his orphan's pension of five shillings a week, a little less so than the norm.

Despite the good intentions, the regime Hughes deplored in *Tom Brown's Schooldays* flourished at Church Farm. Within the strictures of a military-style discipline the strong ruled, and the birch flailed tender buttocks. The Home under-took to carve away the rough exterior of the 'most depraved young specimens of humanity' and achieve great work from their flesh and blood.

Charlie's school had a venerable history of social statuary dating back to 1858. A publisher and freelance philanthropist, Mr George Bell, was the founder. On his daily journeys between 'the Great City and rural Hampstead', he had been galvanized into action by the sight of 'gangs of wild and wandering Bedouins', who 'dragged themselves up' on the streets. 'Poor little Jack' and shoeless Tom were the first young Turks to be drafted. A year later, fifty boys were press-ganged into the Home. 'The destitute, dirty, idle, not seldom diseased – boys who would to a certainty, as they grew up, have fallen into the ranks of the criminal class – these were the specimens of humanity drawn together under [his] care.'

The Boys' Home went from strength to strength largely due to the boys' own efforts. Schools of this kind shut up shop quickly if they failed to become self-financing. In order to succeed they needed cheap raw materials, cheap labour and a market for the low-grade goods the children produced.

If it was a home, as Hughes declared it to be ('I call it a home, a place in which you will find sympathy'), there was one condition he was keen to stress: 'He who shall not work shall not eat.' In those early days of the Home's history there was not much choice but to chop wood.

Charles Dickens paid a visit to the Boys' Home in 1884. He enthused, 'Even the very smallest boys can help, and so this firewood shop is full of life and energy, the gas-engine setting the pace of the work which keeps them all in motion.'

What impressed Dickens most, though, was that almost all the boys reverted to the 'Celtic model', by which he meant they had 'the sallow London faces, the dark lank hair – the type of feature that seems to make its appearance in a single generation of London life'.

Three generations of London lives later, my sallow-faced and sharp-as-needles grandfather met the man he was to revere most in his young life. Nineteen-twenty-four saw another new boy at Church Farm, Mr J. Vaughan Cart-wright, headmaster. He was a softly spoken man – something

Charlie had never encountered before. What is more, he did not react with a vengeance when a group of boys overturned his Morris Cowley in the middle of the night.

Schooling for children under the age of fourteen was not compulsory when Charlie entered the Home. But Cartwright was a radical, and Charlie, for the first time in his life, was lucky. The habits of skill and industry were still habits that needed to be learnt, but education in the arts, history and science were equally necessary for the boys' 'bodily and spiritual' development. There was even an annual summer trip to Dymchurch, on the south coast of England. It was Charlie's first sight of the sea, and he made sure it was his sons' first experience of it also.

What most astounded my grandfather was when Cartwright took the school heavy under his wing, gained his confidence, and turned him around as if by magic. Charlie was impressed – here was a man who did not have to raise a finger to get what he wanted.

There is a grading from 'dirt' to 'well-respected' in the criminal fraternity. The use of violence sends people down a grade, as being 'unprofessional'. Charlie learnt a lot from Cartwright. He did not need to emulate Tots, Harry, or even his father to make his way in the world. There were subtler, more effective methods for self-advancement. Under their new headmaster, the boys' over-active violent tendencies were suppressed. They were given woodwork lessons and coaching in sports to channel unwanted energies. Even the smallest boys benefited from Cartwright's novel experiments with psychoanalysis. To their chagrin, persistent bed-wetters attended his clinic once a week.

When he was not writing essays on Rudyard Kipling, or perfecting his neat and graceful copperplate hand, Charlie was encouraged to take up art. He won a competition organized by the Home Office for a group portrait of his family.

The picture of the funny Taylors cheating at cards in their kitchen ended up on the walls of a civil servant's office.

Charlie was thrilled with the new developments at Church Farm. He got to play sports on the playing-fields of local public schools, and during long winter evenings Cartwright organized whist drives and ping-pong tournaments. He attended concerts, 'socials' and 'dramatic entertainments'. In the process he picked up the social niceties which would stand him in such good stead when charming his upper-class marks.

·

The Twenties were good to my grandfather. Educationalists like Cartwright instilled him with hope for the future as well as correcting the faults he perceived in the 'lost generation'. Unfortunately, his approach to reformatory education was not entirely appreciated by the Home Office. Opinion was divided as to whether Church Farm should be retributive or restorative. Educating delinquents was not the priority. Cartwright was defiant, and took great pains to establish an ambitious curriculum. In 1929 a Home Office conference report concluded: 'The object is not to make learned thieves, but plain honest men.' When considering the use to which Charlie put his education, they had a point.

Home Secretary Sir William Joynson-Hicks took a keen interest in Church Farm. He was not won over by Cartwright's evangelizing efforts. He was a man with whom Thomas Hughes could have done business. He even employed the same language. 'He that will not work shall not eat,' he told striking dock-workers who were protesting against the Depression.

Hard at work in the Home Office, Joynson-Hicks was supervising a project that would prepare the urban un-employed for a new life on the land. Though he would prefer it if he could send them to Britain's overseas possessions. Even the lowest reprobate could carry the flag – even better if they did so in distant countries. Charlie's peers were sent to Canada and Nova Scotia. Joynston-Hicks wanted the great unwashed out of the cities. Church Farm was part of a programme designed to counterbalance this urban blight. England was in the mood for all things pastoral, and small-scale horticulture was very much on Charlie's curriculum.

His schooling over once he reached twelve, he was tending a plot in which he grew marrows. The tradition of chopping and selling firewood still prevailed, taking up much of Charlie's time. He was a big boy now, and Church Farm was too narrow to confine him. Under the duress of the Home Office, the boys sat in files in the lecture hall listening to BBC broadcasts on the latest farming methods.

This little urbanite did not listen. He had found, in that same lecture hall, another source of inspiration. Except this man was strikingly similar to the adult Charlie in that both men shared a disregard for the facts of life, truth and feelings most people cherish. In the winter of 1928 Admiral Evans delivered a lantern lecture to the boys. It was entitled 'Captain Scott's Last Antarctic Expedition'. Charlie never tired of repeating the story of this ill-fated race to the Pole. His own sons were drilled into revering, not Scott, but Evans of the *Broke*.

The admiral's own story would have charmed Charlie even more had he known it. Though not many people did know it, because Teddy Evans, born in 1880, had difficulties recalling it himself.

The man who shaped my grandfather's earliest aspirations was famous for his breezy accounts of polar heroism. They usually starred himself. Brash ambition characterized Evans, a fact that had not escaped Captain Scott. Evans accompanied him on the journey south from the Pole in

1911. Scott noted in his diary that he found his companion a 'queer study', with worrying 'mental limitations'. Others found him abnormally energetic, cheerful and headstrong. Charlie was in thrall. Zest, it seems, blazed from Evans's face. He excelled at useless feats of strength and daring, and outlandish exhibitions of vigour enthralled him.

Evans liked to promote himself as a man who had knocked about. He said he was classless and that his personality was enough to outshine the endorsement of breeding. How Charlie would have rejoiced to hear that, or that his new hero had also acquired his veneer at a 'school for troublesome boys'.

Though his natural gusto caused consternation in polite society, where his behaviour was deemed unacceptable, nothing could stop his rise. 'Evans of the *Broke*' was his nom-de-guerre, and war was his favourite pastime.

On 20 April 1917 Captain Evans of HMS *Broke* sank a German destroyer seven miles east of Dover. The papers were full of it, and the *Daily Express* was ecstatic in its account of his audacity. Charlie, with his keen interest in all things martial, memorized the stirring details.

The conquered Germans were drowning in the Channel. An enemy shell had killed all the men in the *Broke*'s boiler-room, and, as she joined the debris in the sea, Evans was forced to retreat in a lifeboat. He refused to rescue the dying German sailors.

'We're not here to look after midnight bathers,' he joked.

The captain became an admiral and a hero. From then on, he wrote a regular column for the *Express*. Not only did he inspire my susceptible grandfather, but this over-excited, over-grown schoolboy had decided he could best secure 'the fate of our Empire, which [is] in a very critical stage of its existence ... by giving up some of my leisure time to lecturing and addressing schools and young people's organizations'. He travelled tirelessly around the country delivering the same old stories every time. When Admiral Lord Evans died in 1957, he left two sons behind him, one called Broke. Perhaps Teddy realized that no one would remember his story once he was no longer around to keep telling it. So he left it up to his son and men like my grandfather to carry the flame.

·

In July 1931, Charlie, having turned fifteen the previous May, was discharged from Church Farm and sent to work for Mr Lewis's 'Coffee Shop' at Billingsgate Market. The situation might have seemed entirely appropriate to anyone who knew him, but it was not good enough for my grandfather. He had not been writing essays on Rudyard Kipling for six years to end up in a caff stinking of fishmongers. Charlie felt he had more to offer, and that the world should make way for his gifts. He took himself down to St James's Square, Piccadilly, and talked himself into a job in one of the grandest clubhouses of Pall Mall.

The first time Charlie saw the statue of Eros it was submerged in a blur of smog and drizzle. By the time he had arrived at the Naval and Military Club, where he was newly employed as a bus boy, he had soaked up the gleam of opulence and luxury. He wanted more. The reform-school boy from Willesden had arrived at the hub of the Commonwealth of British Nations. He stepped into the club where porters in full evening toilet stood in graceful attendance. The son of rank-Irish immigrants born in the darkest of homes which broke every law of good health was in the England that makes laws and wars, and fears upstarts.

Within the cloistered calm of the dining-rooms, Charlie studied the waiters closely. He watched them pour a pale sherry for the aperitif and a '23 claret with dinner. They played their parts perfectly, maintaining a reverent hush as they paced across the carpeted floor. Charlie learnt that a first-class bearing and serious mien were invaluable camouflage for skulduggery. Charlie's new colleagues were overcharging the club's members and keeping a kitty for their spoils.

Most of the club's members were veterans of the Great War. Charlie had just been discharged from an institution that instructed its inmates in the art of revering these stalwarts of the English shires. And here they were being exploited in their dotage under Charlie's sharp nose. His newly fostered sense of honour was outraged. He could not stand by and allow the discrepancy between respectful appearance and self-serving reality to continue. And, besides, he was not receiving his fair share of the spoils.

Whatever his reasoning, he broke the first commandment of Thomas Hughes's Rugby. He informed on his colleagues, and was sacked forthwith.

'It doesn't pay to be straight,' he resolved. So, at sixteen, disillusioned with society, he set about making his mark.

3 · Empire Builder

Charlie was never a teenager. I never saw him laugh, and it is impossible to imagine him larking about. He was always deadly serious, and always on the look-out for his own gain. It was 1932, and not a good time to be unemployed. Thousands were jobless in the Wembley area alone. The queues outside the labour exchange every Monday morning were immovable.

Katie, however, was coping magnificently. Widowhood suited her, and her troublesome elder sons were safe and sound chipping rocks in various penal institutions. She had settled with Wag, the most devoted of her children, into a nice little house in the Middlesex suburb of Wembley. The stadium, not the masses of hopeless men, was the talk of the town. The Empire Exhibition attracted a stream of gushing crowds from all over England.

On the mantelpiece in her front room Katie proudly displayed a framed photograph of Wag in uniform, on horse-back in Malaya. This was a fitting imperial reference for their new address at Chalfont Avenue.

While Charlie had been reforming himself at school, Katie and Wag had removed themselves from their frantic corner of Stonebridge. Their new house, Number 44, had a pleasant aspect with views on to Monks Park Gardens, Tokyngton Park and the River Brent. It was a fresh start in more salubrious surroundings. Charlie attempted to slot in but soon came up against Wag's military bearing.

Even though they shared the same alma mater Wag was barely literate. He was a brute of a man and as thick as thieves with Katie. Charlie, though he would never admit it, was frightened of Wag's superior bulk and strength. He resented him because of it.

As far as Katie was concerned, Wag knew how to make himself useful. She would send him out on the rob with strict instructions as to what to bring back for tea. Katie was a clever woman, far cleverer than most of her boys, and she exploited to the full what meagre resources were at hand. Heinz's factory was a constant source of sustenance. It was amazing how often 57 Varieties of whatever you fancied in tinned goods found their way into the tea chests which she kept packed to the brims in the scullery.

My grandfather despaired that his hard-won learning had come to naught. Consider Wag: all he had learnt at Church Farm was how to cook and steal. Although his bread-and-butter pudding was a legend in his family's teatime, Wag would never better himself in Charlie's critical eyes. He begrudged his mother's protector all the more for it.

What was worse, Wag had seen action. His glory days began on 19 September 1928. While Charlie was dreaming of Antarctic adventures with Admiral Evans, his seventeen-year-old brother lied about his age in order to enlist as a Private in the Bedfordshire and Hertfordshire Regiment. What he liked most about army life, he later recalled, was the chance it provided to get rid of all that pent-up nervous energy in the boxing ring. He acquired a reputation as a fearless contender. He worked hard at it, and was never a drinker – in fact he was notorious for once getting drunk on two pints of Burton's Ale. Wag had seen what the demon drink could do to a man, not to mention women, and was commended by his superiors for being 'sober, honest and trustworthy'.

On 18 February 1931 his battalion was posted overseas, and Wag's story took a desperate turn.

The place was Malaya and the time was a tricky period in its history. Wag's battalion was assisting the Federated Malay States Police to keep the peace between the indigenous Malays, 'Nature's gentlemen', and unruly Chinese immigrants. Wag once attempted to entertain my mother – and I cannot think of a less appreciative audience than the refined and genteel Greta Ann – with anecdotes about patrolling the island's swampy rivers in prison-boats. The unfortunate Chinese were kept in manacles below deck. Some were unwise enough to attempt escape.

Wag's eyes creased with laughter as he recalled chucking rioting coolies overboard. No one kept count of 'escapees'. But, just like a Taylor, Wag had to go that little bit over the top and into overkill. The day he received the scar that ran from his temple to his chin along one cheek was his last as a soldier.

The story as he told it is brief and to the point. He was engaged on deck in a tussle with a Chinaman. The Chinaman produced a knife and ripped open Wag's face. Red mist engulfed Wag. He wrapped his fingers around the Chinaman's neck and by the time his vision had cleared and his grip had loosened all vital signs of life had drained away.

Since his overall conduct was 'Good' and he was 'self-reliant and cheerful', Wag was given a reasonable testimonial on discharge. He was deemed 'fit for employment in civil life'. The matter of the dead man was dropped. It had been an act of self-defence, said Wag, and his nine months in Malaya were given a lustrous glow in the portrait cherished by his mother. Insult, however, was added to self-inflicted injury. Wag had forfeited his right to an army pension, and his cheerfulness turned to rancour.

On 4 March 1932 there was a momentary blip in the domestic tranquillity of 44 Chalfont Avenue. Wag was convicted of stealing a bicycle valued at £6. Though he pleaded not guilty, he received a forty-shilling fine which had to be paid in twenty-one days. One month's hard labour was the alternative. With two boys already doing time, it would be careless for Katie to lose another. The money was borrowed and Wag fled overseas for more adventures. Charlie was relieved, if a little envious of his brother's exotic lifestyle, but another brother came to his aid.

Brother Will was a foreman on the building site that would become Wembley's Empire Pool and Arena.

·

The places to look for the germs of my grandfather's past are in the arterial roads and light-industry areas of London. Though the Wembley experience was a grand one in his time, today it is depleted and derelict. The Thirties triumph of architecture over humility denotes a long-gone empire that few care to miss. Chemicals from the smoke of factory chimneys have bitten deep into the Portland stone and streaked the white Carrara of the mausoleums that remain. Engineer's Way is a wasteland. Empire Way gets you nowhere, and fast.

Charlie was there when construction started on the Empire Pool and Arena. It promised all the joys of the seaside for Londoners keen to escape the city. It was decided that the North Circular Road would be a perfect way in for pleasure-seekers equipped with a motor car. There would be a covered swimming-pool with real waves, sun-bathing decks and a paddling-pool for children. This was not the sort of place where a man jumped into the water, shimmied about and was off and away. Dotted around the 17,000 square foot pool were fully licensed restaurants, West End orchestras, and heated lounges. There would be gala nights every Tuesday. The pleasure dome would be open from 7 a.m. to midnight every day. Admission was one shilling.

Across the huge car park from Wembley Stadium a two-acre site was cleared, a forest of scaffold poles erected and an army of workmen made busy. Cranes, cement, ropes, ladders, excavators, picks and shovels were thrust into the mix. The construction of the building was of reinforced concrete and glass, without the use of a single piece of constructional steel. Sir Owen William, who had designed the Wembley Stadium for the Empire Exhibition, came up with the radical idea of creating the new building around a giant swimming-pool. It could be used all summer long, and converted to an ice rink in the winter. It would be a light and airy, pillarless structure.

The work, though, was heavy. Floor slabs were six inches thick, and had to be laid over spans of twenty-two feet. The roof was stiffened with planes of concrete twenty-one feet deep and nine inches thick. The dome sat on two six-inch knife-edges of concrete, each carrying a load of twenty tons for every foot of length. Some of the labourers were unlucky, run over by the wagons they were leading to the tip-head. Whenever there was a job vacancy, fifty men would queue for it. The saddest sight was the old-timers, Charlie said. They turned up at six o'clock every morning, rain or shine, hoping to catch the site manager's eye. Charlie never forgot them – his father's generation of working-class men, dispatched to die in their millions for their masters' wars, and they had the dole queue as their reward. He would not, repeat not, end up like one of them.

Brother Will was doing well. He was paid extra because he set the pace for the other men in running barrows of concrete to the mixer. Some over-strained themselves trying to keep up with him. Charlie, always determined to prove himself at the expense of others, challenged him to a race. After a few laps Brother Will turned round and could not see the young rascal anywhere. That was because Charlie had fallen down a ditch with the barrow on top of him.

'Yeah, but in the end I fucked him,' he delighted in telling his sons.

It was not long before he realized he did not have Brother Will's physical capacity or his enthusiasm for hard work. And he did not like the fact that his older brother was earning more than him. But he wasn't Katie's son for nothing. To make up for what he lacked in muscle and sheer grit, he used his ingenuity. It was his sister Doris and her taste for stewed tea that gave Charlie his first bright idea. She kept the kettle on the stove all day to produce endless cups of bitter, strong tea. Charlie proudly set up a stall with her kettle and stove on the site. 'I was making twice as much as him selling cups of tea to 600-odd navvies every day.'

In February 1934, the Earl of Derby laid the foundation stone of the Wembley Empire pool, embossing his coat-of-arms in the concrete block with a die. Scaffolding still towered around him as he pronounced weighty words into a microphone. His photograph appeared in that week's issue of the *Wembley News*. The men – splendidly attired in top hats and frock-coats – who cheered him were drawn from the middle-class enclaves of Willesden and Wembley. Above them, a few hatless labourers can be seen. They are sitting on wooden platforms above the Earl, chomping on doorstop sandwiches and nursing mugs of my grandfather's tea. It was 'an Historical Occasion', concluded the Earl.

Four months later, and another leading light of British society was given a golden key to open the doors of the 'finest indoor arena of its kind in the world'. The Duke of Gloucester pressed a button and 750,000 gallons of water piped direct from Colne Valley, thus bypassing Wembley's less pristine supplies, roared into the chasm. The Duke presided over a banquet for 1,000 local dignitaries and spoke of the Empire Pool advancing the prestige of British sport.

Charlie was out of a job.

4 · Bicycle Thief

When Charlie first met my mother he took her ice-skating. He told her that he had learnt to skate at the Empire Pool and Arena. He held her steady, resting his hands on her skinny hips. He did not like ballroom dancing, its twists and turns and fancy footwork assailed his sense of dignity. He preferred to cut a stiff swathe through the giddy crowd on the rink. To get on in this world a man must be seen to be serious at all times.

After the success of his tea-making escapade Charlie decided he was too smart for the labourer's life. Instead, he would take each day as it came. Sometimes there was money, sometimes there wasn't, in which case he would borrow. It was all the same to him. Only a very foolish fellow couldn't make a pound a week out of nothing. That is the beauty of London. Just by hanging around on a street corner looking shifty, you can pick up some action.

The naïve and sentimental skivvies he met at the ice-rink were taken in by his air of self-importance. He was particularly assiduous in his attentions towards the girls who had Post Office savings books. In between sessions, he would retire, lady friend draped on his arm, to the world's only rink-side restaurant. The ice below them was cleared by a line of uniformed attendants skating in perfect forma-tion to music, rhythmically sweeping the surface as they went. Showmanship was not confined to the staff. Charlie preferred the swagger style in men's outfitting. His shirts had a semi-stiff front, with cuffs and collars in neat stripes. His coat was a single-breasted Raglan number. The bold check tweed was offset with a Prussian collar. He was all the rage.

In the summer of 1934, when the ice turned to water, swimmers shed their inhibitions and squeezed into fusty bathing costumes. Charlie watched them darting around the pool like tadpoles. He preferred to stay dry in the tiered seats, under the embrace of the vast reinforced concrete ceiling.

That July was a particularly hot one. Perhaps Charlie was feeling the heat on his walk home, perhaps he saw something he wanted and knew he could not afford. Perhaps he deplored this hole in his finances so badly he had to do something about it. Whatever the case, it was a lovely day for a bicycle ride, even if it became, as he told it, his moment of no return.

Because when Detective Cashford saw him at 2.45 p.m. coming out of the Exhibition Grounds in Wembley he was on foot. He recognized him, though, as one of a gang of recidivist brothers. Two hours later, he saw Charlie again in the neighbouring suburb of Sudbury, at the top of Harrow Road. This time, he was riding a bicycle.

When he got back to the station Detective Cashford was informed that there had been a complaint of theft. A bicycle worth £1 10s had been stolen from Dagmar Avenue, Wembley. Would it be too fanciful of me to wonder if, like Wag's first dip into crime, the theft of a bicycle represented some overwhelming urge for flight? Probably. He just saw it, wanted it, did not see why he could not have it, hopped on the untended bicycle and cycled off.

Detective Cashford knew where the Taylors lived. Only three weeks previously a member of that 'troublesome family', as Henry Taylor was described in court, had been sent to prison for a month following a scene on a bus in

Harrow Road. He pleaded not guilty (as was always the Taylor way) to charges of being drunk and disorderly, using obscene language, and assaulting a bus conductor, two of whose teeth he had knocked out. The court was told that Henry had many previous convictions. A woman in the gallery cried out, 'Oh no he hasn't!', for all the world as though she were joining in the fun at a Christmas panto.

The woman was Henry's wife, Monk. Wag gave her that name because Henry had met her whilst he was sleeping rough in a shed in Monks Park Gardens. He had been chucked out of Katie's place in Chalfont Avenue for being more than usually fractious, and Monk's family had taken him in. The newly-weds were now living in precarious splendour in Priory Close, Sudbury, just round the corner from Mother Katie's respectable abode. In terms of social climbing, Sudbury was a long way from Stonebridge, and Katie had done well to haul her unruly sons after her.

She had done a moonlight flit from Wembley. Every few months, Katie packed her possessions on to a wheelbarrow, all sons on deck, to avoid paying the rent. It wasn't just the money, however. Flight was also necessary because her family's notoriety was always catching up with the tiny brown woman. She was adept at invisibility, but her sons were determined to make a show. Henry and Monk brought their arguments on to the streets, the neighbours gawped, the landlord complained, and, under cover of night, Katie wheeled out the barrow. But she had high standards, and would not settle for less than a three-bedroom semi with front and back gardens in the cosy new environs of Metroland.

Once electrification had been introduced to the Metropolitan line, the next ring of suburbia was developed. Katie saw that Sudbury had manicured parks and greens. She appreciated the proximity of its red-brick villas to Harrow

School. What was more, a smart new Underground station had been opened in 1931, providing a line into Piccadilly Circus. She was not going to be left behind.

Katie and Charlie were happily ensconced in 14 The Chine when Detective Cashford came calling.

My grandfather was always able to think on his feet, but this was his first time under real, concerted pressure. So allowances must be made for his over-enthusiastic and totally unconvincing protestations of innocence.

'I met a man,' he told Cashford, 'who stopped and asked me the way to Wealdstone. When I told him I did not know, he asked me if I knew anybody who would like a bicycle for 5s. I told him I would give him 5s. for it and I went round to my mother's house to get 2s, as I only had 3s. with me. I suppose it was stolen and he sold it to me because I looked like a mug.'

Charlie so convinced himself of his powers of persuasion that he elected to go for trial. But, if anyone looked less like a mug, it was him, and on 27 July 1934 he received a severe punishment for his insouciance: he was sentenced at the Middlesex Sessions to three years' imprisonment for larceny.

This must have been a terrible blow for my grandfather, who, till his dying day, insisted that he had been unjustly imprisoned for receiving stolen goods. A holding cell at Pentonville Prison is far from the leafy comforts of 14 The Chine, Sudbury. He was kept in a cell and in virtual solitary confinement. Here, under constant surveillance, Jeremy Bentham averred that, in this virtual Panopticon, 'rogues could be ground honest'. Charlie brooded. His position was especially galling since even Tots was on the outside, and seemed to have found his vocation. He was caddying, at which he was a roaring success, at the Sudbury golf course. He had got the job by diving headlong into the course's lake to retrieve errant balls for passing golfers.

Charlie would not be shaken from his improvised fabrication. How could he – so far above the rank and file of the other Taylor boys – get caught for stealing a bike? The shame was so great it blinded him to the shabby truth.

5 · An Independent

After two months the powers-that-be decided that Alfred Taylor had been ground down enough. He was home in time to take part in a rally organized by the British Union of Fascists.

War talk was rife, and my grandfather felt the lack of any real fighting experience. With the importation of Italian Fascism and its gorgeously cut uniforms, his masculinity blossomed. Mosley staged dramatic meetings, à la Hitler. Patriotic banners, lots of marching, dramatic lighting and a dynamic entrance. When he took to the stage, he was surrounded by storm-troopers in black shirts and jackboots.

As early as 1923 advertisements had been appearing in the *Wembley News* for recruits to British Fascism. 'Patriotic residents interested in the welfare of their country and willing to co-operate in work of a definite character in furtherance of the same, are invited to write to D. Bailey, 2 Wembley Way.' I doubt if Charlie, who was only seven at the time, applied to D. Bailey, but he was willing enough to jump on Mosley's bandwagon when the opportunity arose.

Sir Oswald fascinated my grandfather. He was tall, dark and dramatically handsome, and was Charlie's local MP. He cut a glamorous figure in high society but was not afraid to slum it with the lowest of London's scum. At first a Conservative, Mosley had been the youngest MP in the Commons after winning the seat for Harrow in 1918. This was impressive enough. But when Charlie found out that Mosley had crashed out of the Royal Flying Corps in the year of his birth his idolatry was complete.

In 1922 Mosley won Harrow again, but as an Independent. It did not matter – his constituents adored him whatever flag he was flying. He and his lady wife received standing ovations when they graced constituency meetings. During his stint as a Labour MP, when he rose to pre-eminence as Chancellor of the Duchy of Lancaster, he spoke out on unemployment. His opportunism was a papal blessing on Charlie's huge ambitions.

The British Union of Fascists was vehemently anti-Communist – this was one in the eye for Brother Will and his commie convictions. They were anti-Semitic, too, which suited my grandfather fine. They were seething with resentment and sought redress in the wrong places. Mosley was ambitious without being prepared to put in any graft. Just like Charlie. Moreover he incited his followers to destabilize class barriers, to start up street riots and engender unfeasible conspiracy theories. Charlie enjoyed watching the thugs get excited. It made him – a man who would never dirty his hands – feel superior. As for intrigue and paranoia, he liked to spice things up a bit.

All good reasons to be a Fascist in Thirties' Britain. But to top it all, there was Mosley's godlike presence and startling charisma. He was dashing, dynamic and aristocratic – sex on legs to those of a disaffected or criminal bent. For these men, the real hierarchy of the British establishment aligned the aristocracy with the sons of feudal peasants. Just as Charlie worked the bottom end of the social scale, the upper classes were skimming the cream of the economy. Together they attempted to squeeze out the mugs in the middle. Mosley wanted to take on the world, the Jews, and anyone who opposed Free Trade or the Empire. Even if it meant spilling blood on the streets. Especially if it meant spilling blood on the streets.

On Sunday, 5 October 1936, in the East End of London, Brother Will fought the good fight alongside the gangster Jack 'Spot' Comer and the Communists at the Battle of Cable Street. They sent the Blackshirts packing. Brother Will had proved his credentials and was annoyingly triumphant. After their famous defeat, Mosley's forces decided to decamp to more favourable quarters in north-west London.

∎

Charlie was not alone on a Saturday night in 1937 when the Fascists came to Harlesden for a meet. He put on his black polo shirt and smartest black trousers, combed his moustache and made like he was part of the Union. He wasn't, of course; organized politics did not interest him. He just liked to look the part. And he did. Even twenty years later, on a day trip to dismal Dymchurch with his family, he sported the black shirt and bristling moustache of his hero.

Charlie stood slightly apart from the throng which had gathered around the Jubilee Clock in the town centre. Short and inconspicuous, he hung on to his indomitable sang-froid. A black amplifying van bristled with loudspeakers. Enter Sir Oswald. His bodyguards rose as one to make the Fascist salute.

In his smartly cut grey lounge suit – Charlie relished the details – and not forgetting his black shirt and tie, the great man climbed a ladder to the roof of the van. He ignored the chorus of jeers with imperious disdain. He roared, raved and gesticulated the crowd into a stunned silence, his voice echoing down the length of Harlesden High Street. His delivery was superb, his promises wonderfully reckless. The atmosphere was electric.

'Opportunity shall be open to all but privilege to none.

Great position shall be conceded only to those of great talent.' These were words designed to inflame Charlie's heart. The rest was about devoting yourself to the service of the British Nation, upholding the achievements that had existed 'gloriously for centuries before this transient generation, and which by our exertions shall be raised to its higher destiny – the Greater Britain of Fascism'. Whatever, there was something there for every misfit and bigot within hearing distance. Six people were arrested that night, all 'Communist sympathizers'.

When Mosley had finished, a clamouring mob of boys and girls waved their autograph books at him. He was as good as a film star.

He did more harm than he could ever know. Mosley was a star that had fallen. He was out of control – his overweening, unchecked self-confidence had turned him into a tyrant. I say this, because I see Charlie in him. Mosley's perversity of will and lack of self-knowledge legitimized the process of Charlie's dangerous descent into self-absorption. He already knew little of fear or apprehension or regret. Now he could see that it was better to do his worst, rather than suffer someone else's.

And like that other undernourished runt of the litter, Adolf Hitler, Charlie took heed of the power of pedagogy. He had seen the power of persuasion work for his headmaster at Church Farm. Now he was learning with Mosley, he saw how words could be treacherous. Mosley's crude promises spoke to the ignorant as well as for them. He reflected their basest passions. He brought himself down to their level without appearing to patronize them. Not to raise them, like Cartwright, but to debase them. All for his own ends.

Luckily, Charlie was too full of contradictions to be bothered with ideology. He was a monarchist but he despised the Royal Family. He resented the ruling classes, but longed to mix with them. He hated the Tories but was a right-wing extremist. More than anything, he was determined to make his own mark on his own terms. He would not be a foot-soldier for anyone, because he had to be a Mosley himself.

Since life was short and brutish he knew did not have much time. This sad fact had been brought home to him the previous Christmas Eve, when tragedy, in the shape of an omnibus, struck the Taylors. Brother Will, Harry and Charlie had been playing their favourite game on the dual carriageway of the North Circular Road. Although they were men now, they had the high spirits of little boys unfamiliar with their own mortality. Besides, there was money to be won in this game. The winner had to lie in the road until the last possible moment. Like King Canute he would dare the oncoming traffic to do its worst.

·

The North Circular Road had spread inexorably throughout the Thirties, splitting little districts like Stonebridge asunder and laying waste to streets and parklands. It was a road for the future and it promised a wider and happier outlook for every man, woman and child. It was upon these broad highways that the life of the nation would expand. When motorists hurried home from the industrial estates on its northernmost reaches they were travelling at fifty to sixty miles an hour. Houses, factories and schools were clumped together on the roadside, but there were no pedestrian cross-ings. The darkness, blind turnings and bottlenecks added to the danger. Questions were raised at the Commons, news-papers mounted campaigns. The Minister for Transport, Mr Hore-Belisha, said he would consider recommendations to apply a speeding limit. Schoolchildren on their way to Stone-bridge Infants' School lived in constant fear for their lives. All this added to the excitement of the Taylor boys' game.

Harry was the loser on that particularly foggy night. But then fog has a tendency to envelop all dark stories. He stayed prone till the last possible moment, but was hit by a skidding bus that had collided with a motor car in an attempt to avoid him. Somehow he got caught under the wheels, and his head, Charlie said, rolled down the North Circular Road. My grandfather always liked to end his anecdotes with a grisly flourish, like a magician pulling a dead rabbit out of his hat. Harry's death had a devastating effect on Brother Will. The passionate Communist developed a stammer, and won a new soubriquet – 'Stuttering Bill'.

Life and death left my grandfather cold, and he never revealed his true feelings about the death of Piccolo Pete. He did note, though, that Wag made an untimely and clumsy move on his brother's widow. He had just returned from Russia, where he had contracted pneumonia. He was living with Katie in the Tudorbethan Sudbury Court Estate. It wasn't as smart as 14 The Chine, being above a fish-and-chip shop, but the expense of Henry's funeral had forced a compromise.

■

Katie's boys had another brush with the law in 1937. Charlie was twenty years old when he was arrested for the second time with twenty-six-year-old Wag, who was growing more desperate as the years passed. The pair were charged with three offences. On 11 April the brothers had graduated to motor cars as a means of escape. The joy-ride began in Wembley courtesy of a Mr Samuel Gross, and lasted until the following day, when they drove all the way to East Barnet. Church Farm encouraged its old boys to keep in touch, holding annual open days for their reunions. Charlie was keen to join in. He wanted to show Mr Cartwright how well his old boy was doing in his motoring finery. While he was in the vicinity, he spotted an open window. He and Wag broke into the office of Mr Kenneth Henson, from whom they stole a typewriter, a rare and marvellous piece of machinery.

Charlie was arrested on April the unlucky 13th when he and Wag were found in possession of 'housebreaking implements' by night, back in Wembley. That's when the police found the car and the typewriter, and my grandfather was finally done for.

This time he was wise enough to plead guilty. Whereas Wag went the usual route and got twelve months' hard labour, Alfred was sentenced to three years' detention in Borstal.

They left their mother, once again, to fend for herself. But this time she had a grieving widow to cook and clean for her: Monk. All Katie had to do was gaze out of the window on to the Parade – not High Street, mind you – and reflect on what had once been a rural backwater where Irish farm-workers had come each year for the harvest. In the bad old days of the nineteenth century those unlucky Irish had slept in barns. Katie had an indoors lavatory now.

6 · The Quarry

Charlie's favourite stories from Portland Borstal concerned boys who had done a runner. He did not attempt it himself, the odds on being recaptured were too great, but he loved the vicarious thrill of the chase. He gloried in the bare-faced cheek of the boy who walked out of the prison grounds and ran into the deputy governor in the car park who then gave him a lift into town. Another boy, 'Sad Sam', was spotted in the undergrowth crawling his way out of the Quarry Stadium. A police dog was used to flush him out.

'It bit him in the arse,' roared Charlie.

The magistrate who sent my grandfather to Portland had decided that 'a period of Borstal training' was in order. He was wise enough to realize that contamination from older offenders was a problem, and that the stigma of Borstal was adhesive. But what else can be done when, by hook or by crook, a young man's thoughts turn to crime? He needn't have worried about Charlie. There were no basic human values for him. Man was capable of every bestiality; and all moral credos were heroic daydreams, if not the luxury of affluence. Charlie had only to look at the example of Holy Joe – who fled London for Bradford to become a bus driver – to know that he could never work in the conventional way for his upkeep. Those that did must be held in gentle contempt.

Portland was the soft option as far as Charlie was concerned. After sentencing, he was taken to the Borstal Collecting Centre, where he underwent a detailed examination by the Governor, doctors and voluntary Women Visitors. He was good at saying what they wanted to hear. A sob story and good intentions for the future are an important element in any criminal's bag of tricks. He was classified and dispatched to the end of the world as he knew it: Dorset.

■

The prison rose in sinister majesty like a medieval fortress. Its isolation amidst the surrounding rocky hills reinforced its air of impenetrability. Portland Prison had been turned into a Borstal in the Twenties after its large contingent of Sinn Fein prisoners had rioted against the harsh conditions of their imprisonment.

Although Charlie went in with his native cunning intact, his criminal veneer lacked the polish necessary to make it work for him. Thus far, he had been shaped by the clumsy efforts of his older brothers. And they were clearly on a mission to self-destruct. Charlie needed to buff up the sophistication he had acquired at Church Farm.

'If I were a modern Fagin, a professor of crime who wanted to breed hard, ruthless, merciless and desperate killers of criminals, I could not wish for a better academy than a Borstal institution,' said Billy Hill in his 1955 autobiography.

The Boss of Britain's Underworld was one of my grandfather's favourite books, and he bowed to Hill's hard-earned wisdom. He knew that without Portland he would never have learnt how to work the system. There, his elders and betters taught him how to exploit its weaknesses; and how to make up for his own.

In his book Hill describes the horrific regime of Portland. 'If you couldn't put up a good fight, [you'd] be well frigged.'

And if you don't know what 'frigged' means, he suggests you 'ask a sailor'.

Billy was put to work in the quarry. He was seventeen and a 'seasoned burglar and tough guy'. Since the age of fifteen he had been perfecting the craft of 'screwing', or breaking and entering. By the time he was nineteen he had his first mob, recruited, largely, from Portland. In the meantime, though, he was chipping stones.

My grandfather knew what it meant to chip stones, chop wood and work the treadmill. These were the tasks that echoed down the generations as the punishment of poverty. Because chipping stones and chopping firewood were what you did in the workhouse, which was where you were carted off to when there was nowhere else to go. Charlie's first duty as a father was to ensure that each of his three sons read Billy Hill's autobiography. He wanted his boys to know what he had saved them from.

'We had to carry loads of stone in baskets on our backs up a quarry face nearly ninety degrees steep. Every night our backs were washed down with iodine to prevent infection from the cuts, abrasions, sores and scabs. We were harnessed to trucks like horses, and we had to pull [them] along like beasts of burden.'

Charlie was clever, he managed to avoid the physical assaults of authority. But he saw what happened to his contemporaries at Portland Borstal. These boys were his friends, and they had coached him in the ways of the world. When they rebelled against the harshness of prison by running away, the governor sent for a special birch from the Home Office. It was soaked in brine to make it more pliable. The boy would be taken into the prison yard and handcuffed by his wrists, which were crossed above his head, and ankles. He was spread-eagled like a triangle when they gave him the strokes on his bare backside. He did not holler once as the birch sang through the air. He just bided his time in manly silence until he could get out and do his thing.

This kind of brutality was not going to be visited upon my grandfather. He got on board the Borstal train in time for rehabilitation, and made sure he got the best out of it. Even here, his beloved public-school system prevailed. It was just like Church Farm: cross-country running with the colours of his House on his arm, singing songs round the flag, and playing team sports in the old quarry. All he had to do was act contrite and keep his nose clean.

After eighteen months of perfectly acceptable bird, he was released on 'A' licence. The probationary services had decided to release him into the care of his sister, Doris. She could not bear to see her little brother, the first fruit of her nurturing instincts, in a striped uniform in the Borstal yard. She cried for him, and said nothing. They never talked together. They never had what others would call a relationship. They were strangers, always. But when he looked at her, he knew all about Doris. And she, with her trusting heart, knew all about him. And she forgave him. She and her two sons had faithfully made the long journey to Portland once a month, and finally took him home to 97 Aboyne Road, Neasden, on 8 November 1938.

7 · Penny Capitalist

Despite the fact that her husband loathed him, and her sons were contemptuous of his airs and graces, Doris made up a bed for Charlie in the boys' room. Her eldest, Bill, was sixteen, and Albert was fourteen. Bill was working for Harry Neal's building firm on a big contract in Wembley.

'Black Harry' was a highly successful patron of London's labourers. His nickname reflected his customary attire of black Homburg and black coat. He was a stickler for discipline; if you were caught smoking on site dismissal was instant, and he patrolled his territories on the length and breadth of the North Circular Road tirelessly. The Portland stone that had once been hacked by boys like Billy was now being transported in great slabs to the building sites of London. On this particular site, they were being erected into a depot for the Territorial Army. As an apprentice, Bill was earning fifteen shillings a week. Charlie muscled in as a yard foreman on a weekly wage of £4.

He did not spend it wisely. Friday was pay day, and Charlie would hand over a few shillings to Doris for his keep. He would then borrow it back, and buy a cap gun. He spent hours reeling off caps into the garden from the safety of his bedroom window. Bill and Albert were the Indian baddies and their twenty-two-year-old uncle was the cowboy. He threw coins on to Doris's neat lawn to get her boys to break from cover in the shrubs. As they scuttled out to retrieve them, he took fire. Bill and Albert had already worked out that their uncle was bad news.

Despite their youth, Albert and Bill were bigger and stronger than Charlie. They were not ashamed to use their muscle in order to earn their wages. Charlie knew from experience he was no match for him. Without the protection of Doris, his protector, he had to use guile as his means of gaining power. He delved for their secrets, for admissions of an emotional sore point. It wasn't just that he tried to embarrass their girlfriends. 'Do you love him?' he'd ask in a wheedling and knowing voice as the girl blushed to her roots. If he sensed the embers of a genuine emotion coming to light in their hearts he wanted to snuff it out as useless. They sensed that love and loyalty were dead wood for him. But these were simple lads with no time for his deceptively casual investigations. He was wasting his talents on them.

▪

The trouble with Charlie? You could not help but like him. That's what his nephews say, as though he were a naughty child just asking to be loved. But he was worse than that. He wanted your weaknesses; he worked you like a mark. For him, life and the people in it were opportunities waiting to be worked. But at least life was exciting as we basked in his shadow. He was a trickster: he ducked and dived, charmed and insinuated. He assumed characteristics that were not rightly his in order to find the chink in the other guy's wallet. That was the secret of his success. He used carefully acquired social and financial status to give his victims confidence in their transactions with him. More often than not, they would not even know they were involved in a transaction with him. That was the beauty of a really good con.

So Charlie could sweet-talk Doris into giving him more

than his due. She had 2s 6d a day for the family's food, and Charlie made sure he got the best. What was worse, whatever he did, and he did plenty that was bad, he could do no wrong in her eyes. Since she was nine years old she had bathed him, put him on the pot, and cut up his meat for him, as though he were her dolly. Bill and Albert had not seen the horrors of Carlyle Avenue. So Doris ignored the complaints of her husband and sons, and showered infinite patience on the Monkey.

On Saturday nights, my handsome young grandfather would spend hours preparing himself for his big night out at the Hammersmith Palais on Edgware Road. He practised his patter in front of the mirror. Out came the polka-dot bow tie and trilby so necessary to lure the girls out from underneath the palm trees that encircled the dance floor. He relished the chase and derided the conquest. He never brought his girls home; there was no room for manoeuvres in Neasden.

The girls lapped up his heart-warming honesty, and vowed to take him under their wing. He told them about his wild days as a boy who fought six rounds all-comers for five bob a time. How he didn't want to end up like his slap-happy brothers with a pair of tin ears. You've got to keep showing how good you are, he told them, you've got to put on an act.

But this isn't the real me, he lied. Maybe we want the same things. Maybe the demurely smiling Flos and Idas reminded him of what he'd missed. The little house, roses in the front garden, turnips round the back. He'd never had what you'd call a real home. He was so disarming.

Survival made him competitive. By the time other men had worn their shoes out whisking their partner round the dance floor, Charlie had left his in an alley where he had enjoined her to partake in a knee-trembler.

Anyway, he had more important business to attend to. The foreman at Wembley was a mug. Black Harry's accountant travelled round the various jobs on the outskirts of London to audit the cash on site. Each foreman retained the necessary cash to pay the men's wages. Charlie convinced him that, together, they could make a killing on crown and anchor.

The game of crown and anchor, or chuck-a-luck, was a favourite with prisoners, soldiers and Charlie. Its origins lie on nineteenth-century Mississippi riverboats, where moustachioed cardsharps ruthlessly exploited the hopeless odds. All you need are three dice and a cloth, all bearing six symbols: a heart, a spade, a club, a diamond, a crown and an anchor. Charlie would spread the cloth on a table or, more commonly, on the ground. The men placed their bets on the cloth and crouched round it expectantly. They had to decide which symbol would appear on the throw of the dice. Charlie was the bank. He paid even money if the punter threw a single, two to one on pairs, and three to one on three of a kind. He was raking it in because the true odds against the combinations were 35 to 19 for a single, 25 to 2 for a pair, and 215 to 1 for three of a kind. By the end of the game, he had the foreman in his pocket.

Flushed with success, they took the game round the pubs of Neasden on Saturday afternoons. At around closing time Charlie would lay the cloth on the pavement outside the entrance to the public bar. The capital laid down by the foreman in the shape of the labourers' wages was doubled, tripled and quadrupled time after blissfully easy time.

∎

Street-betting was rife in Thirties' London, and 'penny capitalists', or illegal bookmakers, organized sweeps and ran small books for their workmates during the lunch hour before the dogs started racing. Joe Coral, a Polish Jew, was penniless when he arrived in Dalston, east London, in 1912. After a spell as a bookie's runner he realized that 'the English will always back their fancy', no matter how unlikely their chances of winning. He was also quick to realize that the stake money usually stopped with the bookmakers. By the Sixties his shops would be all over London.

So Charlie's next move was to try his hand at illegal bookmaking. The business usually passed on from father to son. But a lone bookie, new to the scene, and unprepared to work his way up, would not gain the support of his rivals. Bookies needed mutual support in order to defray expenses in the rare event of a pay-out. The Royal Ascot meet of 1939 put paid to Charlie's dreams. With such long prices in the betting, one lucky punter who won a few pounds on a rank outsider immediately put him out of business. His guile was getting him nowhere.

·

At last, the sirens that signal war started their wailing on 3 September. Charlie was delighted. He finally had the chance to prove himself – as a gentlemanly scoundrel from a reputable school. He had played on the same cricket fields as public schoolboys so why couldn't he join them at war? He wanted so desperately to go up in the world that his delusions got the better of him, and he applied to the RAF. Within their aerial embrace, he had decided, he could prove his worth as a gunner.

His nephews, who had previously served as target practice, laughed at the news of his rejection. As if the RAF would take on a Borstal boy. Charlie's advances were declined, his criminal record cited.

This was the last time my grandfather's social superiors would rebuff him. When Brother Will suggested he come along to join the Army, he went along for the bus ride into town. He knew Will had some money on him, and hoped he might be able to prise it from him. He didn't. So he left him at the door of the recruitment centre. It was back to Black Harry, whose men were busy building tank traps on the north and west routes into the capital. Invasion was expected any day.

Charlie was deployed at Beaconsfield. Together with Bill, he was building huts for the RAF. How galling it must have been, to be digging the earth as a labourer when he should have been shooting at Jerries in the sky. He was beginning to feel cramped by his sister's neat little house. Neasden was a dead and alive place. Doris was so ferociously houseproud that Brother Will, with his clomping boots and muddy trousers, was too frightened to sit down when he paid a visit.

One wintry wet morning in 1940, Charlie and Bill got off the train at Beaconsfield station, where they waited for the driver to take them to the site. 'It's no go,' he said to the waiting men. 'The site's under water.' They all trooped on to the next train back to London. The carriage was full of office girls. Bill started chatting one up. Charlie moved in on her, mimicking Bill's gruff manners and putting on airs of his own. Bill looked daggers at the Monkey.

'Oh, you want fisticuffs, do you?' sneered Charlie in his pseudo-posh voice.

Bill was slippery as an eel and his boots and fists were everywhere at once. He left his uncle sprawling at the feet of the jeering navvies and office girls. Charlie never went to Beaconsfield again.

Instead, he went back to mother. Katie was still in the flat with Wag and Monk over the fish-and-chip shop in Sudbury. Charlie slept on the sofa in the front room. He went back to the streets with his crown and anchor board, and soon ended up back in court.

This time he was the plaintiff. But then he hadn't studied at Portland Academy for nothing. On 15 March 1940 the *Wembley News* reported that Alfred Taylor, an 'unemployed carpenter's labourer', had brought a summons for assault against two brothers, Daniel and Samuel Springer. The Springers were turf accountants based in Wembley. Charlie claimed that they owed him £15 2s 6d, the profits on a bet he had laid with them.

Charlie went to collect his winnings, the terrifying figure of Wag in tow. Despite Wag's knotty scar and towering presence, the Springers refused to pay. Later that day, they passed Charlie in their motor-car as he was hanging about. They threatened him with iron car-jacks and Samuel sprang at his throat.

Whether his complaint was a real one is hard to say. The defence suggested that Charlie was blackmailing the brothers into paying him money they did not owe. 'No,' he protested, 'I have lost pounds with these men.' The magistrate threw his case out of court. His first attempt to turn the system to his advantage had failed.

■

Elsewhere in London, other members of my family were doing their bit for the war.

Charlie had not yet followed the Harrow Road into west London proper, where the Kinghams resided at Paddington. This was where his future sister-in-law, my great-aunt Dolly, was putting up the shutters against bomb blasts at Lyons' Corner House on Marble Arch. It was here that she served on tables as a 'Nippie'. Her sister, Lily, was keeping house for Special Constable Georgie Vundum in a quiet street off Paddington Green. She had just offloaded her seven-year-old daughter, Greta Ann, once again. This time, my mother was boarding a train to Wales at Paddington Station. Like the other evacuees she was done up like a brown paper parcel to be dispatched from the terrors of the Blitz.

Even Alfred could evade his true destiny no longer. He was called up on 18 April 1940 to serve as a private in the 1st Battalion of the Royal Sussex Regiment.

For the second time in his life he was forcibly removed from his natural environment by an institution indifferent to his plans for self-advancement. He was sent to Newhaven on the south coast of England, where the training of drafts for overseas battalions was carried out. At least he could be satisfied that his regiment had a glorious history of repelling invasion by sea. First it had been Napoleon, now the Germans were the threat. Usually, the choppy waters of the Channel were enough to repulse attack. In case of fair weather, Charlie was there along with the rest of his battalion.

Their camp overlooked Newhaven harbour at the mouth of the River Ouse. The new recruits paraded their weapons and marched in time to the drill. Charlie was bored. Views of the swollen Downs were all very charming but they couldn't help him. After four months in the company of square-bashers he was given some leave and on 22 August he was back in Wembley chancing his arm again.

The complainant was Mr Hirst, the foreman on a site in Alperton where a gang of nine men were employed constructing drains to some ARP trenches. Hirst saw two men who had worked for him previously lurking behind a hedge. Later, he found the window of the contractor's hut had been smashed. He looked around him and saw two men running away with an attaché-case full of the labourers' wages.

Only Wag appeared in court, but he wasn't going to be left in the lurch. He told the court that he had met a friend at Sudbury Town station at 3 p.m. They went, as was their custom, to the Majestic cinema and came out at 6.30 p.m.

Wag told prosecution that he couldn't remember which film he saw, and I believe this is the only truth he ever told. He saw five or six programmes a week, he explained that day. I doubt if any of them had any lasting impact. Cultural artefacts were just that to the Taylors, objects that were not worth retaining because they could not be converted into cash. Wag went to the cinema to be enveloped in comforting darkness – so as not to have to think, and in order to facilitate some slap and tickle with his friend. Mrs Isobel Heydeman was the friend who obligingly appeared in court to confirm that she met Wag every Friday in time for the matinée performance. Since Wag protested his innocence from the start, there was no need for Charlie to get involved, and, for once, the Taylor boys got away with it.

■

No one knows what my grandfather did during the war, because no one was brave enough to ask him. It can be said, though, that in the summer of 1940 Charlie's regiment was waiting it out on the cliffs of southern England. But Charlie had no argument with the Germans. His sympathies lay with the National Socialists, and he admired the ruthless efficiency and go-getting vigour of Hitler's invading forces. In contrast, the men in Charlie's battalion were the sleepy, country-bumpkin sons of Sussex farmers. The straw was literally hanging out of their mouths, he would say, as they took their turns at sentry duty.

They weren't his kind of guy, and this wasn't his kind of action. Passivity enraged my grandfather: he missed the quick-witted opportunism of his London peers.

In October 1940 Charlie's battalion were shipped off to fight in the North Africa campaign under the command of General Wavell. The sandy-haired farmers joined the black-bearded Sikhs in the 7th Brigade of the 4th Indian Division near Cairo. Quentin Reynolds of the *Daily Express* was impressed: 'They were out of a book, this regiment. [The book] might have been written by Kipling. I have never seen fighters like it in my life. Every night they would go out and bring in Huns and Itis . . . The First Royal Sussex showed that they are quite fit to stand with the great British regiments of the past.'

After a few months in the Western Desert they moved south for the overthrow of the Italians in Eritrea and Abyssinia. Their overthrow was completed on 9 April 1941 when 550 officers and 10,000 Italian and native troops laid down their arms. One incident went unreported, but Charlie heard about it from the single friend he made in the regiment, a fellow Londoner – Davey Perkins from Marylebone, tank transporter to the regiment.

Davey Perkins – always keen to get to the kill of a story. 'Half-pint', they called him. He was a jolly little fellow whom Charlie dressed up in a chauffeur's uniform and put behind the wheel of his Rolls. Davey's street-smart wit and frank good nature were invaluable when roping in prospective suckers. He soon learnt to jump when Charlie spoke. He also learnt to turn a blind eye to Charlie's treachery because he knew he was on to a good thing. The story he told his future patron concerned one of the taciturn farmers whom Charlie used to mock.

On the night of the 7th, the Royal Sussex encountered a troop of tanks, which, to their surprise, retreated before their small-arms fire. Charlie relished the irony that this peculiarly dull-witted farmer had captured a three-man tank single-handedly. Slow of reflex and short on imagination, Farmer Giles was more used to implementing rapidly barked orders than using his initiative and taking prisoners. Indecision was more fearful and strange to him than enemy fire. As each man emerged, hands in the air, to surrender, the sudden realization that he was in control of this novel situation went to his head. He counted the three soldiers off with his pistol.

If he hadn't shot them dead he would have got a medal, said Charlie. But these things happen in war all the time, because war does not foster respect for life and death, and a man cannot predict how he will act when his blood is up.

Charlie did not take part in Wavell's famous campaign. He was stationed in a Holding and Dispersal Unit at Folkestone, on the south coast of England. Within sight of the Martello towers built as defence against Napoleon, my grandfather was detained in a camp for reluctant conscripts. As a father of two sons in the spartan Fifties, and the only man on his street with a car, he would take the boys to this dismal spot for days out. He pointed out the rifle range and military camp. They sat on a low wall overlooking the marshland. Charlie gestured at the point where the blustering, grey sky met its mirror image in the sea, and told them the story of the German fighter plane that came in very low, and very fast.

It was a blinding, bright day in his mind's eye, and 'Everything opened up to shoot him down.' But Fritz dodged the ack-ack, using the sun for cover.

'No one could touch him. He shot down two Hurricanes, did a victory roll and went back to France.'

Charlie had given this incident some thought, and had concluded that it was not a reconnaissance flight. He had formed the impression that the daredevil pilot firing the skies with his bravura was drunk, or on a joy-ride. He was impressed with the German's reckless bravery, and triumphed with him as the whole coast opened up but missed.

·

One important feature of Sunday afternoons in the Seventies was Laurence Olivier's sonorous voice doling out the sad facts of war. We watched in hushed reverence as the archive footage showed a scene outside the Polish ghetto at curfew.

A Nazi soldier grabs a little boy by the scruff of his neck, holds him in the air and shakes him until all the vegetables he has secreted under his coat have fallen to the ground. Charlie is enraged at his own impotence and attacks the television with his bare fists.

.

On 2 June 1941 twenty-five-year-old Charlie found time to get married. His bride was nineteen-year-old Evelyn and she had several features that recommended her. She was blonde; she was a WAAF; she was based with the RAF at Hendon; and her father was a motor fitter. She fitted the bill, and her family lived in suburban Greenford, which boasted lime trees and sedate respectability.

Charlie had met her at an RAF dance at Hendon that he gate-crashed whilst on leave from training. His secret compulsion to be part of the élite drove him to loiter in Hendon. So much of his life was spent prowling the streets of London, just biding his time, waiting to pounce.

That night, Evelyn's fair hair was frizzed into sausage curls, and she was tightly packed into dove-grey. When he spotted her, she was dancing with a sergeant. When she spotted him, she noted the glint in his eyes. The bandleader announced the 'Excuse Me'. Charlie made the most of his five foot six frame and three-inch chest expansion.

He tapped the sergeant abruptly on the shoulder. The sergeant muttered an expletive, but custom prevailed and Charlie insisted on excusing him from the privilege of treading on Evelyn's toes. Her hefty partner was replaced by a handsome young survivor of the Luftwaffe's vicious assault on the south coast. That's what he told her, anyway.

For the first time in his life, Charlie took a girl home to

meet Doris in her spick and span house in Neasden. She had nothing, but the house was spotless as only a working-class house can be. Charlie liked things that way. He liked to watch the fussing woman catering to his every need. He did not dare take Evelyn to Katie's, where the tea chests were overflowing with black market tea and sugar.

Doris's son, Albert, was given a shilling to be a good boy and go to the pictures. Giggly Evelyn perched on Charlie's lap in the front room. She fancied him a ringer for Don Ameche. He encouraged her whimsy by adopting the Hollywood film star's trademark moustache, thicker and more virile than Mosley's, and flamboyantly cheeky bow tie. The black shirt was at the back of the cupboard for now.

Charlie and Evelyn's wedding took place at the registry office in Hendon, within sight of the RAF base. Charlie stands proud in his uniform between his mother and his beautiful bride. It was the best day of his life, his new wife believed in him, and if enough people believed in him, the lies he told them would surely come true. Katie encouraged him in his delusions. Girls were there to be gulled, and men to be cheated, so who is to say that Charlie wasn't what he said he was?

Under 'Rank or Profession' on the marriage certificate, Alfred described himself as a man of 'independent means'. Gullible, nineteen-year-old Evelyn was a more modest, and honest, 'clerk'. This wedding was a new beginning for Charlie, who wanted to turn his back on a family mired in squalid petty crime. All Evelyn had to do was go along with it. She must not gainsay him, or challenge him in any way.

There was one thing missing from his calculations, though, the city that shaped his movements.

The joyful couple repaired to 140 Hill Rise, Greenford, for their honeymoon night. A privet hedge marking the boundary of his house showed the working-class motor-fitter had made good. From the upstairs window of the front bedroom Charlie was pleased to see an orderly row of detached houses. Each had its own bay window and porched entrance. Yew trees undulated in the breeze upwards and onwards to Sudbury.

From the window of the bedroom at the back of the house, he looked on to the old, familiar sights of urban desolation. Even here, London's voracious railway lines and their hurtling business intruded on the peaceful scene. To the east, if he cared to look, lay the bomb sites of Hanger Lane and Perivale. Beyond them, he espied the industrial estates of Park Royal where his father had once stoked coal.

Frustration set in. There was no room for a man to manoeuvre when there were constant reminders of his past beyond the wide-open avenues of Greenford, and his country was making unreasonable demands on his future. Evelyn's family became suspicious of their son-in-law's frequent periods of leave from his regiment. Charlie's impromptu evasions and wild excuses did not fool a canny motor-fitter.

Number 140 was the pebble-dashed embodiment of economic security. But Charlie's flight hadn't taken him that far, and his new class status was not strictly his. His wife's family were somewhat disconcerted when they realized that they were expected to provide for him. Before their very eyes, the charming veneer that their son-in-law had initially presented gave way to a core of uncouth resistance to the banalities of daily life. He could not keep up with his own propaganda.

PART TWO · CHARLIE

Before the Romans came to Rye, or off to Severn strode,
The rolling English drunkard made the rolling English road,
A reeling road, a rolling road, that rambles through the shire
And after him the parson ran, the sexton and the squire,
A merry road, a mazy road, and such as we did tread,
The night we went to Birmingham by way of Beachy Head.

· · ·

My friends we will not go again or ape an ancient rage,
Or stretch the folly of our youth to be the shame of age
But walk with clearer eyes and ears this path that wandereth
And see undrugged in evening light, the decent inn of death;
For there is good news yet to hear and fine things to be seen
Before we go to Paradise by way of Kensal Green.

G. K. Chesterton 'The Rolling English Road'

8 · Good-time Girl

All Charlie had learnt from army life thus far was confirmation of what he already knew: look after number one. The girl from Greenford was not prepared to accept her husband's refusal to fight for his country. Besides this, she soon found out why he had not joined his regiment at the Front.

He could just about put up with the cross-country runs in full kit. He quite enjoyed putting on a killing snarl and making a fearsome roar at bayonet practice. But sweeping out the NAAFI was beneath him. And Charlie was irrepressible, even under the strictest regime.

Back at base, the Holding Unit's CO was bemused to find all the taps missing from the washroom when he went to perform his daily ablutions. He later found out that they had been sold to a local builder. The sergeant noted that tins of beans were going walkabout from the mess. The CO's wife was alarmed to find her prize begonias had disappeared from her garden overnight.

She did not see them again until sweaty, breathless Private 6404316 came rushing to tell her that they were on sale at a nearby village's garden fête. She gave him the money to buy them back, plus a small tip and lavish praise for his diligence and concern. From such small beginnings did my grandfather's capacity for conning grow.

Charlie was clever at manipulating the army's rules. Each time he was placed on a course, he would go absent without leave after the first week, making sure he gave himself up by the end of the second. By giving himself up by the end of the second week, he only got seven days' solitary. His reasoning in this, if nothing else, was solid: by failing a course, he could not be sent to fight. And if he could not fight, he wouldn't get killed. When he came out of solitary, and they gave him a job, say painting fences, he made it last. And when they placed him on the next course, he simply repeated the procedure.

In this way, my grandfather spent more time wandering the streets of blacked-out London than at his post, because as a newly married man he was also entitled to privilege leave. (Always remember, by the by, to sell your railway warrant, and dodge the train fare by hiding in the khazi.)

The first eight months of Charlie's war passed quite painlessly. By 1942, Britain had amassed the biggest army it had ever fielded, but she was about to lose one of her six million soldiers. On 22 February Charlie went AWOL, and this time he was not coming back.

An army padre had accompanied him to Neasden in an attempt to patch up his marriage with Evelyn. Charlie had been informed that she was pregnant and used this momentous event to gain compassionate leave. Doris put the padre in the best bedroom. Charlie slept on the couch in the front room. When she took him his morning cup of tea, he had gone.

■

Harrow Road was once a crooked horse track used by the Celts. There is no plan to its meanderings, although it roughly mimics the contours of the Grand Union Canal. It loops and reels from the village green of Harrow to the village greens of Kensal and Westbourne and the lushly forested cemetery in between. The Red Lion Inn, where

Shakespeare was said to have acted as a strolling player, squats on its junction with Edgware Road. Footpads and highwaymen congregated here in the eighteenth century. But the opening of the Grand Union Canal in 1801 and of the Great Western Railway thirty years later, with its terminus in the heart of the parish, brought about an entire change. From here the Harrow Road begins its flirtation with the great estates of Paddington and Marylebone – skirting the corners of Harewood, Cleveland, Colville, and Connaught Squares. It is almost as though the road itself senses it has no place amongst these high-born names, because it finally peters out at the shabby, ancient green in Paddington where the festival of May Day was celebrated.

Jack-in-the-Green would lead a group of youths each enshrouded in bowers of leaves in the ritual felling of trees. Their trunks were erected as maypoles, and the dancing would begin, enacting the triumph of spring over winter's harshness. On this green, at numbers 11–12, my maternal great-grandfather, Alfred Kingham, attended meetings of the Paddington Radical Working Men's Club. For him, May Day was a celebration of the first congress of the Second International.

He would have known Harrow Road as a monstrously tentacled snake that slithered down north-west London. Floodlit factories clung to its shanks, and workers would disembark briefly before being sucked into their orbit. When they came out again they fell into one of the many pubs that neighboured the factories. To his wife and children's chagrin, Alfred Kingham was viciously drunk by the time he had stepped off the Harrow Road. But Alfred Kingham was long since dead, and his political tirades died with him.

The floodlights were dimmed the night Alfred Taylor walked the length of Harrow Road. He found preparations afoot, measurements being staked out. The railroad, the

Underground and the motor-car would soon traverse and make redundant the old byways that ran round this road. Bridges that had barely been begun, he found freshly bombed and desolately reaching across to one another over waste-land and dirty streams. Fragments of embankment had been thrown up, and left as precipices for children to jump from. Along the freezing road, and through the night, Charlie made his way to the west.

By sunrise he had reached Paddington Basin, where the Grand Union and Regent's Canals unite under the umbrella of the Great Western Terminus. This is where I was born, in St Mary's Hospital on Praed Street, which runs outside the main entrance of Paddington Station and leads directly to Edgware Road. From here it is a short distance to a dingy cul-de-sac called Cato Street. Its dilapidated Victorian blocks were set apart from the rest of Marylebone by low archways in the façades at either end. This enclosure, typical of the nineteenth century, was designed to shut off the poor from the more wholesome streets around them. It was a street fit for conspirators and ne'er-do-wells.

My mother was born in a tenement block on this street in 1933, as was her mother twenty years earlier. My great-grandparents, Alfred and Emily Kingham, had converged on these two poky rooms in Windsor Buildings at the turn of the twentieth century. They had high hopes for their new life together. Emily Smith, a lady's maid, came from Southend-on-Sea in Essex, and had seen the world; Alfred Kingham was a house-painter from the village of Flitwick in Bedfordshire.

Paddington Station is the gateway into London from western England, north and south Wales, the Cotswolds and Shakespeare Country. Many a Dick Whittington has gazed up at its oppressive arched roof, then delved into the covered subways and down to the London Underground. It attracts those on the run. Escape routes run parallel at different levels leading on to Harrow Road, the Grand Union Canal and railway tracks. The canal is sunk in silt, the road paved above it dips up and down in time with the tracks. Slums are caught up in the interstices, linked by alleys and footpaths. Their dwellings are lower-middle-class tumble-downs where clerks and grocers lie cheek by jowl with stables.

In 1913 when Lillian Maud Kingham was born, Cato Street was labouring under a different classical reference. The residents of its mews houses had voted on a change of name, so that Cato became Horace for the next 110 years. Their reasons were understandable; they were patriots and tradesmen loyal to their country. So any guilt by association with the Cato Street Conspirators must be expunged. For them at least, the events that had taken place on 23 February 1820 in that unremarkable alleyway never happened.

On that evening, a detachment of the Coldstream Guards left their barracks in Portman Street. Under the command of Lieutenant Frederick Fitzclarence, the bastard son of the Duke of Clarence, they marched up the Edgware Road, turning right before the junction with Marylebone Road. In the deepening gloom, they perceived what seemed to be a blind alley, called Cato Street. This was their destination.

At the other end of the alley, which only seemed blind because its entrance was obscured by an arch, Constable George Ruthven of the Bow Street Runners was also waiting with a dozen other policemen in tow. They watched as, in dribs and drabs, twenty conspirators mounted the ladder leading into the hayloft to join their leader. They watched as a local shoemaker called John Brunt arrived blatantly armed with a sabre. Ruthven and his men crept into the stable. Inside it was pitch-black. As their eyes grew accustomed to the dark the boys in blue realized that the large, shapeless bundles they had nearly crashed into were, in fact, piles of pikes, muskets, hand-grenades, gunpowder, swords and staves.

Upstairs in the hayloft Arthur Thistlewood, an estate agent and revolutionary enthusiast, was preparing his co-conspirators for the slaughter of the entire cabinet of the Earl of Liverpool's Government. Their king was ailing and his kingdom was troubled. Jacobin scares and Luddite fears fuelled the people's discontent with their desperate conditions. The government was fearful of revolution. Worse, there was a new philosophy abroad, and it derived from the writings of Tom Paine and the pamphleteer Thomas Spence. Under cover of night, Arthur and his friends would walk the streets of London, chalking slogans on the walls: 'Spence's Plan and Full Bellies' or 'The Land is the People's Farm'.

At six minutes past eight on 1 May 1820 Arthur Thistlewood, William Davidson, Victor Ings, Richard Tidd and John Brunt were hung by the neck at Newgate Prison. They were spared the ordeal of drawing and quartering, both of which might have proved too provoking for the anti-Government crowd. Thousands had congregated before the gaol and as the doomed men were brought to the gallows a great shout went up: 'God Almighty bless you.' Tidd gave three cheers and carried on sucking an orange. Ings shouted back, 'I'm not afraid to go before God or man.' Davidson bowed, and said nothing. Thistlewood turned to him and muttered: 'We shall soon know the last grand secret.'

So when Lily was born, it was on Horace Street, though her father told her the story. He was proud that his family should be living on a street where radicals had once conferred. His wife was proud, too, though in a different way. Her family, who owned a tea-room on the front at Southend, had disowned Emily for marrying beneath them. She had travelled the world with a lady aristocrat, had been to South Africa, India and Australia. What was she doing in two rooms in a tenement block with a house-painter and six children?

On Guy Fawkes' Night, 1925, she may well have asked herself the same question. On 5 November she went to the yard he rented on Exmoor Street to take him his lunch. She found her husband stone cold dead on the floor. His precious tools had been stolen. Alfred Kingham, the forty-eight-year-old housepainter, had succumbed to cerebral haemorrhage and bronchitis. Emily and her children had joined the hopeless ranks of London's widows and orphans.

All Lily remembered of being told her father had died was the sight and sounds of fireworks dismantling the night. The bare facts were brought home to her, though, when it became clear that Emily could not cope. Lily was twelve and her sister Irene six when they were sent to the Hammersmith and Chiswick Refuge for Friendless Girls.

No one knows what happened to Lily for the next five years, but for the rest of her life she had a horror of institutions, and lived in fear of going mad. It was called a refuge but felt like a workhouse. It spelt the end of respectability. So Emily's dread of poverty and disgrace was visited on her young daughters, and Lily never spoke about it again.

.

When she came out all she wanted to do was dance. And she did. She even won trophies for the rumba and fox trot. Despite the hardships of her childhood, she was a giddy, fun-loving girl. She was pretty and buxom with soft brown hair and hazel eyes which she used to great effect to get what she wanted. Tears were to be her weapon in life.

We all know what happens to girls who like to dance. When Lily fell pregnant at twenty the crying did not stop till the unwanted child was born. The father had fled. Her brother suspects he was the Master of Ceremonies at the Hammersmith Palais – the one who had given her a trophy.

On 4 August 1933 Lily promptly handed Greta Ann to her mother, who had just had her own child, also by an unknown hand. Emily and her seven children plus granddaughter were still living in two rooms at Windsor Buildings. My great-uncle George, who was ten years old, collected and sold firewood to keep the new babies warm. The oldest girl, Dolly, would go round the local bakeries at the end of each day asking for unsold bread.

In that same year there was good news for the elder Kingham girls. The Cumberland Hotel had just risen from a site next to Marble Arch. It was bound on all sides by grand streets – Oxford Street, Old Quebec Street, Bryanston Street and Great Cumberland Place. The venture had been a formidable one. The excavations alone entailed the removal of over 100,000 cubic yards of archaeological relics. But the Cumberland's owners were unconcerned with the dusty past; they were looking to the future.

Every modern notion in luxury and comfort had been studied in earnest. Guests were taken to their rooms in lifts of burnished steel. Dolly was given the prestigious position of silver service waitress. She whisked across the parquet-flooring of the dining-room, balancing silver platters on her sturdy forearms. Sliding round the marble pillars, she kicked open the service door to the subterranean galleys with a jaunty swing of the hips. Dolly sang and whistled while she worked. She was happiest when busy. Lily was more ladylike and dreamy. She adored her smart black uniform with white lace trim. To show it off to best effect, she sashayed around the Grill Room in time to the foxtrot rhythms she constantly rehearsed in her head.

Their youngest sister, Irene, did not take to the performance art of catering. On her first morning as a chambermaid, she took tea and biscuits up to a famous Hollywood star in the Cumberland's bridal suite. She opened the door and found him draped across his bed, stark naked.

'Hop in, why don't you?' he grinned.

She ran screaming from the hotel, and her next job was pulling a baker's cart around the streets of Paddington. Which is where she met Charlie in 1943.

He had been busy, too, since going AWOL the year before. He had no identity card and no ration book. He was on the run from the Red Caps, and constantly on the move. After sleeping in the underground shelter at Paddington Station for a few nights, he got the all-clear from Doris. The padre had gone and the Military Police had stopped calling.

He went back to Neasden for a good night's kip on the sofa. The next day he was walking down Aboyne Road with Bill when they spotted two blokes behind them. They weren't locals, so Charlie told Bill: 'You carry on walking; I'll run home and jump over the fence at the back of the house.'

He borrowed a few bob from Doris and was gone. This time to Sudbury, where Katie had recently made her one and only appearance in court for hitting a policeman. She raised a laugh from the gallery when she called him 'a dirty Gespato'. A small fine ensued and she was back fiddling ration-books and fencing stolen goods.

It was at this point, while Wag was secreted in a dungeon in Whitehall for refusing to join his regiment, that Monk died of cancer. It was the only time in his life that Wag allowed himself to cry.

Katie's flat was too hot for Charlie so he took up with a Sudbury character called Horace Barns. His bad back disqualified him from the Army, and he helped out deserters by renting out his identity papers. He was a kind man who served up powdered egg and fried bread for breakfast for the boys who were resolute in their refusal to go to the Front.

Here they could snatch a few hour's sleep on the front-room divan, and jump out of the back window into the mist of Sudbury golf course before the Red Caps came calling at dawn.

Charlie's new outlook on life was based entirely on observation. His brothers were no use to him, dab hands though they were with the buckle-end of a roadmender's belt. Horace was someone who could be useful. He agreed with Charlie that their country didn't need his sort. Whenever Charlie felt the faint spark of patriotism that faltered within him, he had only to remember his father's generation of unemployed ex-servicemen, some of them legless or armless. Throughout his youth, he repeated endlessly, he had seen them begging on the streets of Willesden, cap in hand. Not that he had ever had a youth, he complained. The Germans and Itis had taken that away. So he pondered his future over Horace's breakfast, and decided it was all out for number one.

.

War suited my grandfather. He soon learnt to duck at the sight of a Red Cap. Soldiers of all nationalities were playing hookey on the streets of London. They had joined up for action, not for wasting their time making daisy-chains in camps where the only foreigners were harmless yokels. Dodging Red Caps gave them an interest in life. You had to know your manor well and lead the MPs a merry dance around the back streets. Once he had given them the slip he would join the congregation of Toms, Dicks and Harrys in a pin-table saloon on the Harrow Road end of the North Circular or the Ace café at Paddington railway station.

Charlie is part of London's folklore. His polka-dot bow tie, burnt-cork moustache and trilby hat marked him out as a spiv. Like a prostitute, he could be summoned from his patch on a street corner. The crown-and-anchor board was whipped out. In no time at all he could gather fifteen to twenty men on Wembley Hill. Inside the smart houses around them housewives were raising money for charity in whist drives. They were willing to do business with Charlie, too. They could trade food coupons for soap, washing-powder, razor-blades, toothpaste and cosmetics. It added a frisson to their utilitarian lives.

Almost everyone participated in what David Hughes, in his essay 'The Spivs', calls 'pale hangdog spivvery'. It took place 'in back kitchens and at the rear of shops'. The risk was worth it, because it was on such a small scale it was untraceable. Everything was in short supply. Household goods, food, whisky, tobacco, wood, cement, petrol. Lily and her sisters were staining their legs with tea-leaves in place of stockings. Dolly, who had the neatest hand, would draw a line in charcoal up the backs of their calves in order to replicate a seam. But you had to be careful if it rained. So it was just a case of people employing their ingenuity and furtively trying to buy that little bit extra. And for those who were cynical and indifferent to others' needs to capitalize on the shortfall.

My grandfather was exactly this kind of man. For him, nothing was any trouble. He was ready to oblige and impossible to offend. The kind of fellow who would swear away his own grandmother for a packet of Woodbines.

So what did Charlie do in the war? He sold you a pup, fiddled your dole and stole your girl in the blink of a flashing eye. He might take her to the dogs, or jitterbugging at the Palais de Danse where the décor was bright and breezy. There was fun to be had in this war. Under the bright lights and with the gentle encouragement of a smooth-talking MC he could wrap a girl round his little finger.

Once he'd got her, his advances were crude: a favour

bestowed, drinks and cigarettes bought, then a lunge. At this stage the girl would act offended.

'Is this the thanks I get?' he would demand.

'What more do you want?' she'd counter.

'Plenty.'

If they were getting serious, he might take her to the spare room in his mother's flat in Sudbury where they could get to know each other a bit better.

To put Charlie's activities into perspective it is necessary to understand a basic economic fact. From spring 1942 one man was allowed to buy one overcoat once every seven years. This would have hurt a man like my grandfather. Threadbare clothes were something he felt he had put behind him. So he had no choice: only the black market could keep up with his demands. As long as Charlie continued to evade the Red Caps he would flourish.

■

By his own admission Billy Hill had a 'fantastic' war. Master criminals had their hands full recruiting deserters with bribes or threats. With Hill's organizational expertise, he had a ready supply of young men willing to carry a gun or act as look-out. By the end of the war, he had so many men working for him on smash-and-grab raids that he had to put them on a rota. He was making £3,000 a week. His closest friend, though, was still his knife, a 'well-sharpened knife with a five-inch blade' that never left him.

Between the wars, the old 'rough house' gangs which had terrorized the poorer districts of the city had been decimated by an increasingly efficient police force. In their place arose more sophisticated gangs, such as Hill's, who paid protection money to the police out of the profits they made from illegal gambling and bank jobs and prostitution. Tots and Harry had been shaped by the rough house model; Charlie believed in organization.

His war wasn't going too badly, despite the birth of a daughter on 20 September 1942. Rosemary Linda Janet was born in Harrogate, where her mother had fled. By this time, though he thought himself perfectly honest, not one of his friends, or family, could trust him. In his turn, Charlie scorned the pipe-smoking, rose-growing aspirations that Evelyn held for him. He wanted a fast life.

He found it in Johnny Miller.

9 · On the Trot

Johnny Miller's all-time favourite confidence trick went as follows. He dressed Charlie up as a civil servant in a bowler hat and wartime utility suit. He directed him to a furniture shop on Harrow Road that was suspected of being involved in the black market. A quick flash of a forged warrant later and Charlie was using his powers of search. In the depths of the shop's musty cellar, he found that he was indeed dealing with a black marketeer. The bright sheen of walnut cabinets and sideboards fresh from the production lines – which weren't supposed to be rolling – gave the shopkeeper's secret away. Charlie was immovable in his admonitions. But deep sighs and a furrowed brow soon gave way to a reluctant grimace, a nod and then a wink, as he allowed himself to be bribed into keeping mum.

Charlie's nephew, Albert, said he got in with the wrong crowd. That's putting it mildly. Johnny Miller was a hard-nosed, grasping villain. He was a flabby man with a moist surface, and dragged a club foot behind him. Everyone who knew him is unanimous in their opinion: he was repugnant – a bogeyman who inspired Charlie to his greatest heights.

In the meantime my grandfather's first mentor was smoking cigars while everyone else was gasping for a cigarette. He had amassed a fortune in the 1930s from robbing banks. Though no one knew it at the time, he had been responsible for blowing up the safe at Edgware Road Station in 1932. The police thought Americans were responsible because chewing-gum had been used to fix the explosive. Johnny was good, but he could not get out of the habit of screwing. His face was too well known to continue breaking and entering, and he was getting on. He knew he had to utilize his guile more subtly.

He employed my grandfather as his right-hand man. If Charlie learnt one thing from him it was to exploit the rules and regulations of the building game. Miller & Sons' construction firm, 89 Olive Road, Willesden, was receiving well-paid commissions from the Home Office to repair buildings suffering from war damage. Brother Will, also a deserter (though conscientious, I'm sure), was employed as a labourer. Charlie and Johnny, he said, were a real double act, just like Abbott and Costello. Except that Charlie was ripping Johnny off.

Will would be sent out to do a job on a house that had been damaged by a bomb. When he came back, Charlie would ask him how much the work came to. Will might reply '£500', in which case Charlie would say, 'Put £150 on top for me.' They would both go into Miller's office where the same question was put by their boss.

'£650,' said Stuttering Bill.

To which Charlie would reply, to Bill's surprise:

'£650! How can it come to that?'

Just to make it look convincing, you see.

■

War was good for Johnny and Charlie because the most serious wartime frauds occurred in the building industry. The 'cost plus' system of payment was particularly vulnerable to their crafty connivings, and the extent of illicit gains enjoyed by firms like Johnny's ran well into the millions. He charged the client – usually a local authority or government-controlled body – with the wages of non-existent workers. This trick was called 'dead men's wages'. All they needed were the National Insurance numbers of recently felled soldiers. Official bureaucracy couldn't keep up with them, and Charlie and Johnny obtained hundreds of pounds a month for the pay of fictitious navvies.

Back in Paddington, Georgie Vundum had set his sights on Lillian Kingham. He met her while she was working at the Cumberland Hotel. They arranged to meet after her shift. She made a special effort to impress him, and was wearing a wool georgette coat over a print Marocain dress with Peter Pan collar. Dolly had lent her a hat in 'English Green' coarse straw and she wore it at a jaunty tilt. She looked a treat. Georgie fell in love with the unmarried mother so prone to tears yet so easy to please. Greta Ann was kept well out of the way in Windsor Buildings. She was seven years old now, and putting up with the jibes of local children. They laughed at her grandmother, who, like Johnny Miller, was cursed with a club foot. Boys would trip Emily as she carried baskets of washing into the boiler-room. She fell head first, club foot in the air. There are two stories that tell how this deformity came about.

The first involves baby Emily falling out of her pram. Her leg was broken and because the nanny did not mention her mishap it never healed. The other involves a tram which ran over Emily's leg when she was little

She was probably born like it. A club foot or a cleft palate were such a terrible stigma for parents they hushed them up, and invented tragic accidents. So Greta Ann was subjected to the cruel jibes of the local children – the unwanted child of an unmarried mother whose Granny hopped along Cato Street on the ball of her right foot. Words cut her like knives. She was easy to tease, always flinching then covering herself up with a haughty air. But each jibe saw another layer of protective skin peeling until, in the end, she was raw. All she wanted was respectability, because it was crucial to the poorest of the poor. It was the only thing that stopped them from being outcasts.

The biggest stigma of all was being black, and Georgie Vundum was of mixed race. They called men like Georgie 'Cape Coloured' in those days, when they mentioned these things at all. He was lucky in that his complexion was fair and his nose was straight. The Dutch invaders spoke through him. His sister Ida, though – she was as black as night. No one in the family ever mentioned that Lily was so ahead of her times when it came to miscegenation. But she kept it quiet, too. Anyway, Georgie was a handsome man with a motor-car. He worked as a chauffeur for Sidney Landau's clothiers on Berwick Street, Soho. His tuberculosis kept him out of the Army, so he could supply Lily with all the lace and organdie she needed for nights out at the Alhambra, on Edgware Road. But all anyone really remembers about him is the irony that Lily should be involved with a War Reserve Special Constable, and then end up with a spiv.

Georgie was a 'utility copper' assigned to Harrow Road police station. Every night he went out in search of blackout transgressors. One of his colleagues, John Reginald Halliday Christie, was so zealous in his duties that the locals called him 'The Himmler of Rillington Place'.

Georgie and Lily were living in a dank little house on Oakington Road, Paddington, and tuberculosis was on the increase in London. Dampness, darkness and ruination lay around them. Paddington Station was a particular target for the Luftwaffe, its lattice-work steel roof glinting in the darkness. Their windows were boarded up; litter was left on the streets, weeds that had not been seen since Jack-of-the-Green's days were growing between the cracks on the pavement. Rats were having a field day. When Georgie handed his oxygen mask to a fellow sufferer on the contagious diseases ward at St Mary's Hospital, Praed Street, it was his last generous deed.

Georgie died a blameless death on 19 February 1942, two days before his successor to Lily's hand went AWOL. Ten years later Christie was condemned to death by asphyxiation on the Pentonville gallows for the murder of seven women.

·

A few miles away, and Charlie is in Sudbury. A regulation British Restaurant has opened on Court Parade. He is feasting on soup, roast beef, mashed potatoes, apple tart and a cup of 'gnat's piss' coffee. There are no street lights outside, and it is amazing what you can get away with in the dark. A figure who calls himself 'Flash Harry' but who is, in fact, my grandfather is offering to change £350 in 'white notes' for £280 in one shilling coins. He is chased on to the street. He has no ID card, since Horace won't lease him his medical card – the cops know Charlie Taylor too well by now.

He was making it as a contact man. He introduced men who needed something to men like Miller who could fulfil that need. Deals were struck in corner cafés over Formica tables. The scene was straight out of the flicks so Charlie felt quite at home. Sovereign rings flashed as palms were smoothed over brilliantined hair. The mood was larky – tough, hang-it-all humour – in the face of real hardships and possible death. Charlie and Johnny dealt in lorry-loads of anything – fresh salmon one day, toothpaste the next. Whatever it was it had to be disposed of at high speed and at the highest price.

And he was always on the move – as quick as a flash he could be stalking the Marylebone Road, London's first bypass, built north of the congested roads nearer the river. It was one of London's finest shopping streets, with several blocks of smart, modern flats on the Paddington side. It was in these genteel surroundings that Charlie finally met my grandmother in the run-up to Christmas 1943.

They made a date to meet at Lyons' Tea Shop in St Marylebone. It was said to be haunted by the ghost of Oliver Cromwell. The building marked the spot where the Protector was hanged, drawn and quartered after being disinterred from his tomb.

Lily was fed up with the miseries of war and death. She wanted to take a chance on life. When Charlie 'No Questions, No Cheques, No Coupons' Taylor came along, he offered just that opportunity. Here was a chap who never worried and whose pockets were overflowing with chocolates. It wasn't even black-market, he told her, just surplus stuff to sell on the street. Lily may have had her doubts about Charlie. She knew that when she turned her back on him leaving her purse on the sideboard it would be lighter on her return. But she said nothing. She carried on serving him cups of tea and let him sit in her front room hogging the meagre fire, hatching his plans.

Her sisters knew straight away that Charlie was dangerous. Especially when he tried to seduce vivacious Irene. He picked the wrong one there. Clearly, no one had told him about the Hollywood film star at the Cumberland Hotel or her fear of masculine effrontery. Lily, though, was more game, and hence susceptible. She was excited by this compact figure who bristled with energy and an electrifying malice. He was quite a guy when all the other fit men were at war.

The times dictated a climate of furtive ingenuity, a quality they both had in buckets. He breathed the spirit of wartime licentiousness, and Lily was essentially a good-time girl. Besides this, she possessed that chameleon-like quality of blending into the background, perfect for a conman's mate.

My gentle grandmother was invaluable. She excelled in warmth and good nature that reassured her lover's flustered mugs. If necessary she could summon up those tears that were so effective in melting the sternest of hearts. She was flowing water to Charlie's staunch earthiness. The shadings of her personality continually bled over the cosy contours of her frame.

Everybody in London was in love because they didn't know how long they had to live. Lily definitely was, and Charlie saw her as his perfect foil. She had the manners of her super-refined mother and the mores of the social-climbing Smiths. Like Charlie, she had been to 'boarding-school', and they had both been let down by their fathers. Lily knew what it was like to walk to the public baths in shoes with no heels. More importantly, neither of them cared for home-grown turnips or roses. They wanted chocolates and furs and fast cars. Charlie had some good connections and promised her the latest fashions and drawers full of silk stockings.

Despite her reservations, my great-aunt Dolly invited the new couple to her house for Christmas. This was especially convenient for Charlie – in the guise of eager lover he could count on several new billets. Irene had decamped to Southall, Lily had her own place on Oakington Road. Her other sister, Ann, lived down the road. Christmas Day was consummately prepared if a little frantic. A frenzy of Christmas decorations greeted them as Dolly opened the door.

'You couldn't see the ceiling for tinsel,' Lily joked.

Dolly's bright red hair and lipstick matched the festive silk dress she had made from a pattern in *Woman's Weekly*. She was an excellent seamstress, and until Charlie came along Lily was always borrowing her frocks to go out dancing. Even as a seventy-year-old woman, Dolly festered with bitterness at the amount of dresses her sister had ruined. She regaled me, her sole auditor, with lamentations for lost gowns. The chiffon pleats that had been singed with a carelessly discarded cigarette; the virginal lace collar stained with ruby port. No amount of costly dry-cleaning would render them clean.

Whereas you could always get a laugh out of Irene, Dolly was subject to funny turns. Sometimes she could be boisterous. But on a full moon, her sisters knew they would find her sitting mute in a corner with a doleful expression on her face. She was rapt in ineffable misery. As her mother's closest companion she had felt each jibe and deprivation the family had had to endure. Emily spared her no details of the awful degradation she had suffered in order to become the Kinghams' mother. Dolly was midwife for each birth and chief mourner when baby Johnnie and Father passed away. She was the repository of her family's misery. While Lily was living it up Dolly remembered them all as children sleeping top to toe in two beds.

At the age of twelve she was taken out of school where she had shown great promise – even winning an essay-writing competition involving the entire Commonwealth. Mother needed the money, and Dolly went into service. She never married, having been jilted at the age of twenty-two. After her cruel desertion, she could not bear the thought of any more intimacy. When a young man took her out dancing and expressed too much interest she would excuse herself outside the public lavatory on Marylebone. He waited in vain, as she climbed out of the window and sprinted home. Dolly expended her energies on working: cleaning, cooking, and serving. Except for those occasions when her system could bear the hardship no longer, and shut down. A full moon might be the cause or, more often, the tensions within her family. They pressed in on her so deeply she had to escape. Since physical escape was impossible, she retreated inside her head.

Lily's brother George was on leave from the Army, and strumming mournful chords on the piano in the parlour. Greta was sitting close by him, humming along. She could not help noticing that her uncle was crying on to the keys. Fear, asthma and obsessive sadness ran through the King-hams like the three-minute mile. Like Dolly, George did not see the bright side of life, but then he was on his way to a Japanese prison camp. Lily took a puff on her inhaler and begged him to buck up and play her favourite tune. It suited the mood and she would sing it.

> 'Music, Maestro please!
> To help me ease the pain
> That solitude can bring.
> He used to like the waltzes
> So please don't play a waltz.
> He danced divinely.
> And I loved him so.
> But there I go.
> Music, maestro please!'

For some reason, Dolly was sparked into a rage. Things were not going as she had planned, perhaps Charlie had not placed his glass on the coaster provided. He was the son of Irish peasants, this man, not good enough for a Kingham. What would their mother say?

Dolly had her own special term of abuse for the Irish, of whom Charlie was an especially untrustworthy example. 'You fucking potato-face,' she screamed. It was a harmless enough insult that would become more apt towards the end of his life. When his virile features were bleary with age and drug abuse, and his black eyes had scorched two dirty great holes in the starchy white blankness of his face.

·

On 15 March 1944 a boy, Edward Charles, was born to 'C. Taylor, Cashier (Civil Engineer)' and 'Lillian Maud Vundum formerly Kingham'. Charlie was now officially Charlie and in a flamboyant gesture worthy of Admiral Evans named his son after his hero. Lily, in deference to her lover, and possibly to remind him that the child was his, suggested Charles as back-up to Edward. The mother and father give separate addresses on my uncle's birth certificate, Charlie still using Katie's flat in Sudbury as his official residence, but living mostly with Lily, the new baby and Greta Ann on a back street in Paddington.

My mother was brought out of retirement to look after her new baby brother. She was ten years old with fluffy brown curls and hazel eyes that gave off a wary smile. Self-preservation had made her fierce.

Lily tried to pass off her mysteriously olive complexion as a living remnant of Georgie Vundum. Charlie was not the only one adept at spinning a yarn. I do not know if he saw through the deception – my mother's illegitimacy was a secret that no one must ever know. But he sensed it was a sensitive issue and used it to puncture Greta's reserve. 'Vundum, my arse,' he sneered when she turned up her nose at his crudeness. Lily was beginning to see his nasty side.

Charlie was indifferent to the Kinghams' social distinctions – he was too busy chasing young girls and married women. At first, three years older than Charlie and dressed in widow's weeds, Lily had represented the older, moneyed woman for him. She was ripe and *au fait* with London's lowlife. But after the birth of her second child, Lily was putting on weight and, at thirty-two, her hair any old how, she assumed the blowsy looks of a harassed mother.

Charlie's lone friend from the army, chirpy Davey Perkins, met his wife while visiting Lily. She was a merry and dapper little Wren, who had grown up alongside Lily on Cato Street.

Charlie never could resist a girl in a uniform. When Davey was sent back to the Front, Charlie seduced his new wife and had affairs with her two younger sisters. But the one he really wanted was Adele. She was eighteen and terribly thin. Her sisters were concerned because she had not started menstruating. She was such a slip of a girl, and a gratifying conquest because she was Greta's best friend. 'Are you going to play with Adele?' he would mock, doing his nasty, insinuating best to upset her. 'Yeah, well, I've fucked her,' he'd boast.

.

The war in Europe ended on 8 May 1945 for everyone except my grandfather, who was still wanted as a deserter. When London's streets, shops and public buildings were lit up once again Charlie could no longer rely on the darkness. He had a good scam going though. He had been collecting sets of insurance cards which he stamped himself. When he had enough to go on the dole, he gave Johnny Miller's name as his employer's reference and went up to the counter to collect his money. It was risky, and it kept him hopping around London. But if what he said was true he was collecting eight lots of dole each week. When two policemen spotted him and Brother Will, who was genuinely signing on, at the Praed Street labour exchange he ran round the back of the building. Brother Will was left to fend off the cops.

Charlie successfully stayed in the shadows for the next two years, living off Lily's rations when funds were low. The grim winter of 1946–7 was a turning-point in the Government's fortunes. Severity and crises ensued. The *élan* of 1945's celebrations mocked the party-goers as climatic and economic misfortunes came thick and fast.

Bread rationing in 1946 was the last straw for people no

longer pulling together under threat from the Blitz. Fuel shortages paralysed industries and stolen petrol coupons were at a premium, so there was more money to be made for Charlie. Britain had become 'the land of the well-greased palm. We've developed into a nation of bribers. Everyone is on the game, from the big shot who buys the motor dealer's wife a fur coat and gets delivery of a new car in a week, to the housewife who slips the fishmonger a packet of cigarettes once the queue has gone,' deplored the leader-writer of the *People*.

In the same newspaper gossip columnist Arthur Helliwell was charting the activities of Pop-Up Ted, Wicked Bill, Playful Pluto and Ben the Bandit, habitués of the sleazy cafés of Notting Hill. Charlie was one of them; flashily handsome in a sharp suit, mooching around on the off-chance for hours. His female equivalent was the good-time girl, which Lily longed to be if only Charlie would let her.

But he was the kind of man who remembered your age and forgot your birthday. That wasn't the only joke doing the rounds. My great-aunt Dolly, when she emerged from her catatonic state, loved to tell me old jokes: 'A young spiv shot his mother and father so that he could go to the orphans' outing.' She probably had Charlie in mind. Tennis on the television sparked off memories each year and she would repeat: 'Spivs heard dozens of new racquets were opening up in Wimbledon.'

Clothing, sugar and milk were still on coupons, tinned foods and dried fruits were on points, chocolates and sweets on 'sweetie coupons'. Lily's weekly allowance for herself was 13 ounces of meat, 1½ ounces of cheese, 6 ounces of butter and margarine, 1 ounce of cooking fat, 8 ounces of sugar, 2 pints of milk and one egg. Though Charlie was trading in ration books he had none of his own so Greta had to share her allowance with him. She was thin and unhappy. My mother doesn't like to talk about the war.

It was a time when you had to 'shiver with Shinwell and starve with Strachey'. The only people unaffected by Lord Shinwell's electricity cuts were night owls like Charlie; the gambling-joint spivs and the Piccadilly layabouts who went to bed with the milk.

'Cuts? What cuts?' queried Charlie when Lily complained about trying to care for a toddler without water or electricity. Every evening my resplendent grandfather left Oakington Road for Civvy Street, a nightclub in Soho which was five rooms and a basement hosted by a lady friend of Miller's. She engaged a band and got in drinks which she mixed with water. Charlie's job was to go round the pubs at closing time and give away free invitations. He wore his best spiv's jacket – a belted, zooty sports affair with a yellowish green check, pumped-up shoulders in the style of the boxer Joe Laksi. He rounded up the girls of easy virtue, who hired the club's upstairs rooms at five bob a time. They brought in a profit of four or five pounds a night. It was a meeting place for the underworld – screwsmen, conmen, dragmen, pimps, prostitutes, *tout le monde* was there. There was a good trade in tea and coffee, but the sideline was buying hot stuff from the boys, and peddling a bit of dope now and then.

But you could not afford to stay still. Charlie got complacent and the Red Caps caught up with him in a filthy mews flat off Paddington Green. On 26 February 1947, he 'rejoined his unit' and they managed to hold on to him for two days.

During his absence Lily gave birth to Victor. Charlie escaped from his unit and carried on doing what he was best at. He was good at living off his nerves, and liked to test himself against all-comers and prove his worth. He was a true freelancer, and the insecurity of continual improvisations was what he lived for. The birth of a second son did not alter Lily's precarious relationship with Charlie. She stayed because she was in thrall to his danger.

She sympathized with his need for excitement. Like most crooks, Charlie saw himself as a rebel from everyday slavishness. Respectable people were slaves to the clock, with nothing to brighten existence until they died. It wasn't that he objected to work itself. It wasn't the wages, the conditions, or the hours. It was all three. His objections were understandable given his overwhelming fear of boredom. He passed on these objections to me.

10 · The Glasshouse

In 1610 King James I decreed that in every county a House of Correction should be built. Shepton Mallett, the only prison in Somerset, was soon packed with men, women, children, rogues, vagabonds, prostitutes and idle apprentices. In 1944, the oldest prison in the country had become a Military Detention Barracks behind whose grimy, barred windows American GIs gazed at the observation towers manned by armed guards. The World's Grimmest Glasshouse, as it came to be called, inspired a book called *The Dirty Dozen*. It was here that unwanted soldiers were brought to be shot.

The regime was tough. All movements were done at the double. Charlie was brought to the charming old village by train then marched half a mile to the prison shackled to his fellow deserters. He had been in Southall, visiting Irene, when he was collared on 26 June 1948. Once inside, he lost his formal rank and name and was stamped with a number on his arm. Cigarettes were rationed, two per day, to be smoked at specific times. The butt-ends had to be returned. Illegal smoking went on during the period set aside for ironing clothes. Charlie would scorch the cloth of the board to hide the smell of his cigarette. The punishment for this infringement was a beating administered with batons. Charlie liked to taunt his gaolers by holding a piece of chalk to his mouth and exhaling imaginary rings of smoke into the air.

Work consisted of boot repairs, coir-mattress-making and furniture production – old hat to a lag like Charlie. At night, warders brought dirty trays or rusty tins to the men's cells. They had to be cleaned and polished by the next morning. The clattering of tins, the rending cries of condemned men – Charlie was surrounded by the most desperate criminals in the country, and he was screaming the loudest. When morning came, Charlie heard the firing squads at work.

Glasshouse prisoners were routinely kicked to death. Charlie relished telling these stories to his sons. Of the prisoner who was held in solitary confinement for nearly six months, during which time he was beaten three times and had a bucket of boiling water poured over him. One sergeant was particularly sadistic. My grandfather hated Sergeant Connolly who spoke with a rough Belfast accent. The fact he was Irish compounded Charlie's already ambivalent antipathy towards his compatriots. When Sergeant Connolly found a pound of lard hidden in a man's cell, he sent for a spoon and forced him to eat it. He then had to clear up his own vomit. This was lenient compared to another inmate who accidentally splashed Connolly with urine when slopping out. He was never seen again. Or, as Charlie conjectured, 'He was served up for dinner.'

Shouts, screams, moans and mumbling – Charlie took childish tantrums to hellish extremes. When an array of distractions failed to gain the attention he needed, he attacked the prison vicar. Then he turned on himself. He poured paint over his head and laughed wildly. He barricaded himself inside a cell and set it alight. He tried to hang himself when in solitary confinement with a piece of wire he had secreted in his sock. When he was foiled mid-dangle, he smeared his shit on the walls.

He eventually convinced the warders that he was insane and was sent to a psychiatric unit in Banstead, Surrey. It was here on 20 November 1948 that he got his 'ticket' home. It came in the form of a dishonourable discharge, and the recommendation that he was 'permanently unfit for any form of military service'.

■

On 15 November 1948, Lily went to the divorce courts to obtain her lover's decree nisi from his wife. Evelyn had brought the proceedings, citing adultery, and warned my grandmother: 'Have nothing to do with him. He's mad.' Five days later Charlie was released from the psychiatric hospital where he had been declared insane. Two verdicts against him but Lily carried on loving him regardless.

She was living in one room above a shop with fifteen-year-old Greta Ann, four-year-old Edward and one-year-old Victor. Their address was 40 Bourne Terrace, Paddington. All around them were the bombsites and slums that, twenty years later, were to be buried under the colossal Westway. The boys slept with their mother and sister, Kingham top to Kingham toe, in a brass bed under the patched-up panes of the room's only window. Four families lived in this house, packed tight in a deep canyon between towering factories and the spectral form of a gasworks. The goods lines passed on embankments all around. At ground-level where the viaduct fought for space with the railway lines and the canal, soot-stained grass pushed through the cracks in the pavements.

Nettles stung Lily's tea-stained ankles. Edward played with the other war babies in the trampled heaps of earth, dog muck and ashes that had once been houses. Their cries and shrieks were shouted down by the noise of factory hooters and trains shunting. Lily cooked their rations on the landing, where a single stove served as a kitchen for all the occupants.

Rent was kept low by legislation, so the landlord did not bother with repairing the window or the wallpaper that was hanging by threads from the mildewed walls. Lily washed the boys in a tin bath in front of a meagre fire. Steaming nappies hung on a line across the room, adding to the cloying dampness of the atmosphere.

Charlie came home to the maddening claustrophobia of impoverished family life. He saw again the dull, grinding poverty of the type peculiar to London with its grimy pubs and whey-faced drinkers negotiating narrow back streets. Even the spivs were feeling the pinch. They could be found on street corners selling winkle shells minus the winkles at 1s 6d a pint. Charlie heard that Davey Perkins had been reduced to snatching logs from the fire at the Lord Nelson on Harrow Road. Housewives were struggling to feed their burgeoning families. On one thing the whole of London agreed: austerity was a hard price to pay for victory.

11 · New Futurist

More than 100,000 houses had been destroyed in London, and another million needed war damage repairs. At the same time there was a dramatic increase in demand for housing due to demobilization and the postwar baby boom. This was good news for Charlie, who resumed his double act with Johnny Miller.

The more obvious types of criminal at this time were the safe-breaking gangs, receivers, protection racketeers, and 'jump-up merchants' who stole loaded lorries. In 1947, Charlie read in the papers that a man called Edwin 'Teddy' Machin together with the infamous Billy Hill had stolen a Manchester bookmaker's safe containing £9,000. Machin was a chiv man. He could gouge a man's cheek in one fell swoop. The following year, along with the rest of the country, Charlie read about London's other contender for the title 'King of London's Underworld', Jack 'Spot' Comer.

The *Daily Herald* reported that eight bloodstained men had been arrested during an attempted robbery at a London Airport warehouse. It was said to contain £6 million worth of diamonds and £3 million in gold. It seemed that the man who had led Communists, Jews, gangsters and Brother Will in the battle against Mosley at Cable Street had been brought bang to rights.

A huge central terminal had been completed for the new London Airport. It came to the attention of Sammy Josephs, a thief, that valuable cargoes were being kept overnight in flimsy, temporary huts. Jack Spot's team did their homework. Each man went on the guided tour for visitors to the airport in order to familiarize themselves with its layout. Opportunities such as this were constantly dropping into the laps of dedicated criminals.

Someone grassed them up, though. Police received 'information' that something was to happen on the night of 24 July 1948. By 11 p.m. the roads leading to the airport were being kept under observation. A million pounds' worth of gold ingots was the bait. Thirteen policemen lay in wait. At 11.30 they heard a lorry drive up. Three policemen disguised as airport officials lay down pretending they were asleep. Masked men – Franny Daniels and Teddy Machin (who was on loan from Hill) – entered, tied them up and took their keys. Machin decided to cosh one into unconsciousness as a safety measure.

The glorious Flying Squad came to the rescue. They jumped out of the shadows, and gave chase. Teddy ran blindly and fell headlong into a deep trench. Knocked unconscious by his fall, he lay there all night, and was never arrested. Smart move. Franny hid under a Black Maria and clung to its underside by toes and fingers. He was driven all the way to Harlesden Police Station, which was handy since he could bunk up at that well-known villain's, Johnny Miller.

But Miller was too old for this kind of racket. He had a new business based in an old knackers' yard on Kensal Rise. The straw from the horses' stable still lay on the ground; their halters and saddles hung from the walls. Amidst these relics of the days before the motor-car, Johnny set up business with a Canadian engineer who had patented the design for a folding pushchair. The first of its kind, Miller named the new invention 'Miller's Monarchs'. Men were dispensable to Johnny once they had served their purpose. As soon as the factory was equipped to produce the folding mechanism, chassis and wheels, he dispensed with the Canadian by playing on his New-World primness.

His sprawling bulk and gammy leg were kept obscured behind a massive roll-top desk in his office. Its size matched his ego and his appetites. Miller was sexually incontinent. When he was not robbing Paul to pay Peter he sat in his office being entertained by prostitutes, or teaching his son to swear at coppers. Fastidious Charlie was revolted when his mentor urinated in the sink in his office while talking on the telephone. One day, Charlie recalled, Mr Miller as he reluctantly called him ordered two 'toms' at once. But, said Charlie, 'He couldn't control them.' He offered one to his Canadian partner. The man refused. Miller docked £5 from his wages anyway. The father-of-three returned to his native country, leaving his pushchairs behind him. As for the other men, Miller sacked them just in time for Christmas so that he did not have to pay their bonuses.

·

Crime is like any other business, you have to keep improvising new methods to improve your turnover, or you go under. Charlie admired the older man's capacity for self-invention, because he knew that in effect it was self-effacement. It was like one of Admiral Evans's lantern lectures. You never saw through the display of endless transformations because ultimately, underpinning it all, was a great big, fuck-off nothing. Johnny was versatile, always keen to learn new tricks. His days were spent thinking of the best way to earn fresh revenue, and the surest way to do it without being arrested.

In postwar Britain a dodgy load of metal could be worth a fortune. Johnny showed Charlie how to extract the best price by applying a little pressure. A man who drove up to the yard told Miller he had £500 worth of lead in the back of his van. Miller had a look, agreed the price, then told him to unload. Once the lead had been decanted, the grateful vendor, eager to be rid of his ill-gotten gains, asked for his money. Miller turned nasty: 'That's bent. I'll get the coppers on to you.'

The man had no choice but to accept £100 – one-tenth of its worth. Johnny did not care who he turned over, as long as he could keep the show on the road. He was canny, too. He invited the local bobbies to his yard: they came for free pushchairs for their toddlers.

Charlie never liked to stay in one place for too long. Something he learned from Katie. Once he got the hang of a place he grew bored with it; and there were always creditors to be slipped. So he moved on – preferring to start from scratch somewhere else. If he took rooms it was only for a few weeks, but he stuck to the Harlesden area so as to be close to the yard and Miller's constant supply of brand new ten-shilling notes.

·

The streets of Harlesden were longer and broader than those of Paddington, lending an air of respectability to its inhabitants. From Kensal Green station the ribbons and ropes of criss-crossing rail tracks have obliterated the old route into Harlesden. In the 1870s Charlie would have jumped the stile at Stonebridge, sauntered across the dairy farms and entered the snoozing hamlet at the wicket gate, the last streaks of a russet sunset settling on tarred barns and sheds.

Sometimes things happen so fast they take your breath away. My mother would often tell me things about Charlie that left me reeling. So it was safer to lock myself away in the deepest recesses of my mind, where I told myself comforting stories. I liked the Victorians – they made sense. It was, of course, Victorian engineers who brought the railway, and Victorian architects who implanted a civic centre. Harlesden was pleased with itself; it had a town hall and clock tower around which streets were thickly laid with red-brick villas. They were not infested with inner-city poverty; plane trees and privet hedges were dotted along the avenues, filtering the sooty air and smog. Away from Lily and the boys, Charlie could house a string of girlfriends to work the tapper and sucker racket.

Lily and Greta and Dolly turned a blind eye to Charlie's goings-on. But there are others who are always prepared to tell a good story. A tapper is a typewriter, and a sucker is a vacuum cleaner. Charlie would go into a 'tapper shop' and tell the manager that his wife was thinking of buying a typewriter but that she did not know what sort to get. The salesman, always keen to oblige, would suggest sending a man to his address to display the workings of the latest model. When the salesman arrived, the lady of the house would accept the item and the salesman would leave it on approval for ten days.

Then Charlie would get on the phone and ring up all the other tapper and sucker firms making the same arrangements with them. As soon as one machine arrived he would cart it off to a fence. He and his lady wife were gone before the first mug started to squeal.

For the next eighteen months Charlie was bringing in good money. He was in charge of handling the complicated fiddle of filling in time-sheets and paying wages to dozens of labourers. Some of these men were his brothers. Will, Wag and Ted the painter, as well as his nephews, Albert and Bill. Familial loyalty resided solely on their side, since they were aware that Charlie was often cheating them out of their rightful pay-packets.

Miller's Monarchs were doing well: they were, as Miller

proclaimed, so convenient for the modern mother. Britain had to maximize its exports, so production was essential. Men like Miller were able to thrive in favourable economic conditions. Industry was re-asserting itself, and tuppenny-halfpenny factories were going up all over London. These locally grown, well-to-do businessmen were beginning to blur the distinctions of class. One who employed many, such as Miller and his underling Charlie, could almost pass for middle-class. Charlie was on the fringes of respectable society, which was just how he liked it.

The Conservative Party, currently biding its time in opposition, was packed with small businessmen: property developers, investment brokers, men from the new communications industries. Petrol rationing had just ended. Building controls were about to be abolished. Boom conditions arose from a seller's market at home and abroad. When the Tories came in, their erratic fiscal policies made life easy for the money-makers. The country was a speculator's paradise as hot money moved in.

•

Charlie received his decree absolute on 7 January 1949. In theory, he was free to marry Lily, who was pregnant with his third child. But his family was a burden to him. He was thirty-three years old and bitterly resentful of what he considered as his lost youth. He wanted to make up for it even if it took a lifetime. In the meantime he would have to make do with living at 143 Buchanan Gardens.

It was a back-to-back in Harlesden, and it is still there, holding its secrets tightly. There are three bedrooms and a bathroom on the first floor, one through room on the ground floor, and a scullery at the back, opening on to the yard. Railway lines and the Harrow Road come up sharp behind. The road itself is pleasingly long and broad.

Lily was thrilled when she walked into the narrow hallway, dimly lit by the stained-glass panels of the front door. She did not mind that the first floor reeked with the melancholy, unloved air of a house permanently let to tenants. It was her first proper home. The first thing Charlie did was to knock down the wall separating the front room from the dining-room because he needed space to stride around his castle. At five foot six inches tall, weighing 144 lb and with a chest span measured by the army doctor at thirty-six inches, he was master of all he surveyed and that included my mother.

Within the walls of his castle I am finally on to him. He ducked my gaze and dived down London's alleyways but I have found him. The family secret is not going to be kept by me. He wanted blind devotion, he is getting exposure.

Greta was sixteen years old, and Charlie was in love with her. She had won a scholarship to a grammar school in Kensal Rise. She was studious, pretty and well-spoken. He could not resist her innocence. Especially since it was undermined by the flamboyance of her features. She had the look of a Fifties' starlet but she was determined to hide her voluptuousness. Her stepfather's gaze followed the startled look in her hazel eyes straight down to the dimple in her chin. The green skirt of her school uniform inflamed him. His mouth watered when its demure swish revealed rosy knees. The sweet, round concave of her plush and peachy mouth drove him wild. She was the fairy princess who goaded him into wickedness. So he hated her, too.

Dictators need enemies to bind their subjects close in abject fear. Hitler invaded Poland. Charlie invaded his step-daughter. Her hands rush to her mouth, it hollows in despair. The words do not form, he makes her do things she does not want to do. He says he will pick a fight with her mother if she does not do what he wants. She has to protect her mother from his vicious attacks. Anything is better than witnessing the blows, the blood and the screaming. Anything. And then, to compound the shame, he gives her ten bob.

She was what he did at home. Outside home, Charlie dug out his enemies' weaknesses. It might be fear, sex or gambling, but he made his marks feel his guilt, and then dangled his knowledge of it over them. The methods he used were the same. The effect he had was similar. His perversity was focused on snuffing out any hope of redemption his victims might enjoy through their own efforts. After a while, they reckoned they were bent to his will, and if they were then so should everyone else be. He was their fate, and it was inescapable. He made them as bad as he was. That was the source of his strength; only he knew their deepest secrets. Men like Charlie are almost overburdened with motives for their cruelty. It is just a part of the pattern of their lives.

On 26 January 1950 Lily gave birth to Charlie's third son. With his wife's cries ringing in his ears, he climbed the stairs to my mother's bedroom. This was where she passed her lonely evenings. He leant over her bed and whispered his demand. She did not allow her fear of him to stop her spitting out, 'How could you?' For once, he looked ashamed and left her alone.

■

Greta spent her days in Kensal Rise Library, reading her way out of misery. It provided refuge for her and covert inspiration for Charlie. Its red Suffolk bricks with Doulting stone dressing, mullioned windows with leaded lights and casements were to be repeated in one of his and Billy Hill's ventures in the 1960s. As Greta trod the hallway paved with mosaics and looked above her to the pediment arch supported on Ionic pillars, she little thought she would see them again in a casino.

Mark Twain opened the library in September 1900. He had come to Europe to flee his creditors after losing a fortune in a printing-press venture which failed. Seventy years later Charlie was in a similar predicament.

For now, though, he was in the enviable position of having creditors evading him. He had done some freelance building work for a neighbour and when the man didn't pay him, he stole his lorry. The police came knocking at Number 143 and Charlie admitted to the offence, but told them he wouldn't give it back until he had been paid. The policemen were amused, and the matter was settled out of court. Bravado such as this, as well as a run of wins at White City Stadium, meant that the Taylors were the first family in Buchanan Gardens to own a car.

His Alvis TB 14 Sports Tourer was the only bright spot on the road's horizon. The crimson bodywork offset by ivory leather upholstery was startling enough in those penny-pinching times. But when the model was introduced at the Earls Court Motor Show its streamlined, swooping lines had drawn crowds to a standstill. The same show saw the introduction of the Jaguar XK 120, Morris Minor, Standard Vanguard and Land Rover but Charlie only had eyes for the Alvis. Its 0–60 mph speed was nineteen seconds. So it made for an exhilarating ride as Charlie loaded the boys into the two-seater and took them on tours of his old stamping grounds. From Stonebridge they whizzed up to the Empire Pool, then out to East Barnet and back into town to visit Pentonville. He rehearsed the stories of his life along the way.

He took Lily to see her sister Irene in Southall. Irene never forgot the sight of his fabulous motor skidding to a halt outside her house. It drew a crowd of neighbours who cooed and marvelled at its frivolous sleekness. When Charlie emerged bearing chocolates and stockings for Irene they were overwhelmed. They clustered round as Charlie – his chest puffed up like a courting peacock's – boasted to their drab menfolk about Miller's Monarchs and commissions from local government.

Lily basked in their admiration of her fox fur. He treated her well, they gushed, or at least she never complained in company; but always kept up a flashing smile. When she had black eyes and he had no money Irene and her friends saw sight nor sound of the Taylors. Though they would not have been disturbed by the sight of Lily's bruises. Battered wives were no big deal.

One thing surprised them though. Charlie would give anyone the keys to his car. Their husbands and sons queued up – some of them couldn't even drive, but Charlie didn't care, he waved them off as they took turns behind the wheel. Once it was his it was as though he had lost interest. He did not even mind when, in 1959, a young aristocratic type wrapped the Alvis around a lamp-post. In fact, Charlie was rather proud that he had such good connections.

He brought another dash of colour to Harlesden in the shape of his new friend Fred Scuse. Fred was a magnificent six-foot black man, and the neighbours stared when Charlie brought him to his door. Lily screamed when she opened it.

Black Fred was the son of a polygamous chief. He had arrived in London from Ghana during the war. Charlie always maintained they had met in the Army – thus they mutually supported each other's claim to patriotic duty. In truth they met on a train coming into Paddington Station.

The ticket-collector asked Fred for his ticket. Fred, who spoke immaculate English, having been educated in a missionary-run school, declared with a white-toothed grin: 'Me no ticket.'

The bewildered official asked: 'Where have you come from?'

'Me come from Africa,' Fred exclaimed.

It was love at first sight. Fred was a proud, fine-featured man with an impeccably dignified bearing, but he was happy to trade on prejudice to get his way. He was a showman – a fire-eater and snake-charmer with a troupe of dancers and musicians. His stage name was 'Prinz Nikizolo', and he was continually being arrested for being black.

'You black bastard,' the arresting officer would say. 'You stand to attention when you're talking to me.' He would then set about Fred with truncheon and boots. No one stopped to help him.

∎

Charlie and Fred loved good clothes. Davis the Gentlemen's Outfitters on Edgware Road was their first hit. Charlie introduced his friend as Nigerian royalty.

'Step this way, Your Highness,' and he was ushered in.

Once they were safely installed, Charlie managed to negotiate a suit of clothes for his royal friend on tick. Royalty never carry cash on their person, and Charlie and Black Fred never paid.

Fred and Charlie strolled the streets of a newly rejuvenated London – the Festival of Britain was in full patriotic force. Charlie did not visibly partake of the enthusiasm displayed by the steamers (steam-tug = mug), preferring to stand apart, the disdain etched on his face. They may have enjoyed the feeling of being at the heart of something new, but only Charlie, or so he felt, could read the symbolism inherent in the New Futurism of Skylon. From the bombed-out wreckage of the South Bank, the reusable space plane soared like Cleopatra's Needle. As if conjured up by a magician, it floated in the skies above the mud-disposal machines on the South Bank of the Thames. It was a tall thin structure with no visible means of support. It was, went the joke, 'like the British economy'.

Lily was stuck indoors with her inhaler. She was becoming increasingly wearisome to her fiancé. She whined and grumbled about the thick, yellow pall of smog that had descended with winter. The killer fog seeped into houses and covered every surface with a film of dust. It clung to her face like a wet cloth. At times it caused a fifty-foot mantle that choked the air and inflamed the lining of her throat. Love of an open fire was the official cause, but in truth it was the power plants that the government had encouraged to be built on the wastelands of inner London. The noxious fumes they emitted caused 12,000 lives to be lost in a single year. Sometimes it was easier not to breathe. So Lily held her breath and waited for something to happen.

She was let out of confinement on 29 July 1950 for her wedding at Paddington register office. It was a hurried, ungracious affair. Lily's aunt came specially from Southend-on-Sea to be one of the witnesses. She took such a dislike to Charlie that she was never seen again. Emily had just died of breast cancer so missed out on the better-late-than-never legitimization of her grandsons. Her granddaughter, Greta Ann, did not assume her new stepfather's surname. She loved her mother dearly. But more than that, she pitied her for the fate that lay so clearly ahead. Since the country was a 'speculator's paradise', Charlie and Black Fred were rolling in it. They decided to try their luck at Jack Spot's Botolph Club in darkest Aldgate. They couldn't see the green baize for greasy fivers. East London was never Charlie's idea of a good time – and he didn't like mixing with rough shop-keepers, so Black Fred suggested a tour of Bayswater's nightspots. It was more uptown, more Charlie. The passwords and rendezvous changed each night. But Fred was always in the know. He lorded it at the Slippery Sam, over the Trinidadians in their zoot suits and sombrero hats. The ska music was full on and girls were grinding themselves into the ground. Fred was wearing an ankle-length wool overcoat with astrakhan collar. In deference to his regal bearing and association with a white man, the card-players handed him the dice.

·

As the son of Stonebridge detritus Charlie's attitude to money was strangely ambivalent. It was his sole object in life to gain it, but when he had it, he despised it. He liked nothing better than an evening at home by the fire throwing bunches of notes into the flames and watching them burn. They had lost their allure so they had to go.

Charlie lusted to thieve, and did it not just because he was compelled by hunger or poverty, nor did he bother to enjoy what he stole, but he wallowed in the joy of the theft and the sin itself. Which is why the Christmas after he acquired the Alvis, as well as Buchanan Gardens' first television set, Charlie was in dire financial straits. So much so, that he was forced to take a job as a relief postman. He kept the job long enough to enable him to steal parcels containing presents suitable for three growing boys and their mother.

He spent his nights hunched over the fire, bemoaning his lost rolls of fivers. Greta was upstairs in her bedroom swooning night and day to Frank Sinatra, who crooned tremulously on her Bakelite radio. The fog outside was so thick visibility was no more than one foot. The sounds of the street lost their echoes and lamp-posts emitted a yellow mist. When Greta did go outside she felt she was walking on a cloud.

Bad news came. Even Katie Taylor in sylvan Sudbury was extinguished by the Killer Fog. She died of pulmonary bronchitis. Charlie arrived at the funeral in Johnny Miller's black Bentley, which was more appropriate than the open-top Alvis for a grieving son. He looked like Al Capone in a Burberry raincoat, and was armed with an ostentatious wreath.

At his mother's grave he caught up with Tots, who was in the grips of a tumour that had rendered him half-insane. He was cracking jokes as Katie's coffin was lowered into the boggy ground. But young Alfred, the prodigal son, was forced to leave early, when Doris's husband threatened to kill him. The reason? His son and his new daughter-in-law had given Charlie £130 in key money so that they could move into Buchanan Gardens. The trouble was, so had a lot of other people. Charlie scarpered, and his brothers and sisters were not at all surprised when his cheque for the share of funeral costs bounced.

12 · Deb's Delight

On losing her home in Buchanan Gardens, Lily paid a tearful visit to the housing department of Paddington Council. Before long the weeping mother, her three boys and their father were moved into a bed-sitting-room that had once been the attic of a Victorian mansion on Hyde Park Square. Greta was removed to Irene's safe house in Southall after a few quiet words with Lily. Thus my grandmother resolved her family's problems.

Lily's new home was a slum but the location was promising. The Taylors were planted on the corner of Connaught Village and Hyde Park. They looked on to a square dotted with plinths, hydrangeas and luscious shrubs.

Charlie had progressed from Stonebridge through the great forest of Middlesex to a deep valley called Marylebone. Its endless rows of monumental houses built from massive Portland slabs stood around him. They were not ready to admit him yet.

He had nothing, and this suited his temper. When you have nothing but your ambition it is surprising how relaxed you feel. All his fine clothes had been pawned so he went shopping at Portobello Market. He found a pair of boots suitable for navvying. After the first week's work digging up the miry shopping track of Oxford Street, he cut holes in the leather to make room for his blisters. This was the first time his sons had seen him consistently cheerful. The sudden swings into enraged furniture-throwing and obscene cursing failed to materialize. The hard physical work rid him, albeit temporarily, of his demons.

Edward felt the hardship more acutely. It was his job to go to the coal merchant on Edgware Road. On his way he walked past the pawnshop and saw his mother's fox fur wrapped round the throat of a shop dummy. Once he had purchased a twenty-eight-pound sack of coal he would lug it up the damp floorboards of the stairwell to the attic. At ten years old he already had the physique of a builder, although he had taken his father's injunction never to reveal anything, not even your name to strangers, literally. He was strangely mute. When a teacher asked his class to write essays about their fathers, Edward felt compelled to leave the page blank. With his lazy eye, which he refused to correct by wearing spectacles, he seemed backward to Charlie. This first son was turning out to be a disappointment.

The bailiffs followed Charlie from Harlesden. When he was stopped on the stairs of his new home, and asked point-blank, 'Are you Charles Taylor?' Edward heard his brusque denial, and retreated further into the safety of silence. Shivering fear and the smell of decay that rose from the aged lino muffled any spark Edward might have had. His slow, unsteady responses to his father's cajoling were more reminiscent of Holy Joe than a Taylor boy. He hoped for better in seven-year-old Victor.

And he was not disappointed. One day it was Victor who answered the door and said by rote to the man outside, 'My dad's not in.' As he closed the door the bailiff edged his foot between it and the doorframe. Victor could not shut the door, and quickly said, 'All right, mister, he is in.'

With that, he opened the door a hair's breadth. The bailiff pulled his foot back and Victor slammed it shut, laughing at his own bravado. Charlie was proud. And Charlie was indifferent when Victor came home with a bunch of tulips he had pulled by the stalk from Hyde Park. 'So what?' Charlie countered to Lily's reprimands.

He was making new friends. Old Man Moses was one of them. He was a Jew who carried with him the Hasidic pall of history, thereby provoking the taunts of local children. Crowds would gather round him to peer at his graveyard pallor and undertaker's bearing. He and Charlie talked late into the night about religion, history and the building game. Moses was making a small fortune on development, and his son, Ephraim, was training to be an architect. Charlie had his eye on this promising lad.

It was a slow-thinking world in the late 1950s – Jews, blacks and queers were still just that, but they were neighbours, too, and Charlie could always find a use for them. Even so, he preferred to gravitate towards rich people, because, like him, they were looking for life's perks. They do not want to spend their money, they want to make more. And just like the rich, the aristocracy, and the Royal Family, top-class villains are in a narrow one per cent of the population. The established one per cent bamboozles the rest of the population. So Charlie decided that, at some point in his life, it was up to him to bamboozle them.

·

Once the building work dried up, in the depths of night, he developed an idea for his greatest scam. Charlie suffered from insomnia, and had not forgotten his nemesis at the dogs. He sent Lily in a taxi to Fleet Street to buy six months' worth of back issues of the *Greyhound Express*. Even at my family's poorest, public transport was anathema. We do not like to be at the behest of others. We cannot bear the physical proximity of others' bodies or to be subject to the whim of their demands. We need room to operate. For two months

Charlie spent night after night, unwashed and unshaved, sitting at the table poring over old newspapers. No one could reach him, said Edward.

The hard grind of life carried on around him as Charlie studied the form of each winning dog. He kept notes in folders full of figures. Although he knew the dogs were nobbled, he was looking for a winning pattern in each track.

He found one. There always seemed to be one trap that produced a winner more often than the others. On average, he found that trap six, say, at White City stadium, would release thirty winning dogs out of every hundred. After trap six, the next one might be trap two, giving an average of twenty winners out of every hundred. Then he started betting. He always sat in the working-class stalls – some inner resistance to being exposed as an impostor forced him to keep to his own kind. And he never bet on horses because 'the horses are got at, and the jockeys are too', so you are contending with two lots of form.

On the night he put his theory into practice, he chose the second favourite at 10 to 1. The floodlights came on; the skittish hounds blinked as they were paraded on the garish green. Charlie sat back and the money rolled in. For the rest of his life he took delivery each morning of the *Greyhound Express* and *Sporting Life*, always counting the winning tracks. And he kept on winning, so much so that the bookies refused to accept his bets. He was forced to send Brother Will, Wag, or Black Fred to place them for him and share in the winnings. In the 1970s when he was an hotelier in south London he persuaded the sergeant from Streatham police station to act as his runner, for a cut. Charlie was confident he could trust a plod not to cheat him.

The dogs represented Charlie's greatest achievement; through them, he beat the system, and with them, he could reach the winning line. He still needed Lily, because she also knew a thing or two about working the system.

In 1956 her tears wrought miracles once again when she negotiated her family into a smart modern council estate in Bayswater. There were only five cars on Hallfield Estate when the Taylors moved in, but Charlie added a pink Vauxhall Cresta with fins and silver horns to the collection. He had the horns customized especially. They cost £20 when the average weekly wage was £7.

·

Bayswater is a confusing place which once had great expectations. Queensway is its strung-out main street, in a shallow bowl that inhibits any views of the city beyond. Although Kensington Gardens forms an airy open space at the south end, it has no presence from the street. I am surprised Charlie chose this place as his HQ. At the north end, the road is abruptly halted by a sharp bend. East and west the sense of enclosure is reinforced by chaotic street patterns. To the west, Moscow Road and Porchester Gardens connect to Notting Hill Gate, but they pass through a tightly knit enclave of squares and mews. The whole offers no hope to those bent on free movement.

I would have liked to see it before its development. Queensway had been a favourite ride of Queen Victoria, who rode in state from Kensington Palace to the popular beauty spot of Westbourne Green, and its name of Black Lion Lane was changed accordingly. The empress's presence and stucco-faced mansions attracted Bayswater's first residents in the 1830s. Upper-middle-class merchants, bankers, lawyers, diplomats and army people moved into the crescents whose colonnades reminded them of Nash's work in Regent's Park. The order and stateliness were exemplary.

In 1885 the area around Queensway was described by

the *Bayswater Annual* as 'pasture and common ... green fields, and blossoming gorse, and old hedgerow elms, under whose shadow the holiday-maker, or wandering botanist or ... suburban bird-trapper would take his rest', but within a very short time it had become a busy shopping street known for its cosmopolitan population. The first horse-drawn tram in London ran along the Bayswater Road in 1861. Two years later, William Whiteley opened his first eponymous shop on Westbourne Grove. His boast was to supply everything 'from a pin to an elephant at short notice'.

The *Bayswater Annual* of 1890 depicts the new sights to be found in the teeming byways: 'In Bayswater we are largely an Oriental people. In India, as well as in England, Bayswater is familiarly known as "Asia Minor" ... From the Ghats of Kensington-gardens Square to the Ghats of Calcutta, the storied boarding-houses of Bayswater to those on the banks of the Hugli, the change is but little thought of by the wives and children of an imperial race, to whom the Suez Canal becomes even more familiar than the Canal of Paddington.' A new, exciting phase of its history was in the offing.

When leases began to expire in the 1930s, the Church Commissioners who owned great tracts of land hereabouts began to tear the mansions down. Individual developers did their best to ensure that cut-price stuccoed terraces went up in their place. A substantial area bordering Bishop's Bridge Road was cleared and redeveloped and in 1952 work began on Hallfield Estate. These clean-cut blocks with winged balconies were designed by Sir Denys Lasdun, the architect responsible for the concrete slabs of the National Theatre. According to Bayswater's electoral register, it was Henry and Annie Taylor who moved in. Henry was listed as Master Builder; and this was the first time I caught my grandparents lying.

The interior of Number 1 Lynton House was cheap-and-cheerful contemporary. Bright colours, snappy designs, thin wood a man could put his foot through. Charlie lay in bed till two in the afternoon, ignoring the beckoning rays of the sun as they stirred the nylon curtains. When he did rouse himself it was to visit the demolition sites of Park Lane. From the luxury hotels that were being pulled down he and Brother Will struck deals with the demolition gangs. At a knock-down price they bought discarded boilers, cast-iron radiators, chandeliers, doors and parquet flooring. More often than not Charlie could blag a job from the Church Commissioners on the strength of his second-hand boilers.

Soon after moving into their all-mod-cons flat, six-year-old James was getting ready for school. Lily had laid out his tailor-made silk Italian suit on the bed when there was a knock at the door. She opened it, and two men wearing Sam Spade trenchcoats and trilbies walked in. They were policemen moonlighting as bailiffs, and they had come for money.

Lily started crying. When that did not work she became hysterical. The men ignored her. James flew to the kitchen and returned with a carving knife.

'Listen, you fuckers, I'll fucking stab you if you don't fuck off.'

Lily found her cool: 'Be a good boy, put the knife down and go to school.'

But the knife act had worked. Female histrionics they were used to, but not a maniacal six-year-old. Just as the bailiffs were leaving, however, one of them trod on Nicholas the poodle, who leapt up and yelped. Edward, who had stood by pursuing his usual policy of saying nothing, was galvanized into over-reaction. He grabbed hold of the offender by his collar.

'You bastard!' he screamed, and punched him in the face.

Luckily, Charlie was awoken by the barking poodle and weighed in to heal wounded pride.

He gave the two men a drink and a tenner each. 'Here's something for you. Come back next week and I'll settle the debt.' They gave him a week's breathing space, and came to know and respect him, and learned to turn a blind eye to his wild, uninhibited sons.

■

The poodle was a tribute to Billy Hill – a man with refined tastes in life. Charlie had been following his progress in the popular press. He read with interest that the snappy dresser who sported diamond rings on his fingers and was a ringer for Humphrey Bogart had retired to Bayswater. Just like him. Unlike Charlie, however, Billy Hill was being fêted with iced champagne cocktails.

It was 1955. The location was Gennaro's restaurant on Dean Street, Soho. The occasion was the publication of his autobiography. Its purported aim was to act as a warning to delinquents of the perils of crime. In reality it was used as a primer for would-be cosh boys. The fun started with a shrill blast on a police whistle, and a stampeding entrance of men in black masks bearing jemmies. Johnny-up-the-Spout and Three Pints Rapid, heavy-set fellows in drape suits, were joined by Billy's new friends, Sir Bernard and Lady Docker. The latter was so taken with Johnny, Rapid and Billy that she invited them to lunch on her yacht.

She also found time to consult Billy about a £150,000 robbery that had recently taken place at her Hampshire country home.

'The world could do with more men of his ability,' she told the *Daily Express*. 'There are certain things I love about him. He would always go for the big stuff – banks and things. Oh, it is rare that I come up against a gentleman like Billy Hill. We are so alike in many ways.'

Sir Bernard was more moderate in his praise: 'He said he did not want a penny for his work – not even for his bus fares.'

My grandfather noted how easy it was to take these gullible aristocrats for a ride.

The Dockers found Hill's knockabout humour refreshing and full of vitality. Spoof telegrams were read out: 'Hope you have a topping time – Britain's No. 1 Hangman'; 'Will you send us back our mail van? We miss it – Postmaster General.'

In the middle of the back-slapping fun, battle-scarred Billy announced his retirement.

'Villainy and crime is a young man's game,' he declared. He reflected on his life of crime as though he were a managing director delivering his swan-song. The Dockers listened as he expounded on his trademark – a V-sign for Victory carved on the side of a man's face. He described his methodology.

'I was always very careful to draw my knife down on the face, never across or upwards. Always down, so that if the knife slips you don't cut an artery. Cutting an artery is usually murder and only mugs do murder.'

His last verbal flourish was greeted with theatrical sighs.

'I am on my way out,' he lied.

■

At the same time, things were picking up for Charlie's little gang of men. This development came about through his growing dependence on sleeping-pills. Drugs were, quite simply, something you got from your doctor. Doctor P had a surgery on Harley Street from whence he dispensed sleeping-pills, appetite suppressants and black bombers to his fretful patients. In the postwar years, his middle-class clientele were fast becoming chronic pill-heads.

In return for some building work, the doctor provided Charlie with a steady supply of barbiturates for himself and diet pills for my grandmother. She was growing increasingly plump. On her fortieth birthday Charlie had told her she was too old for sex. With her asthma, headscarf and spectacles, she was not the good-time girl he had married. So he turned to Dr P's daughter, a débutante who always wore gloves and a hat. She was not of the hunt-ball variety but one of those debs who occupied the pages of social glossies. And what she lacked in maturity she made up for in readiness to turn a bit of Willesden rough into a Bayswater deb's delight.

•

The Fifties were about barbiturates. They were prescribed in their millions to housewives because they round off the rough edges of life. Barbs close your mind rather than expanding it. They make the confines of home somehow softer and more bearable. Because of their association with weepy housewives barbiturates do not have the glamour of heroin. There is, however, a thin line between an effective hit, addiction and an overdose. The déclassé pill of the drug world is also the most lethal street drug ever. It was my grandfather's drug of choice and I can understand all too clearly why he made that choice.

Things were happening fast for him. Through the socially adept Miss P Charlie met the newly married Lord and Lady Colwyn. She was the former Mrs Mortimer Reddington, the widow of a Harley Street surgeon. Lord Colwyn was a divorcé twice over. Like Charlie, he saw sex as something that occurred outside the family home.

He had only just been divorced by his second wife,

Hermione Sophia O'Bryen Smith, when he married the forty-three-year-old widow in January 1955. Hermione had been granted a decree absolute the previous November, just two years after marrying him, on the grounds of her husband's 'refusal to consummate the marriage and incapacity'.

Born on 26 November 1914, he succeeded to the family title in 1946. Shortly afterwards, the loyalty of his first wife was sorely tested when Lord Colwyn was court-martialled by his regiment. He pleaded guilty to acts of gross indecency with Italian youths while serving with the Central Mediterranean Force. He was cashiered without further ado.

His solicitor explained his conduct as follows: 'Severely wounded in the Normandy landings with subsequent illnesses and separation from his wife, this man with a latent tendency to homosexuality went to the island of Ischia, the morals of which had been notorious since the days of Tiberius.'

His wife told the court: 'I am prepared to take him back and make a home with him and our children.' She did until 1951, when the marriage was dissolved.

Lord Colwyn's proclivities were useful to know. But scandals happen to the best of families, and what was more important, in Charlie's eyes, was the new Lady Colwyn's keen eye as a property developer. She was always willing to exploit her connections with the Crown Estate. The graceful, and empty, houses of Connaught Square were in her sights. Lady Colwyn needed help from someone who could provide work at the lowest cost, and was happy to be paid cash in hand.

Connaught Square is one of the remaining bastions of Tyburnia's early nineteenth-century stylistic reticence. Tyburnia proper is the city that sprang up between the Edgware Road and Westbourne Terrace in the reign of William IV. It was admirably suited to the needs of yesterday's men, mushroom aristocrats and ex lord mayors. History was irrelevant when it came to doing the houses up. But it is interesting to note that wherever Charlie turned he could not escape his sordid past or hints of his doom-laden future.

At Number 49 Connaught Square the two uprights and crossbeam of Tyburn Tree gallows had once stood. The houses opposite had great iron balconies because that was where the sheriffs sat to watch the last act of a criminal's life.

What was now a garden enclosed by wrought-iron railings had once been an amphitheatre in the shadow of the gibbet. The 'last dread penalty' was enacted in the shade of the 'Deadly Never-Green' Tree. Seats were sold to spectators in open galleries like those of a racecourse. The key to the theatre was kept by Mammy Douglas, 'the Tyburn pew-opener'.

The first execution is supposed to have taken place in 1196; the last in 1783. The tree derived its name from the little River Tyburn, a brook bordered by elms, which meandered down from Hampstead to the Thames. These elms were used to string up the condemned. Criminals would make the long, straight journey from Newgate Gaol to Tyburn in an open cart, with the Chaplain and their own coffins as witnesses. Pepys remarked of the victims 'drawne towards the gallows at Tiburne . . . that they all looked very cheerful'. And it was a festive occasion, in which a life was celebrated and young girls handed out nosegays to the 'gentlemen of the road'.

Charlie's procession to Tyburnia was equally triumphant, with Brother Will his faithful foreman in tow, bearing boiler-sections from the Park Lane hotels plus the plumbers to fit them, and brother Ted to paint over the joins. The latter was used to turning up to work lacking the essential builders' materials. That is how he got his reputation as a thief.

He would take a door off its hinges, place it on two tea-chests and use it as a pasting board for the cut-price Sanderson wallpaper Charlie provided. If he needed a ladder he would nip round the corner and steal one. To paint the cornices of ceilings with the gold-leaf paint Charlie insisted on he'd use a brush attached to a broom. Sadly, the ingenious and imperturbable Ted did not last long. He died some time in the Sixties of painter's colic. No one is sure of the date of death. There was far too much else going on.

Part of Charlie's brief as dictated by Lady Colwyn was to supply the fixtures and fittings needed in a modern house. This brought him into contact with the demolition men who were currently making a fortune out of London's re-emergence from the ashes. One of these cronies offered him twenty second-hand radiators. Charlie bought them with the idea of selling them off to Moses, who was in the process of refurbishing a couple of houses in Bayswater. He went to Moses offering him the radiators at an inflated price. It turned out that they were the exact same radiators that had been stolen from Moses the week before. Not surprisingly, he was enraged when Charlie offered to sell him back his own property. Charlie had to give in and return them to their rightful owner. It cost him £300, which was lot of money in those days, but it was always the source of a good laugh.

As well as the building work, Charlie boasted that he was, in his manner of speaking, 'carrying on with' Lady Colwyn and her friend Mrs H, the sixty-year-old sister of an earl. Both were flamboyant women, married to 'difficult' men. One or other of them would ring Lynton House late at night and drawl down the line: 'Charlie, I need you. I'm so bored.' In the case of Mrs H, Charlie would rush to Queen

Street, Mayfair. In her penthouse flat, they explored the relative merits of sex and champagne. She became somewhat of a bore, though, when she came to find her lover amidst the scaffolding on Connaught Square. Her dress was décolleté and she had a bottle of champers in her hand. Charlie was outraged by her immodest display in front of his men: 'How dare you come here dressed like that?'

The highlight of my grandparents' social calendar in the year 1958 was a gilt-embossed invitation to a wedding reception at the House of Lords. Charlie was thrilled. Although he was ripping off Lord and Lady Colwyn right, left and centre, and diddling my good Lady and her female friends in every way, here was written proof that the act was working. Lady Colwyn's son Gerald Reddington was the groom, Valerie Gaunt, the Hammer-Horror actress, his bride. Charlie can be seen in a photograph that was intended to be of the erstwhile star of *Dracula* and several episodes of *Dixon of Dock Green*. There he is, in forbidding profile and pearl and grey finery, the new Mrs Reddington's snowy tulle skirts billowing around him. He had gone legit for the occasion, hiring top hat and tails for himself and reclaiming Lily's fur from the pawn shop. The cross-over between disparate sections of society had begun. Entertainers and crooks schmoozed their way into the confidence of the rich and, usually, titled. It can only have been at their invitation; perhaps they sensed that their vitiated stock needed new blood.

On Sunday nights Charlie would watch his Rediffusion television where he could catch up with Black Fred, live at the Palladium. Prinz Nikizolo appeared thumping wildly on bongo drums, his pet snakes writhing around the set. Black women in leopard-skin bikinis undulated in time to the jungle rhythms, jangling shark's-teeth necklaces round their necks. Men in loincloths brandished spears and shields and pretended to fight to the death. Black Fred and his tribal ensemble were a hit.

Through haunting the demolition sites of Park Lane, Charlie met the rabid fighting dog called Teddy Machin who patrolled the area as Billy Hill's enforcer. Charlie told him about some ornamental lights he had recently acquired. Machin told Billy Hill, who turned up at Connaught Square in his Mercedes. The deal was done.

■

The 1948 Criminal Justice Act made preventive detention more widespread. So, as an habitual criminal, Hill could expect an extra ten years to be added to any sentence he might incur. He gave up screwing and opened spielers with the help of Jack Spot.

The black market's illicit profits caused a boom in clubs in the 1950s. Poker, faro and rummy were played for high stakes. Gambling-mad burglars like 'Taters' Chatham would absent themselves from the table for a few hours and return with funds after a foray into the mansions of Mayfair. Then they would lose it all over again in the same night.

Hill set a tone of play and conduct that was unparalleled. Charlie was dazzled by the sophisticated mix of Hoorays and hacks, and the sleeker variety of criminal. It was in his basement dive at Soho that Billy just caught sight of my grandfather. The skimpy and undernourished body had pumped itself up into an appealing and lethal maturity. As for Billy, he was a crook, a villain, a thief, a thug, a genius and a kind and tolerant man, said Duncan Webb, the journalist who ghosted his memoir. And he recruited men with all sorts of talents.

Under Billy Hill's orders, Charlie converted a private house in Green Street, Mayfair, into a successful gambling club. For Ronnie Dice, who borrowed the money from Billy

Hill, he built the first gay club in London, which featured coffins and toilet seats around the dance floor, and was frequented by the son of a cabinet minister. The club closed down when Dice had to leave town in a hurry, Billy Hill in hot pursuit.

On the proceeds Charlie bought a flashy Rolls-Royce, and was able to convince people that he was wealthy. He flashed large bundles of notes around, but most of the time he was desperately broke. He was beginning to see crime as a trade, with greater rewards and dangers than that of a master builder. His extravagance, addiction to boasting, impatience of conventional morality were driving him into the arms of Billy Hill. One important venture for which Billy supplied the capital was renting a castle in Scotland for a week. He did this especially to strip the roof of its lead.

When Charlie pulled off a big job he liked to celebrate ostentatiously, to go out on the town with his comrades-in-arms and burn money. In my family, if you have money you spend it immediately because we refuse to believe in the future. Something else we learned from Charlie. He was a wide boy who did not care that his wife had been forced to take an evening job, waitressing at the dog races. There were endless violent quarrels, over money and other women, from which she emerged covered in bruises. Edward would take himself off to the hush of the cinema on the Edgware Road. He liked thrilling re-enactments of bloody wars, because the hurt was contained by the silver screen.

•

Violence was part of the backdrop to west London. Bayswater was becoming notorious. Rival groups staked their claims on gambling, prostitution and rent rackets. Drinking clubs were being burnt out by petrol bombs and toughs shot at each other from moving cars. Just past the Edgware Road, it was said a whiff of 'old Chicago' hung in the air. Charlie was more than a passing bystander, though he did appear as just that in *The Blue Lamp*.

In the dark alleyways and stairwells of Paddington, George Dixon, later of *Dock Green*, hunts down Dirk Bogarde's desperate delinquent. Charlie claimed that he could be spotted laughing wildly in the scene that takes place outside the Coliseum Cinema on Harrow Road. In fact, it is the merest suggestion of a smirk. Bogarde, dressed in a black roll-neck sweater with slicked-back hair, is being questioned by a colleague of Dixon's. My grandfather saunters past the action – his contemptuous jeer the exact mirror image of Bogarde's own unwillingness to respect the Law.

The trademark black shirt and moustache of my grand-father make another appearance in a photograph taken by Victor at Dymchurch. He sits on a low wall, the grey sky hanging like a shroud behind him. The view is bleak, and Charlie's white face reflects the landscape's harshness. His eyes burn holes in the viewfinder. My grandmother sits further along the wall. She is windswept, yet solid and com-forting, and smiles in the face of his distaste for her.

Charlie was proud of his ability to squander money on his sons. He would give them anything, even the money to buy drugs. But what he really enjoyed was the adrenalin rush of being scared, of constantly having to look over his shoulder. It made him think more quickly; it got him keyed up. It was like sex with a minor or another man's wife.

In what is a chilling portrait of a man surrounded by his loved ones, my grandfather can be seen in yet another snap-shot from the family album. In each successive shot he is so carefully poised it is as though he were begging to be exposed. The blustering air of the seaside features once again as it ruffles my grandmother's thinning hair. All those perms and dye-jobs are taking their toll. This time she is flanked by her two younger sons, her sister Dolly and brother George. They make a complacently cheerful, blow-the-weather family group. But Charlie is determined to provide a sour note. Like a sulking child, only far more virulent, he is provoked by this show of solidarity. He stands slightly apart, his body at right angles from the rest. He is wearing a grey pullover with a white shirt and a cravat tied neatly at the neck. His hair is slicked into place with brilliantine. His eyes are narrowed with suspicion, his lips set in grim contempt. He does not want to be there. This is not me, his eyes are telling Edward who wields the camera. I am not really here.

•

As bulldozers knocked down the low-rise streets north of Kensington, West Indians, many of them working for London Transport, moved into the remaining terraces. Perec Rachman was one of the few landlords who allowed Irish, blacks and dogs into his properties. An estate agent's clerk, he started his business from a Bayswater phone-box. A local prostitute encouraged him to set up a flat-letting agency in order to sub-let properties to her and her friends. He began by renting flats for £5 a week, sub-letting them at £15 to working girls.

Soon Rachman's flats were let, sub-let and sub-let again to prostitutes, burglars, murderers and desperate immigrants. The lively presence of Trinidadians, Jamaicans, *et al* – who were used to spirited congregations on sunlit streets and booming ska music – incensed the under-privileged, more reticent whites, who saw them as competition for jobs and accommodation. There was a reason for my grandfather's new black shirt. 'Little India' was already home to an intriguing mix of Russian-Polish Jews, Cypriots and Maltese when it became known as 'Brown Town'. Landlords started charging a few pounds extra for allowing relatives and friends to camp on the floors of the original tenants. Soon it made sense to charge per head rather than per room. Rooms were split into six sections, the inhabitants sleeping in shifts.

Charlie, surprisingly, despised Rachman. Perhaps because Rachman's chocolate-and-coffee-cream Rolls PR 23 was more visible than his salmon-pink pride and joy.

Rachman's presence led, in a roundabout way, to the resurgence of a ghost from Charlie's past. In 1956, Sir Oswald Mosley entered his living quarters once again. Fascist splinter groups proliferated in Notting Hill, Ladbroke Grove and Bayswater. Charlie had time for them all. The White Defence League had its HQ on Tavistock Road, from where a swastika flag was flown and military marches broadcast into the street. Ronnie Kray was paid to 'knock off' the League's leader, Colin Jordan, but never got round to it. The League of Empire Loyalists had their base in a hotel on Connaught Terrace, just round the corner from Lord and Lady Colwyn. Once again, Charlie was in the middle of the action.

After the war, which Mosley had spent in Brixton Prison, he had recuperated abroad, only to return to the latest hotspot as soon as his country demanded. He made his first 'The Blackshirts are on the march again' speech to a 600-strong crowd in Kensington Town Hall. He recruited workers from the coal and coke wharf near Ladbroke Grove and local Teddy boys. Again, he provided instant solutions, pinpointing blacks as the cause of poor housing and low wages. Again, his powers as a demagogue proved successful at rabble-rousing.

From January 1958 his Union Movement held meetings on street corners outside Kensington Park Road synagogue. Charlie went along to listen to his old favourite. As he drove home in the dark, his Rolls was attacked by a mob. In the darkness a group of men standing outside the synagogue mistook his black hair and polo shirt for the skin of a West Indian. They threw a bottle of HP sauce through the window, and Charlie roared with laughter all the way home.

His allegiance to Mosley was in no way incommensurate to his fondness for Black Fred or Old Man Moses. They were friends, close contacts. Charlie was broadminded in that respect. Besides, Black Fred and Moses despised the West Indians, their raucous shebeens, happy-go-lucky appearance and games of dominoes on the street.

And in the words of Mosley himself: 'The word of honour is sacred; that is the very basis of European values . . . Once honour in dealing with all men, and complete loyalty to each other are set aside, the end is not only an abyss of horror but chaos and final disintegration.' It is strange that Charlie did not take his words literally; they might have helped him later on in his life. But Mosley's fine talking struck a more superficial chord with my romantic grandfather, who held the word of upper-crust men in sacred trust.

The Union Movement's membership increased to 1,500 and the August issue of its newsletter, *Action*, declared: 'Times have changed. The people are waking up. Once again our critics can't take it. But stick close, boys, and hang on tight. There's a lot more coming . . .'

Perhaps they were referring to the race riots which occurred later that month. For four days gangs of white youths roamed the streets attacking black people and their property. Black youths retaliated. Charlie cruised the streets, but not in his Rolls. It was too conspicuous for this lark, and he wanted to watch the mob at work. It made him feel so superior. A house in Paddington was petrol-bombed and the canal towpath in Kensal was blocked by rioters. Milk-bottles and dustbin-lids became missiles, as well as bottles of HP sauce. Posters went up showing Mosley's face in messianic relief with the legend 'He Is Coming' printed beneath it. They were defaced with graffiti of penises and the words 'Lucky old him.'

Mosley's Union Movement then issued a leaflet with a cartoon of a black man with spear and grass skirt. It read: 'People of Kensington act now. Your country is worth fighting for. Fight with the Union Movement . . . Take action now. Protect your jobs. Stop coloured immigration. Houses for white people – not coloured immigrants.' Action! How my grandfather loved that word.

The aftermath was more shocking than the actual events. Alexander Marshall from Mosley's Union Movement received a conditional discharge for inciting a crowd of 700 to riot, and a £10 fine for distributing Fascist leaflets. The judge described the leaflet as 'very reasonable' but deplored the term 'coloured invasion'. The police commended Marshall as 'the most amenable and courteous arrestee that Notting Hill has seen in a long time'. Fascist involvement and government incompetence were ignored by the media. Instead the *Daily Mail* printed a cartoon of Teddy boys standing on a bloodied Union Jack. As usual, Charlie noted, it was the working classes who took the flak. More fool them, he decided.

▪

Another politician friend of Charlie's was in the news a year later. Lord Colwyn, who much preferred talking to working, resigned as the president of the Marylebone Liberal Association on the eve of the December 1959 by-election. Whenever Charlie was spotted through the bay window of his house on Connaught Square the cry went up: 'Look out, here comes Charlie!' But Colwyn and his extended family of stepchildren could not help liking the cockney rogue.

Colwyn held court in Connaught Square every night, and

Charlie duly attended. He was there when the great man dictated his letter of resignation only twenty-four hours after volunteering to distribute leaflets. He had been president for eighteen months but complained: 'I am unhappy at some features in the Liberal by-election campaign in St Marylebone. I have not yet resigned from the Liberal Party, but I am sending a letter to Lord Rea, and in future will sit on the cross-benches in the House of Lords.'

Charlie listened and nodded sympathetically. Like his Lordship he had a profound distrust of the Labour Party. Lord Colwyn explained that 'at the present time a vote for Liberal is the same as a vote for Labour'. Since the Conservative majority in St Marylebone was 14,771, and Labour hadn't a hope of getting in, it was a strange position to take. But his colleagues were not too surprised, since he had resigned from the party once before. A party spokesman summed up Colwyn's erratic behaviour: 'This seems to be a habit, and one is forced to wonder just how permanent the present situation will be. Only on Monday night, Lord Colwyn was anxious to speak from the same platform as Lady Violet Bonham Carter.'

His resignation was not expected to influence the voting. But Charlie was very impressed at all this, and only too happy, a short while afterwards, to lend his lordship several thousands of pounds. As with his politics and his sex life, Lord Colwyn's finances were a movable feast. No one knows what he needed the money for, but I doubt if Charlie cared. The significance of the loan came in a rush to him – here was a great lord indebted to yours truly. Charlie thought he had the lord and all that a lord brings with him in his pocket. He was not to see that money again for a very long time.

13 · The Major

Moscow Road was completed in 1812, and named in celebration of the Muscovite blows that destroyed Napoleon's
forces that year. Its red-brick blocks of luxury apartments,
which arrived in Queen Victoria's reign, reflect the triumph
of communal might over despotic self-aggrandizement.

The wealthy Levantine merchants who first inhabited
Windsor and Burnham Courts caused the Greek Orthodox
Cathedral of St Sophia to be erected on their road. It is still
there, its striped yellow and red bricks and terracotta walls,
the marbled interior decorated with mosaics, successfully
evoking the Byzantine influence on Bayswater. This was a
street along which men who looked suspiciously like Peter
Lorre prowled.

At the Bayswater end of Moscow Road, fronting on to
Queensway, is another grand edifice. This one houses 'the
universal provider'. In 1851, William Whiteley and his family
travelled down to London from Leeds to see the Great
Exhibition at Crystal Palace. He was so impressed with the
commercial enterprise and innovation on display that he
moved to London *toute suite*. The great chancer opened his
first shop on Westbourne Grove – called 'Bankrupt Avenue'
back then – and sold ribbons and fancy goods. By 1872 he
had bought all the neighbouring premises, despite riots by
the local traders who burned an effigy of 'the most hated
man in London' on Guy Fawkes' Night. When he opened a

butcher's department, the local butchers went up in arms, standing outside his stores – marrow bones and cleavers at the ready. His store suffered a number of mysterious fires, the most spectacular lasting for several days despite the efforts of thirty-four steam fire-engines.

The next shop he opened was the one that still stands on Queensway. It is also where he was shot dead on 24 January 1907 by a young man who claimed to be his bastard son.

Lily loved Whiteley's. Like Eliza Doolittle in *My Fair Lady* she sang its praises, especially the haberdashery department's. She and Charlie moved into Number 4 Windsor Court in January 1961. They started the new decade in style. Moscow Road was an exciting place to be – full of call-girls and warring minicab drivers, oriental tradesmen and beatniks.

It had been a long time since a new decade had been greeted with such buoyant enthusiasm, especially in the economic world. The stock markets in Wall Street and London had both finished the old year at new peaks. Share prices in London had risen over fifty per cent. Gone was the dollar shortage; gone were the currency restrictions that had hampered trade. International cartels had taken on a new respectability under the cloak of the Common Market, so the man from *The Times* said. The European economy was a world force again.

There was a new idealism about. Charlie and his sons were convinced that at last their lives, by rights, should be better. After the great depression of the Thirties, six years of world war and fifteen more of austerity, they were hungry for fun. National service had been abolished, the Clean Air Act of 1956 meant that Lily could step out without her inhaler. Everyone could have a job for the asking. But not Victor. Lily smothered her boys with love and fear. She did not see why they should have to be exposed to life's misfortunes – such as work.

As for Charlie, 'You don't want to work there,' he would say, 'not for those fuckers.' But Victor insisted on thinking for himself; his parents' authority was, by their own admission, questionable. In the end, Charlie was forced to give Victor money not to go out to work. He received ten pounds a day to slouch around the flat. One day he stumbled across some gas cylinders and an oxygen tank in the spare room. Victor knew, from his father's demolition sites, that these were essential tools of the trade. He knew that if you mixed the ingredients and lit them they would burn into metal. But he did wonder, a few days later, when the local paper was reeling from the shock of an audacious attack on the safe at Barclay's Bank on the corner of Moscow Road and Queensway. The burglars had rented the flat above the bank, drilled a hole in the ceiling, and then, in the dead of night, burned through the walls of the safe with the aid of oxygen and gas. They fled from the scene of the crime with hundreds of thousands of pounds – never to be seen again.

Victor registered these seemingly discrete facts but let them be chased away by his own preoccupations – such as where he might find the next good time to be had. James, however, was more alert to his father's activities. He knew that Charlie had provided the equipment for the raid on Barclay's Bank's safe. And he was thrilled when his father – to keep him quiet – gave him his first driving lesson at the wheel of his brand-new Silver Cloud II. The new motor, with a top speed of more than 112 m.p.h., and acceleration to 100 m.p.h. within 38.5 seconds, which was 12 seconds quicker than the previous model, was a present from the grateful burglars for his ability to keep quiet. 'At 60 m.p.h. the loudest noise in this new Rolls-Royce', went the sales slogan that Charlie cheerfully repeated, 'comes from the electric clock.' James was not the only one to be paid off. Victor received a larger-than-usual cash sum that day for doing absolutely nothing at all and took himself off to Soho's espresso bars and jazz clubs, and Chelsea's discothèques and boutiques. On his relentless quest he found exciting company. Smoothies and swingers, like Black Fred who was hanging out with Brian Epstein, were using their cool to calculate their every move. The imperative was summed up by John Lennon: 'to live now, this moment'. Victor and James soaked up the new optimism. Listening to the warbling voices of the Beatles and Bob Dylan, they were liberated from the poverty of Hyde Park Square. But it was not just about freshness. It was remarked that there was a strange, psychopathic energy abroad. More than Epstein and the Beatles, the ruthlessness of Andrew Loog Oldham and his Rolling Stones energized my over-stimulated uncles. Mean-eyed and foul-mouthed, they groaned about satisfaction. And when they got it, they still were not pleased.

If anyone felt the new vibe, it was Charlie. He was living it up in his latest establishment, emerging from its vast oak door in businesslike pin-stripes and bowler hat. When they saw him ambling up the road, his new friends, the Kray twins, would giggle: 'Here comes the Major.'

Although the East End was hypnotized by the randomness of the twins' ferocity, Billy Hill and Charlie were more circumspect. They thought the Krays were fools. After all, violence is so unnecessary when you possess a truly great criminal mind. From the windows of Number 4 Charlie could watch two of these minds in action.

Jack Spot, Brother Will's old fellow traveller, paraded the Edgware Road in his brown fedora and sharp suit, immaculate and fresh from the barber's. Personal hygiene was so important to men with not-so-metaphorical blood on their hands. After much perambulating and regal waving to passers-by, he took his seat in the tea-rooms of the Cumberland and sat there for the rest of the morning. From here he dispensed advice to anyone who asked for it.

Davis the Greengrocer's was directly opposite Charlie's window. On his daily tour of his high-rent empire, Perec Rachman would help himself to plums from the display before walking on by without paying. His black henchman walked ten paces behind. Charlie became friendly with Mr Davis, who had a son with whom James also struck up a lively friendship. Although James was only eleven years old he was privy to the older boy's hectic love life. Pepe was romancing the Welsh chanteuse Shirley Bassey. He took her out every night, Pepe said, and helped her to chase her dream. Once Shirley achieved fame, though, she left Pepe for Kenneth Hume. He was more high-profile; a television producer and chronic gambler who attended Charlie's chemin de fer games. To prove he still loved her despite everything, nineteen-year-old Pepe visited Shirley in her suite at the Cumberland Hotel. Once he'd bullied his way in, he took a gun to her head. James's young friend died in prison.

■

Shirley Bassey was not the only popular entertainer to grace Bayswater. Alexis Korner, the blues man, lived at Burnham Court, and Charlie's sons often saw the thrillingly scruffy Rolling Stones paying him visits. Brian Jones, the blond poster-boy, had even worked at Whiteley's. Vic and James really were part of the in-crowd. James was precociously suffused with the sense of his own power. Adrenalin pumped through his well-fed frame as he ran up and down Moscow Road brandishing a machete. It belonged to Teddy Machin, who had left a store of weapons and ammunition at Number 4 for safekeeping.

Charlie gave up building work in favour of gambling

because it was far more exciting and glamorous. He knocked down the dividing wall between the two reception rooms, and installed a baccarat table. He placed a mirrored bar at one end – he liked to watch himself pouring drinks for his friends. It was a crescent-shaped affair, lit from beneath, with richly coloured Venetian glasses on glass shelves. Gangsters were asked to leave their guns on it. Albert Dimes, an old villain who was now a spent force, Jack Spot, who soon would be, and Billy Hill, still sitting pretty, assembled around his table carving up London. The Krays, they decided, were a major irritant but Billy knew he had to befriend them. It made sense to keep on the right side of up-and-coming youngsters. Deals, secret meetings, pay-offs and broken promises all took place under my grandfather's nose. And all the while, he was learning new tricks.

Billy Hill had learnt to play baccarat and its variant, chemin de fer, at Monte Carlo. There he met the swells of the gaming élite, men like Major Stoop, John Aspinall, who founded the Clermont Club, and Tom Holland of Crockford's. Billy had ostensibly retired to a villa in southern Spain. But his white Lincoln convertible was still to be seen cruising his various interests in London. These interests were the gambling clubs that my grandfather helped to run. In them, Billy and Charlie fostered the illusion that in just one night a miracle might be worked – something that would change a man's life for ever. The younger sons of great families cheated by the curse of primogeniture sought to change their luck with a roll of the dice. But the lucky break is a dangerous misconception. It teases a man into losing his reason.

Illicit gambling was the cornerstone of crime in the Sixties, when gambling fever was rife. Charlie was convinced that this was where the fortunes of the future lay. In 1960 the Betting and Gaming Act was passed, which for the first time allowed the working man to place bets outside a racecourse.

Its main purpose, though, was to restore credibility to the police by legalizing street betting and gaming clubs. Its architects assumed that their Act would damage criminal interests, but Charlie's new mentor, Billy Hill, saw it as the legalizing of his criminal empire. As the racketeers moved in on the clubs, he proved his gift of foresight. By 1964 Britain was in the throes of the biggest gambling boom outside Nevada.

In order to fund their activities, Charlie and Billy went to Crockford's, the oldest and most exclusive gambling club in the world. A portrait of its founder, the Duke of Wellington, graced the dining-room, where venison and Burgundy *jus* were served under the Wedgwood ceiling. Their first mark was a dummy to practise on – Johnny Miller, too old and slow now to recognize his former protégé's duplicity.

In his dotage, Johnny Miller was softening up. He caused much amusement *chez* Charlie with his extravagant acts of kindness towards children. At Christmas he loaded his car with toys and chocolates, and dressed himself as Father Christmas to entertain the sick kiddies at Paddington Hospital. But Billy was disgusted by Johnny's coarse manners. He slurped his food as though he were in a transport caff, mopping up the Burgundy *jus* as though it were ketchup. Billy raised his eyebrow at Charlie, who promised to do better next time. Their revulsion at Johnny did not stop them robbing him blind at poker.

They had a system. It is hard to believe that Johnny did not see through it. If he did, it is just about conceivable that he was resigned to being ripped off by his friend. That was what friends were for, after all. Each convoluted bluff was predetermined weeks in advance. Charlie and Davey Perkins, his cuckolded mate from the army, practised with marked cards, nods and signs in order to beat their opponent. Charlie and Davey were inseparable. My grandfather fed off Davey's indefatigable good humour, which Davey was happy to deploy in return for ready cash. They practised at Moscow Road for hours on end under the expert tutelage of Billy. By moving his hand across his hairline, Charlie could indicate to Davey, who was dealing, 'I need a king.' By rubbing his right eye, 'I need a queen.' Charlie bit his fingernails to the quick in his anxiety at memorizing the signals. He was as absorbed in his craft as an actor preparing for his début appearance on the West End stage.

·

I am told that a good attitude at the table is vital. This was why my grandfather was so good at playing cards. Furthermore, each man is engaged in close observation of his opponent. Charlie had been doing that for years. How is the dealer shuffling the cards, how are the players laying down their chips, what are they saying, how are they looking at their cards? Was he forcing them to guess his class, or did they have some kind of read on him? These were the questions Charlie had to ask himself. The strength of a player's hand, confidence in his strategy, were summed up in one word: 'class'. Charlie was concerned that his chewed stumps were a sign of nerves, that they would show his class. So he sent Lily in a taxi to Selfridge's to buy false finger-nails.

Since the Seventies Poker is no longer played at Crockford's. Because of cheats who act in concert, like Billy and my grandfather, it is not deemed a game of equal chance. But chemin de fer is. Billy set up Charlie with a mark – Boyd Williamson, the heir to a Scottish cooperage firm. Billy had first met him in Monte Carlo, where he had borrowed £500 from him at the roulette wheel.

'Don't you know you should never lend money to a stranger?' Billy asked him. He never paid him back because he knew a mug when he saw one.

Charlie and Davey sat in Crockford's lobby waiting for

Boyd. Black Fred was the wrong colour for this game. But Davey Boy slotted in smoothly. He was charming and made people feel important, always ready with a joke and an ingratiating smile. They sat in the leather armchairs, where they happened upon the splendidly turbanned and berobed Gaekwar of Baroda. The founder of the gracious Gaekwar's dynasty was Damaji I, who had risen to power in 1740. Strangely, the last Gaekwar, Sayaji Rao III, died in 1939. But this most enlightened of the Mahratta princes of the Gujarat state insisted on being taken at face value. And who was Charlie to argue with that? Out came the weapons to disarm a rich oriental: army stories, off-colour patter, a subtle deference, and they enticed him into the game.

The croupier was in on it. The inspector had been nobbled. All they had to do was lead Boyd and the Gaekwar to the table. The banker dealt one card each to the players and one to himself. The players were eager to see what fate had dealt them. The banker repeated the operation. The tension mounted. The cards were exposed. If any pair of cards totalled eight or nine the holder of that pair would win. Not one of them could beat the banker, so he offered a third card to the player on his right, and the shoe was passed around again.

Bank takes a card, the player takes a card. Is punto going to win or will it be banco – or even égalité? The drama was enacted under lampshades that hung low over the table and emitted a discreetly flattering green glow. The furniture was Louis XV. 'The Battle of Waterloo' was taking place on a canvas on the opposite wall.

The players were each given the opportunity to shuffle the cards. When it came to Charlie's turn he inserted a batch of prearranged cards, the sequence of which he had memorized. The croupier stacked them in the sabot, taking care not to disturb the order. All Charlie then had to do was wait for his cards to appear, and place his bets accordingly. Once Charlie and Davey had made their nightly profit, they stopped playing. That night Charlie came home with plastic bags full of chips and notes. They added up to a quarter of a million pounds.

·

Charlie's day started very pleasantly. Lily brought him a cup of tea in bed with his copy of the *Greyhound Express*. He placed his orders with Black Fred, who would go to the track that evening. Fred had been displaced from the Palladium by a beat combo, and was in need of the extra cash to supplement his earnings. He was pimping his bikini-clad dancers and selling marijuana in Bayswater's clubs and cafés. No wonder my mother was wary of him. Sometimes he would put the frighteners on people for his old friend. Especially if they were Jamaicans. Like the ones who worked as tailors on Berwick Street. When Charlie's suits were not made to his liking he sent them back, demanding free alterations. When the Jamaicans demurred, Black Fred paid a visit.

'Your suits will be ready tomorrow,' he assured my impatient grandfather.

Once he was suitably attired, Charlie hit Moscow Road, and the first thing he would see was his brother Tots, the Stonebridge King of the Gas Meters. Tots waited on the pavement outside Windsor Court every morning, knowing that Charlie would give him ten pounds to put on the horses. Lily often invited him in for breakfast but he always refused, preferring to wait on the street outside. He was on his own now that his wife had left him. In 1945 his daughter had married a Canadian GI who took her to start a new life on a new continent. As soon as she could, she sent her mother a plane ticket. Mother told Tots she was going to visit their daughter.

'That's nice, dear,' he said. What she didn't tell him was that the ticket was one way. He never saw her or his daughter again.

After handing some folding stuff to his decrepit brother, Charlie made his first call. Davey, who had been waiting in the kitchen for his boss to make an appearance, drove him to his barber's on Jermyn Street. Inside the wood-panelled enclosure of Trumper's, the perfumers, Charlie's creeping grey hairs were replaced with black. From within the soothing balm of hot towels he held forth on the previous night's successes. How he had been at Crockford's and found himself next to the Marchioness who owned the estate in Cork where his grandmother had worked.

'My grandmother broke her back for you,' he thought to himself. 'I'm going to get a lot of money off you,' and he did.

•

Charlie and Black Fred still chanced their well-tailored arms in the outfitters of Piccadilly and Soho, more for the fun of it than through need. It was the time of the Kenyan uprising, and Black Fred put the conflict to good use. He and Charlie entered separately. In the presence of a junior assistant and other customers, Charlie muttered 'Mau Mau bastard,' throwing his voice so as to cast suspicion on the salesman.

'Did you call me a Mau Mau bastard?' asked a haughty, upper-class Fred. The ensuing fuss was such that the master tailor was grateful when Fred walked out with a free, off-the-rail pin-stripe suit.

Afternoons consisted of mooching from one post to another acquiring information from men in belted raincoats. London's population shifts too much for there to be a Cosa Nostra. So there are just temporary alliances in its under-world. That way, Charlie could work with Billy, the Krays,

Teddy Machin, whoever was around at the right time in the right place with the right skills for the job in hand.

He would join Teddy Machin and another hitman, Ray Rosa, outside Billy Hill's club on Green Street. Mrs H lived round the corner, and Charlie had long since ditched her, so if he was twitchy it was understandable. But there were other, more palpable reasons for an attack of the nerves. Billy's men were patrolling the streets of Soho tracking the movements of the baby-faced Kray twins. Although Billy and Charlie were contemptuous of the terrifying twosome, if they were in the vicinity a runner rushed to the club. He would warn the shuffling men, 'The twins are coming!' and they would scatter in all directions.

Another stop-off point was the Bank of Valletta, deliberately spelt wrongly so as to be confused with the Maltese string of banks. The bank, on Shaftesbury Avenue, was a front for non-existent businesses that needed a trading account. It was run by Cyril Green, the man who sold a fleet of Routemaster buses to the Indian government. He drove the delegates round and round a field in Sussex on which six buses were parked. Each time they drove up to the field Cyril took a different route. The Indians did not realize that they were seeing the same buses from ten vantage points. So they paid for sixty and took delivery of six.

Cyril had the dried-out look of a man who had seen better days but whose expertise was still considered a valuable commodity. So people took him seriously. They respected him because his tweeds were old, like his manner. He was all too happy when unsuspecting members of the public opened an account with a cash deposit. But it was another matter altogether if they made a withdrawal. When one customer asked for £50 in ten pound notes Cyril made his excuses. He ran upstairs where various villains were assembled and asked them to empty their pockets to the tune of a 'tenspot' each. The bank was essential to my grandfather.

∎

According to the experts, long-firms must start straight and end with a twist. This was how Charlie liked to do business. Billy Hill was the backer; he put up the money to finance the fraud. He approved of my grandfather: here was a fellow who knew how to dress and behave, who was soundly connected, who understood and appreciated what Mr Hill was trying to do. Because Mr Hill recognized intelligence when he saw it. That Charlie was profoundly untrustworthy did not deter him one iota. For one thing, so was Billy himself. For another, he preferred working with like-minded men. The great thing about men like Charlie, he figured, was that they got on with the job if the price was right, and did not ask damn foolish questions.

So Charlie was the organizer; he directed operations from the background, and selected the cast to help him run the firm. The most important member was Teddy Machin. He was the minder, and minders must have the right credentials for the job. Since Teddy was an efficient killer who was expert at glowering in the background, he was an effective deterrent to potential informers. He was put in by Billy and Charlie to protect their interests and to ensure that their instructions were performed to the letter.

Charlie also had to find other sources of finance. These could be bent bank managers, retired villains or businessmen with 'black' money; men like Johnny Miller who thought they had money to burn. He was especially useful since he could double up as the 'fix'. He was paid in advance for his contacts. If the firm ran into trouble Johnny was prepped to pay off the police, lawyers and judges.

The front man was crucial. In this case, it was pipe-smoking, genial Cyril. He nominally owned the business and, should things go wrong, it would be him who took the rap. But he rarely did, he was so slippery.

Cyril's great strength was his discipline, and his ability to deal calmly and collectedly with 'screamers', or angry creditors. The Bank of Valletta was an excellent means of authenticating the numerous firms the cast created. From the sanctity of his desk at the bank Cyril could order goods from suppliers known by those in the know as a soft touch. He could write his own credit references in unnaturally glowing terms, using Bank of Valletta headed notepaper.

The kidology of sales reps is an essential factor. Cyril relied on his suppliers taking him for a mug. You must start with small orders, then slowly increase them. Pay promptly. Place one large order. Keep paying. Order nothing for a couple of visits. The rep will be worried. Then place another large order to coincide with a half-page advertisement in the local newspaper. Do not pay for it. Place another large order on trust. Disappear.

My grandfather became known by his peers as a top-class long-firm fraudster because the skills needed came naturally to him. He could judge within moments the strengths and weaknesses of the people with whom he was dealing. He could sense if his partner was trying to con him – all con men know better than to trust their partners. He could improvise schemes and stories for the benefit of creditors, backers, and front men. Perfect timing was needed to know when to speak and what to say. He learnt this from going to the tailor's: he was well known, he collected and paid for his goods on time, he would say he was coming back tomorrow with an African chieftain, together they would order more goods, go to fittings, is sir pleased?, the bill can wait. Fraudsters are businessmen who can make large amounts of money from crime without becoming known as criminals.

Charlie had another reason for spending his afternoons at the Bank of Valletta. She was eighteen, beautiful, and straight off the boat from Cork. She was an Irish girl, but there her resemblance to Katie O'Sullivan ended. Tall and skinny, just like Twiggy, mini-skirted, wide-eyed Kathleen had come to London for an abortion. If she hadn't, the former convent girl would have ended up in Cork's 'Magdalen laundry'.

In order to understand the motivation of an eighteen-year-old girl who embarks on an adulterous relationship with a conman, and since no one was prepared to talk about her, I did some digging. From the 1800s Irish girls who had committed the sin of bearing children out of wedlock were virtually imprisoned behind the walls of convent laundries. Once there, they spent a lifetime of penance laundering army uniforms in the service of the Sisters of Charity. Unlike their prostitute namesake they were not rewarded with forgiveness or love but were treated with unrelenting harshness. In the 1970s, church property once held by the Sisters in Dublin was sold back to the Republic. Some 133 unmarked graves were uncovered in a cemetery on the convent grounds. They were the graves of women who had worked in the laundries all their lives.

The guileless Kathleen with her guilty secret was smitten by my forty-five-year-old grandfather. When she became pregnant by him, he 'paid her off', she had another abortion and he moved on to the next girl. But Kathleen had not given up on him.

·

Charlie could not sit still long enough to enjoy his love-nest with his colleen, he had business to attend to. Putney Bridge was the next port of call. Billy Hill and Charlie had bought the demolition rights to a row of Victorian houses that were being replaced by office blocks. They got Miller to invest money in the project. Having given him a bit of money from their first demolition job – the *Illustrated News* building on Fleet Street – they were going to knock him this time. But Johnny sent his henchman to work on the site. He suspected something was up. Charlie wanted Johnny's minder off the job so he told Brother Will to start a fight with him. They duly fought, and Charlie rang up Miller to complain that his man had been fighting.

'What can I do?' he asked. Johnny agreed that his minder must be sacked. Needless to say, he lost all his money. Charlie explained it away. 'There wasn't as much steel as I had reckoned. I've lost money, too. Don't worry, we'll make double next time. There's another building I've just heard about. Come on, we've got to get our money back.' Johnny was losing his touch.

Evenings would find my grandfather hosting a cocktail party at Windsor Court. Johnny and his corrupt police friends would be guests of honour. Pretty girls were laid on for entertainment. Charlie offered every type of drink, although because he did not drink himself he had no idea what measurements to give. He handed out tumblers filled to the brim with Scotch and finished off with a splash of soda. Lily's plump form was coaxed into a silk dress and her hair carefully crimped as she wheeled her hostess trolley around the guests' legs. She tried to keep smart for Charlie's sake, whispered her platitudinous sister Irene, even taking slimming-pills – though they were bad for her asthma.

Lily had baked the tartlets and sausage rolls that were being scooped and speared on to cocktail sticks. She handed them round while Charlie flirted with the girls, kissing and cuddling them indiscriminately. They wore their hair loose and their skirts short and were very decorative. One of the girls who came with Johnny Miller pointed to the club-footed villain and confided to Greta: 'It makes me wet just to look at him.' This was the context in which my mother grew. She saw the new sexual freedom wrought by the Pill and *Lady Chatterley*. She saw that Johnny Miller did not even have to pay the wretched, un-idea'd girls any more, just give them cash presents. Greta was appalled but kept her mouth shut. She retreated to the back parlour, where she showed Victor how to do the *Guardian* crossword.

Irene busily admired the flock wallpaper and tile sur-round. When Johnny gave her the glad eye, and Charlie whispered in her ear, 'Mr Miller would like a word with you,' she promptly left. Not before Mr Miller had promised he would be round with a Miller's Monarch for her new baby.

Boyd Williamson would arrive on the dot at eleven when the chemmy table opened for business and Lily was sent back to the kitchen. He was the handsome younger son of a Scottish family who had made their money from a cooperage firm. He was married to a society hostess and worth around £3 million. He was a regular at Moscow Road, where Billy and Charlie took all his money over a series of nights at the chemmy table. Charlie won his second open-top Alvis from Boyd.

'Banco', 'suivi', and 'neuf à la banque', he said, were the most expensive words in any language. Hostesses wrapped in furs and feathers plied him with drinks. The stake started at £750. Playing against him were Charlie, Davey Perkins, Stanley Baker – the actor who modelled his gangster imper-sonations on Albert Dimes–Kenneth Hume, and Percy Horn, who specialized in the demolition business. Percy was at his peak – trading in battleships for scrap iron. He had sixteen Flying Squad officers in his pocket.

Charlie enjoyed the feeling of being a bystander in his own home. He watched the tawdry excitement of winning a shoe light up his guests' greedy faces. When a player was allowed to win, his face would shine with exaltation. He would fill with conceit and a feeling of omnipotence. Every gambler thinks they have a system, but the only good system, as Charlie knew from his apprenticeship on the Crown and Anchor board, was to be the Bank. It is an old, old story, as the 'Scrutator' states in his 1924 treatise *The Odds at Monte Carlo*: 'Le Noir gagne quelquefois; le Rouge gagne quelquefois; mais c'est la Banque qui gagne toujours.'

Boyd Williamson would lose thousands in a single night. But Charlie was always warm and gracious; lending Boyd money, taking him further into his debt. He was generous to a fault. He could hear his marks thinking, 'We can't lose money to this upstart little man,' and on they went, laughing. It almost felt as though they were donating money to a lost cause. So they hurried back to lose some more. In fact, Boyd was addicted to losing money. In the mornings, as James was getting ready to go to school, he would be full of despairing confidence. He would quote his favourite line from Rudyard Kipling: 'If you can make one heap of all your winnings. And risk it on a turn of pitch and toss . . . You'll be a man, my son.'

Thus armed, he convinced his host's son to join him in a game of three-card brag. They played for threepenny stakes. Boyd lost, his shoulders sagged, he let the cards fall to the floor, and his head flopped into his hands. But he did not give up, and was still there when James returned. This time, they played for Boyd's collection of matchbooks that he had collected from his travels around the world.

·

James himself had been running a card school since the age of ten. He knew the score. Within the school playground, he was the one to be in with. He started bunking off at twelve and by the time he was thirteen, he gave up altogether. Charlie got him a job on the demolition sites he ran. He loaded up lorries with scrap steel and was making lots of money. At fourteen, he started taking pills.

·

The Sixties were far too hectic for Johnny Miller, and by 1964 he decided the game was up. He was past his safe-cracking prime, and was lonely despite a new wife. 'Isn't she gorgeous?' he'd say to Charlie. 'Like the back-end of a bus,' Charlie would say to Davey Perkins. Miller's need to feel part of the action, for the companionship and excitement it brings, made him vulnerable. Con men are 'wide'; they are used to cheating each other with consummate artistry. It is called 'fair dealing', and can be summed up thus: 'Make sure you do your partner before he does you.' Johnny Miller could not face up to the reality of what he had become. The old pro had turned into an old fool. Even I could have told him not to be so naïve. Fair dealing was ingrained in me when I was little, because Charlie did not just use shady businessmen as backers. He used his family. In so doing, he ruined my great-aunt.

Dolly was living in a neat little house of her own on Kensal Rise. She would tell me all about it. The rooms came off a corridor she had painted canary yellow. The kitchen had a tin bath for her weekly wash. The parlour was where she received visitors. She grew busy lizzies in her window-boxes. Charlie asked his sister-in-law to invest the savings she had gleaned from years of skivvying in a demolition job. He gave her the taster. She made a little profit. He persuaded her of the advantages of ploughing it back into his next business venture. Dolly thought she was canny, but she lost everything to Charlie.

At the same time as Dolly was sleeping on a bench in Holland Park, Johnny Miller tried to hang himself from the rafters of the old stable on Kensal Rise. He was found in time and resuscitated. He told Charlie that he still wanted to die, but he did not know how. Charlie did not need to give the matter any thought but silently handed his friend a bottle of Tuinal. There was no need to dissuade his old friend from his desperate course. Charlie knew Johnny's time was up. Death was incidental to my grandfather – Stonebridge had seen to that. On finding Johnny dead in his bed, his glamorous new wife pulled up the floorboards in the bathroom. She found £250,000.

Johnny was not the only old pro to go down to barbiturates in the Sixties. When neighbours raised the alarm the policeman who forced entry into the flat in Sudbury found Wag dead in an overflowing bath. Brother Will decided that it was Charlie's fault that Wag died. He had also asked Wag to invest in the demolition site at Putney. Wag put all his money into the project, never to see it again. When Brother Will returned to the flat to retrieve Wag's last effects, he found that someone had been there before him and stripped the place bare. That was Charlie. He needed the real Charles Taylor's uniforms, birth certificate and army documents to accessorize his fraudulent past. There was nothing of Wag left.

▪

Boyd Williamson also lost everything, largely thanks to Charlie. His wife divorced him, and he started to drink heavily. His ruddy complexion had been enlivened by an incipient purple bloom around the nose. His features had coarsened, his hands shook. Such was his distress that

Charlie felt sorry for him. So sorry that he found him a job in his new venture with Billy Hill.

Windsor Club House on London Road, Virginia Water, was an attempt to marry the atmosphere of a club house with the decadence of an aristocratic country home. Its initials spelt out William Charles Hill – and the marriage of minds between Billy and my grandfather.

Charlie was in charge of the refurbishment of the derelict garage they had found near the Ascot racecourse. He chose the 'Instant Stately Home Look'. It was perfect; the half-baked Tudor pageant style – evoking the greatest period of English history – anchored his punters' unfulfillable desires. There were antique Turkish rugs, exotic lighting and classic furniture with marble coffee tables. There were the requisite young and eager-to-please hostesses, and discreet, murmuring waiters. These contrasted sharply with the doormen, who all looked exactly what they were – heavies, some of them murderers. This despite the green livery made to order from Soho.

Ray Rosa was one of the minders. It was said of Ray that he liked his razor to be rusty. That way, when he made a cut in a man's face, it would be prone to infection. Even Teddy Machin called him a psychopath. He once slashed a man about the face and body after finding him in bed with his wife, but that was the least of his exploits. He and his brothers were the terror of Elephant & Castle. They were friends of Billy Hill's, on whose behest they had performed acts of general mayhem. Ray was a good man to have around should anyone need a seeing-to.

Sixteen-year-old Victor was given a uniform to wear which consisted of a tunic and military trousers with a sharp red line down the side. His job was to brush the tables after each shoe. On spotting the svelte young man, Ronnie Kray asked him: 'What do you do, son?'

'I work here,' was the brusque reply. Victor's mother had warned him about men like Ronnie.

'All right. Good boy,' soothed the homicidal maniac.

•

Kathleen was allowed back on the scene. She excitedly wrote home that she was waitressing in a grand new casino, with a smart restaurant and debonair clientele. The former convent girl with wild eyes and a fashionably undernourished body was trying her best to be sophisticated and unshock-able. Her hair was styled by Raymond at Vidal Sassoon's new salon. Charlie paid for it, just as he paid for the stiletto heels that snagged in the deep-pile carpet in their love-nest above the Bank of Valletta. Although to say he paid for these consumer desirables is an exaggeration – he got everything on hire purchase or 'off a friend', because he never really paid for anything. Kathleen did not care how he paid for it, because older men were Kathleen's meal ticket. She was surrounded by the latest in everything. She was grateful because Charlie had rescued her from the oppression of Catholicism and the bogs.

The croupiers at the Windsor Club Hotel were French and let everyone know it. They had been recruited by Mr Hill in Monte Carlo. The band was the Harmony Hawaiians playing soft and rhythmic music, 'so seldom heard today'. The hostesses wore gowns in the new Tricel mixture – which was handy for its crease-resisting, stay-fresh properties. The style was very simple – low necklines, side-fastening and tie belts. They were as fresh as flowers in their wash and drip-dry garb of delphinium blue and coral pink. The card players, all from different backgrounds in all shapes and sizes, had one thing in common – a fierce, hungry look in their eyes.

Boyd was installed as the manager – so upper-crust he would give the right first impression, and the Windsor Club

House was set to open in May 1963. His Royal Highness, Charlie's old friend the Gaekwar of Baroda, had promised to do the honours. The mailshots which were sent to well-known gamblers were posted from the Bank of Valletta. The club was to open in late spring to chime with the first Ascot meeting of the season. Unfortunately it caught fire just before the grand opening night. Apparently offcuts of carpets were left by some radiators which caught fire when Brother Will forgot to turn the electricity off. But the other torch artists could have been the Krays, who were peeved because they had not been offered a piece of the club. Anyway, damage was estimated at £10,000 and Mr Williamson told the *Bracknell News*: 'The damage was confined to the upstairs rooms which were very luxuriously furnished. We believe it was caused by a short circuit in the electrical system.'

Perhaps he was telling the truth. But, as Evelyn Waugh once remarked: 'The debonair duke living by his wits soon grows to resemble the plebeian crook.' Whatever the case, everyone pulled together and it opened on time. This time, the Krays were paid in advance for their troubles. They were also paid £1,000 each time they arrived threatening to 'cut' my grandfather. They were very polite about it, he joked: 'We're really sorry, Charlie,' cos we like you. You've got a good head for money.'

That first night was a roaring success. Prince Philip was there with his Thursday Club pals (ex-Guards officers and dissipated toffs), as well as an exotic array of Far Eastern potentates. Their surroundings were conducive to losing money. The walls hung with tapestries, or painted cloths, wherein diverse histories were stained. Hinged panels opened at the windows, which overlooked Great Windsor Park. The fireplace in the main banqueting-room was made from four pieces of roughly carved hearthstone that had fallen off the back of a quarry. It was a triumph.

The club lasted until the end of the year. The bigshots stopped turning up once Charlie started charging them for their drinks, gaming chips and Dover soles. A series of 'dodgy' cheques did their damage, as did the regular £1,000 payouts to Ronnie and Reg. Boyd Williamson took the casino's failure personally. There was no break to his luck.

He had already broken the cardinal rule of gambling. If you have enough capital you must come up trumps in the end. It stands to reason that you can't lose for ever, even if you keep losing for an awfully long time. Whether or not he realized he was being duped by my grandfather, and that he was not playing a game of equal chance, the point of his life was to end it as sordidly and traumatically as possible. One morning, after Lily had cooked him breakfast, Charlie drove Boyd to Paddington Station. He handed him a one-way ticket to Australia, paid for by 'yours truly' and Billy Hill. It was the least they could do.

PART THREE · CHARLES

Gee Mary, this London's a wonderful sight
They're digging for gold there by day and by night
At least when I asked them that's what I was told
So I tried out my hand at this digging for gold
But for all that I found there, well I might as well be
Where the mountains of Mourne sweep down to the sea.

Irish folk song

14 · Son of a Gun

Lily lost her daughter to Charlie, and she was beginning to wish her two younger sons had never been born. Life was not meant to be like this. Her husband had stopped paying her the attention she needed to thrive. He was pursuing the good life alone, and it hurt her. But if Charlie had been married to the Queen of Sheba the chains of matrimony would still have made him resent her. So Lily was left at home each night, where she was prey to introspection.

She wandered around the great rooms of the Kensington mansion bemoaning her fate. But I loved that house like a mother. I cherished everything about it, down to its most intimate details – the scent of Pears soap as I wallowed in the claw-foot bath, the breeze of trees rustling through the window, even the wooden toilet seats. I marvelled that even the most basic, lavatorial items had the patina of age. It was as though I knew the house and its contents would not be ours for long. My grandmother picked up on my obsession with detail, and encouraged me to ignore the larger picture. She would take me by the hand to the little girls' room and paper the seat as though it were Christmas. Nothing unseemly must make contact with her precious grand-daughter.

Outside, London was a dream of swirling fog, startling spotlights and rude speed. But inside Number 1 Inverness Gardens I found a haven of lush female properties. Two women – past the fresh flush of youth, as they were constantly reminded – cared for me. Mad Dolly rocked me to sleep. She lullabied me repeatedly with a magic formula which consisted of only two words: 'Mummy's baby.' Fast-fading Lily gave me my bottles, before handing me back to Dolly who was in charge of dirty nappies.

It was Lily's job to lavish me with stuffed toys. Charlie gave her wads of cash that he had earned at Crockford's, and Davey Perkins drove her to Hamley's. I had the very best of everything a child could want. Victor and James had felt the fierce heat of their mother's passion and fear. She would not let them gain their majority. But she had cooled by the time I was born, and I was treated to a more mournful and detached mothering. If I was wise enough to realize my luck was in, I was also aware that babies do not make a woman happy.

Lily needed stimulation and thrills. Instead, she had jealousy, disappointment and disillusionment. She cried at least once a day for the next twenty years. But the confusing thing about Lily was that her moods were never constant – they passed like clouds in the sky, with occasional moments of irradiation when the sun broke through the cover. It is fair to say, though, that this was not the life she had wanted – and it was not the future she wanted for her boys. In a way, her two older children had benefited from her neglect. At least Greta had grown up to be an air-hostess. She wore a smart uniform and spoke several languages. She was like her doughty grandmother before the children came.

Greta travelled the world on a BOAC jumbo jet but could not find lasting happiness or peace of mind. When she came home to her mother and half-brothers, she found them in a haze of drugs and tears. Victor was the one most like his father – but instead of exploiting his quick wits and charisma he was overwhelmed by his own sense of potential. He knew his family expected great things of him but he refused to comply with their demands. He had a strange habit of shutting down his face from inspection as though he were fending off the effects of a bomb blast. I remember as a child I would stare and stare at him – he was handsome, with his mother's eyes and black hair. Occasionally he would acknowledge my interest with a rueful smile. It was as though he did not dare to open up. So Victor remained self-sufficient – he was there, but not palpably so.

James was more like his mother – at least when she was in her good-time mode. He loved to laugh, and drugs were just another prank to be indulged. He was fun to be with, especially for children. We would play hide and seek for hours. He would tell me stories about my beautiful mother and handsome father. His enthusiasm for the high life was even more tireless than mine. But both Greta's wayward halfbrothers were in awe of her aloofness. They wanted her respect but she could not give it to them. How could she when she had none to give herself? So she blamed them for their drug-taking and narcissism. It seemed to her that their troubles were self-inflicted. But what really rankled was that no one had made a fuss over hers.

This was because, to everyone in the family, my mother was goodness incarnate. She was inviolate. James told me that she always remembered to take an apple to her teacher. Even then – especially then – she longed for approval and respectability.

But she married my father. When I asked her why, since he made her so miserable, she replied that it was because he was a good dancer. She loved to jive at the Two I's on Old Compton Street. The dancers would make room for my parents as they executed complex moves in perfect harmony. She would share jokes with the other regulars. They were smart and interesting people, like George Melly and Millicent

Martin, while my father hovered at her elbow, as self-contained and inert as his native Adriatic Sea. Greta was no longer adrift in his impassive presence, and he respected her quick mind and eloquence in his own tongue. His silence was stability, she thought. She knew his story, and it moved her.

Pino had been orphaned during the Second World War, and had survived by running errands for American GIs. Italy's saviours brought new life to bombed-out Ancona, the capital city of the Marches. Pino scrabbled around in its ruins, fighting off the other boys to curry the Yanks' favours. He was impressed by their good-natured coolness. It was such a refreshing contrast to the dour fatalism of his compatriots. The GIs paid him in cigarettes, bacon and chewing-gum. Which was more than he ever got from his local priest.

Ancona was dead in the water for Pino. After just about surviving a bout of TB, he abandoned the old port town for good. The journey took in most of Europe, where he plied his rusty accordion. He serenaded Austrians, Germans and the English with arias from the operas of Rossini, a more illustrious son of the Marches. Like Greta, Pino never knew his own father, who had been long-married when he met his mother. But at least he knew his name. Ippolyte Tomado, he told Charlie, had been a pilot – one of the few Italians seconded to Hitler's Luftwaffe. He had bombed the lights out of his future grand-daughter's birthplace.

Charlie could not help but be jealous. Through Ippolyte, my father could lay claim to Fascist stock. He was the real thing to Charlie's blackshirt impersonation. And Pino's eyes mesmerized where Charlie's skewered. Furthermore, he was tall and handsome with elegant limbs and devastating self-possession. His mohair suits clung to him like a spurned mistress – and he had plenty of both.

Charlie wanted to make amends to my mother. He wanted

her to be thankful for having such a stepfather. So he found her new husband a job as a croupier in a smart casino. Pino was happy enough for a while. He worked till the small hours and then he hit the town. Once his shift at Ladbroke's Casino on Oxford Street was over, he hightailed it to the White Elephant in Mayfair, where white-lipsticked girls wrapped themselves around his long limbs. At around four in the morning, he settled down to a game of poker at the AM private members' club in Soho. He was an exquisite and liked to impress with extravagant gestures. If a man complimented him on his silk Hermès tie, my father would send it to his address in a taxi. It was the Sixties, and there were girls, card games, and dancing a go-go. His friends called him 'Lucky' because he always won at poker. 'But I'm unlucky in love, Lily,' he told me.

My father had already worked out, without Charlie's help, that life was a racket. Neither did he need this old guy to tell him about long shots, hot shots, side bets and spread bets. What my mother mistook for stolidity was in fact a corrosive cynicism. Given the circumstances of his childhood, it was all he had ever known.

In August 1965, three months after I was born, Pino left England for the Bahamas. London was too big for him; he did not like it – the fast-talking, incomprehensible jargon foxed him. He did not feel he could thrive in such a hostile and competitive environment. More than anything he wanted money and status – as for everything else . . . well, in Italy he would have been called a *menefreghista*. Which Charlie accurately translated as 'one who does not give a fuck'. You see, Charlie saw straight through him, and what did he find but himself – a *cafone* – a crude peasant, not from the mud of Willesden, but the marshy borderlands of the Holy Roman Empire. And this one was also keen to make his mark.

But first he needed to find a new world – one that made

room for inarticulate and hungry foreigners. He got a job at Il Casino in the town of Freeport. It was built as a playground for rich Americans on the bare, brackish island of Grand Bahama.

It was all because of Charlie. Because my father was him all over again – an extravagant peacock to my mother's spry sparrow. Since he needed to impress the sense of his own importance upon the rogue male in his household, Charlie told my father of a recent meeting he had had with the Jewish-American mobster Meyer Lansky. Because it was to his advantage, Pino listened carefully.

Lansky ran gambling operations in Florida, New Orleans and Cuba, where he arranged pay-offs to the dictator Fulgencio Batista. He was also involved in narcotics smuggling, pornography, prostitution, labour racketeering, and extortion as well as having control of such legitimate enterprises as hotels, golf courses, and a meat-packing plant. Monies were secreted in Swiss bank accounts. By 1970 his total holdings were estimated at $US 300,000,000.

He met Charlie on a fact-finding mission to London, where he wished to extend his gambling empire. Since Charlie was a main player in London's gaming circles, and the Krays were blatantly psychopathic, it was only natural that Lansky should make his inquiries at Number 1, Inverness Gardens, Kensington. It was a far superior address to Vallance Road, Bethnal Green.

His London concerns did not flourish, however, and with Fidel Castro in power in Cuba, Lansky turned to the Bahamas. He built casinos on Grand Bahama and Paradise Islands after nurturing government cooperation. These jerry-built pleasure domes were Meyer Lansky's Caribbean front for laundering money.

My father sent for my mother and their ten-month-old baby just when London was the place for hipsters to be. For the next five years we had miles of sand and a Fiat 124 Sport Spider with which to play. It was a blur of red, and little boys clamoured to be my friend. Pino was the dashing wide boy of the island as he whizzed us around in his flash car. But memories pulled my mother up short: 'Yellow Submarine' was playing on the car radio. She sighed for the town where she was born. She languished in the heat, and refused to come out from under the shade of palm trees imported from Miami. At night, I heard her cry herself to sleep, which made me wonder what went on before and after I was born.

·

In 1963 a lavish party took place in the front room of Number 1 Inverness Gardens. Charlie had moved his headquarters from the seedy demi-monde of Bayswater to the Royal Borough of Kensington and Chelsea. The marble pillars that had graced the dining-room of the Windsor Club House were installed on the ground floor, and the baccarat table found a new home.

This party served a double purpose. It was a housewarming and it advertised that Charlie's new premises were open for business. The star of the show was Miss World – my grandfather's latest mistress – Rosemary Frankland.

The Miss World contest had been the brainchild of Eric Morley, an early exponent of corporate PR, who had been asked to think of an idea that would publicize the Festival of Britain. His big concept was to televise a worldwide beauty contest direct from the industrial miracle that was London.

Miss Sweden won the first contest in 1951. Miss Sweden won the second contest, too. So when Rosemary – the first English contender to take the title – wept into a borrowed handkerchief on receiving her crown, the UK press was jubilant.

The new Miss World was a 5ft 6in eighteen-year-old. Her vital statistics were 36–22–36 but, even more vital, she had the naïveté of a child. Even as ten million TV viewers were applauding her apotheosis it was rumoured that Bob Hope, the compère that night, had rigged the results in her favour. He was the first middle-aged man to want to wallow in her unalloyed freshness. She was perfect; her blatant, bouncing fertility offset by a wide-eyed look of helpless wonder. To men like Hope, it was lip-smackingly obvious that Rosemary was not in full control of her body.

Imagine, then, the effect on my grandfather. As she stepped, like a goddess, from the podium of the Lyceum Ballroom into Charlie's front room the applause of ten million viewers rang in his ears. They were cheering and whistling for him.

Because she was a coup. Just a little larger than life, and certainly more lustrous, she was a dazzling addition to his soirées. Men like society photographer Terry O'Neill and pop star Dave Dee were competing to squire her around London's happening night spots. After her coronation, Bob Hope whisked her off on a two-week tour of the American forces in the Arctic. On their return, he declared, 'She's so hot we were in danger of going through the ice.' She was screen-tested for four film studios, including Warners and MGM. She was sure a place could be found for her on the silver screen.

'The most beautiful girl in the world' was the daughter of a hospital cleaner and a factory foreman. She had been raised by her grandmother in North Wales, and was working behind the counter at Marks & Spencer when she started entering beauty contests for a bit of fun. But her good looks became big business, and before she knew where she was, she had been hailed Miss Lancashire, Miss Lake District, and Miss Wales. She went global as a runner-up in Miss Universe, before setting her stall as Miss UK.

'Everyone thinks this beauty-queen business is a picnic,' she told the man from the *Daily Express*. 'But it's not, it's hell. You have to become an automaton. We walk mechanically to music – and smile to music.'

What her men did not realize was that Rosemary was angry. What is more, she did not want to play the game. She resented posing for the cameras, right hand on right hip, left foot forward, holding her breath and gritting her teeth until they snapped her. But she could not give up the attention. With nothing to offer but her grace and vivacity, she stuck to what she knew, enlivening London's first nights with her smile.

By the time she met Charlie she was going out with the well-known roué, Maxwell Brown, and married to photographer Ben Jones. She was exhausted but was pinning her hopes on finding the man who would make her feel unassailable. Charlie was that man for a brief, glorious time. He stroked her vulnerability as though she were a velvety and enigmatic pussycat. When she purred he could not tell if it was from pain or pleasure. Miss World and my grandfather made an exciting couple – with her looks and neediness and his power and vitality they delighted in each other's hollow aims.

Rosemary's glamour attracted more fame-hungry television personalities to Charlie's chemmy table. Each brought a recently acquired veneer to the game. To her left sat a trend-setting disc jockey who suffered from *le vice paternel*. Even Rosemary was too old for this guy. He wanted flesh that was untouched by human hand. Davey Perkins was recruited to supply him with under-age girls. With his merry blue eyes and ready smile, Davey was good at soothing fretful and rapacious egos. However outrageous, illegal, or sickening the demand, Davey's easy-going charm made it perfectly reasonable.

'She's caught my eye,' the DJ would confide to him. He had a weekly music extravaganza on television and the pick of the kids who followed him around town. From behind his long-player which was spinning the latest in poptastic hits, he pointed to a girl in the crowd. It was up to Davey to sound her out: did she want to meet the man whose catchphrases made her feel part of the in-crowd?

Next to the DJ was Maxwell Brown. He was a war hero and at least twice Rosemary's age. He carried his six foot two frame like the guardsman he once was and commandeered her for champagne and entertainment. He arrived bearing gifts. James was festooned with Nazi war medals that Maxwell had snatched from German corpses.

Class boundaries dissolved at my grandfather's table. Because sitting next to the war hero was a tiny tough from Glasgow unencumbered with social graces. As a merchant sailor, and still called Angus Murdo McKenzie, he had achieved early notoriety in Rhodesia, where he was known as 'Boaty Maseteno', or the 'brother of Satan'. But this was 1962, and Karl Denver the pop singer had reached Number 4 in the UK charts. 'Wimoweh' was a Zulu chant and Karl's greatest achievement. His falsetto voice, insistent yodelling and souped-up Cuban heels filled the gap between Cliff Richard and the fast-approaching Beatles.

Karl was taking time out from summer season at Great Yarmouth. He was high on fame and buzzing with the latest news: next year his Trio would be getting their own Light Programme show. It was to be called *Side by Side*, and among his guests would be the Beatles. Charlie and his guests lapped it up. This was exactly what they wanted to hear. Karl was one of them, after all. He had some talent and he had found an outlet for it. He was in the money and he was squandering it on cards. They were all on the up and up, and the new, permissive society was making way for them. But what really linked the members of this magic circle was that each and every one had a secret. And only Charlie knew it. Karl's was alcohol.

The elderly down-and-out boxer Ted Kid Lewis was also there. As well as the middle-weight champion of the world, Terry Downes. In truth both he and Rosemary had had their moment two years previously, but no one was going to tell them that.

Lewis was the only man there with credibility. Pound for pound he was the greatest fighting machine England had as yet produced. A non-stop, all-action, relentless attacker, he brought his style to the chemmy table. Where he lost all his prize money. Terry Downes was overjoyed to be in the great man's company, but to Charlie they were all the same. Punters, and he creamed a hell of a lot of money off them. The chest-of-drawers in his bedroom was filled with bank notes. James would help himself to a couple of hundred here and there. No one was counting.

.

I doubt if any of Charlie's guests realized the drama being enacted deep in the basement. In the self-contained flat of Number 1 lurked Billy Hill's mistress. She was young, black, and determined to make it as a singer. She was to commit suicide in 1979. Billy's wife, Gypsy, was a different kind of woman altogether. She kept her early history quiet, but reliable sources linked her with an ageing Maltese pimp known as Tulip. She was violent, too, having once appeared in court for slashing a man's face with a knife.

Gypsy suspected that Billy was keeping his mistress in Charlie's new house. She rang up demanding to speak to 'the tart'. She said she would be round with a knife. My grandmother took the call and consulted with Charlie. They decided to go out for the afternoon, and to take the young singer with them. They left my mother alone in the house. As they suspected, Gypsy kicked up a fuss but left the clueless young woman unscathed. Greta was useful: her determination to see or hear no evil saved the day. Charlie knew he could count on that.

Nor would his guests have been aware of Charlie's former willing victims. But he was so skilful at keeping his assets close to his chest that no one really knew what was going on in his life. Not even his own family. Lily and her boys could see, though, that Wing-Co Eaves was down on his luck. His Dormobile van was permanently parked outside Inverness Gardens. There was nowhere else for him to go. As a mark he had been particularly easy to bilk. He was quite ready to participate in extra-legal money-making schemes, which required a hefty investment. Davey Perkins and Charlie bounced Eaves between them so effectively he merely registered his loss as a gambit that failed.

Lily often cooked him dinner and kept him company. She felt sorry for Charlie's marks and fussed over them. Neither was her husband indifferent to the pain he caused. He welcomed men like Eaves and Boyd Williamson to break bread at his table, as long as he sat at its head. It was almost like having an extended family, only it was better than that, because every one of them was dependent solely on him.

Nineteen sixty-three was also the year of the Profumo scandal and the Great Train Robbery. The police and politicians had lost their moral authority. The young Ted Heath exemplified a new classless affluence. He was tough, superefficient and his father was a master builder from an ordinary terraced house.

Eaves was part of the bewildered old guard who were suffering from the new economic conditions. Retired officers and crumbling gentry felt betrayed by the death of the imperial dream, and Charlie understood their disappointment. Their servants had gone, their money had gone, and they could not afford to keep up their land or houses.

But the dapper Eaves still had schemes to recover his millions. He asked Major Stoop to buy Lord Vansittart's 100-acre estate in Denham. 'You buy it,' he urged his friend, needing a cover because his own reputation was shot to pieces. 'And I'll turn it into a supermarket. It's within driving distance of ten million people.'

All Eaves wanted was fifty per cent of the action. He needed it to cover his gambling debts. But Stoopie didn't bite, and Eaves was left to dream his impossible schemes in his Dormobile van.

Life had been different when he had first met Charlie. On that occasion, Davey had pretended to be the rich man in a hired limousine chauffeured by Black Fred. He took him to lunch, introduced him to Charlie, and together they obtained the lease on the house in Kensington through driving him into debt. It seems everything my family possessed was ill-gotten gains. On first moving in, James was delighted to find that Wing-Co had left his RAF gear behind him. He could add a dinghy and flying kit to his collection of Second World War memorabilia.

In fact, James's entire collection of historical artefacts came from his father's past marks. Including a stamp album which was passed on to me. It once belonged to Nicholas 'Van' Hoogstraten, a shady property developer and erstwhile philatelist. The 'Van' was added for effect in the Sixties, and the stamp album was just one in his million-pound collection. Charlie had helped him out with a competitor in the stamp trade. He sent Ray Rosa down to a shop in Sussex with a can of petrol and a lighter. Soon afterwards Van Hoogstraten was sentenced to four years in Wormwood Scrubs for employing criminals to mount a hand-grenade attack on a former business associate. The judge described him as a 'sort of self-imagined devil who thinks that he is an emissary of Beelzebub'.

Wing-Co invested £20,000 in Charlie's demolition business. He even drove the van that supposedly carried the loot stolen from demolition sites to a scrap yard in Teddington. He swung the great truck viciously round the bends of Harrow Road until the tyres shrilled and the men shrieked in alarm. The truck was in fact empty, the goods having been disposed of long before Wing-Co had waxed his moustaches and surfaced for the day's business.

He enjoyed the company of men like Teddy Machin, Davey Perkins and Charlie. Ted's battle-scarred face and my grandfather's coarse humour reinforced his wavering hold on his masculinity. Davey told the jokes, he could do a marvellous impersonation of Johnny Miller. His audience cried itself hoarse with laughter. Teddy Machin had his moments, too. He kept a human finger in his coat pocket, and would wave it at Kensington's matriarchs to make them gasp. Wing-Co sat behind the wheel of the van with a cargo of desperate characters in the back. It was fun. The van had the same engine as the tank he had driven in the Second World War.

·

If Charlie had taken time out from the *Greyhound Express* to read the *Sunday Times*, he would have found an article in its new multi-sectioned layout brazenly extolling London's modernity. A much-remarked-upon fact was that 130 London property developers had been converted into millionaires. Nothing surprising there. As the M4 motorway sneaked out of London Airport, and the Post Office Tower made its neighbours look like child's play, men like Charlie were bound to be raking it in. He was at his zenith. His energies were finding their release in the pulsating atmosphere of the swinging metropolis. He was enjoying secret rendezvous with the former Miss World. He was a go-between for Billy Hill and the Krays.

The telephone would ring. It was Reggie.

'Tell that fat cunt I want £5,000.'

'Yes, Reggie.'

The receiver slams down. Charlie makes a phone call to Bayswater 5609. Billy Hill picks up the receiver.

'Bill, the twins have been on the blower.'

Five minutes later, a car arrives at Number 1 with a package for Mr Taylor. Davey Perkins drives Charlie in his new, black Bentley to Reggie's club somewhere in the depths of the East End.

He certainly had his uses. Sadly for Rosemary and the other innocents who crossed his path, Charlie had the opposite of the Midas touch. Their promise failed to deliver success. Shortly after that night in 1963 when he had been pushing the shoe round the chemmy table, Karl Denver was seriously injured in a car accident. His son died in another crash that year. There were financial problems, too. He could not keep up his divorce payments to two ex-wives, and was declared bankrupt. Finally, he was committed to Strangeways prison.

Rosemary fled the scene after her second nervous break-down and a disastrous bit-part in a Bob Hope vehicle called *I'll Take Sweden*. Despite a walk-on part as a showgirl in *A Hard Day's Night*, the invitations had stopped flooding her letter-box. Her lustre had faded, and her husband divorced her on the grounds of adultery.

She went to live in Bob Hope's house in Palm Springs. She married again in 1970, to Warren Entner, who rose to brief fame singing 'Feelings'. They divorced soon afterwards. She stayed in Beverly Hills, to be close to the big time, until her death in December 2000. When the fifty-seven-year-old ingénue, addicted to sleeping-pills and one-night stands, was found dead on her bed, two bottles lay by her side. One was for sleeping-pills, the other Tequila. They were both empty.

When I was born on 14 May 1965, the most beautiful girl in the world had just left my grandfather for Bob Hope. But there was always Kathleen, still in her twenties and, despite the abortion, still clamouring for Charlie's attention. He found her a job in his new hotel, where her dark Irish looks and white Courrèges boots charmed the customers. Her jangled nerves had not yet given the lie to her bid for coolness.

•

Charlie had to keep up with the youngsters, so he took uppers during the daytime and downers at night. Black Fred always knew where to get the latest drugs. He kept abreast of the latest developments: first amphetamines, then pills and capsules that excite the central nervous system, then the psychedelic maelstrom of LSD and, last but not least, the needle drug, heroin. The Taylor boys did not bother with LSD, they didn't need hallucinogenics to open their eyes to the surreal. All they wanted to do was to keep going, to soak up more of the action, to consume bigger and bigger quantities of whatever was going. So although Fred tried to turn them on to cannabis they turned to heroin instead.

Amyl nitrate and black bombers were what kept Charlie going. He needed them for the rush of energy that fifty-year-old men so sorely miss. He wanted the feeling of go, go, go to be never-ending. He had so many long-firms and businesses to occupy him that his family could not see him for the dust.

The little black bottles of amyl nitrate were for sex. Straight sex had always been something of a bore for my grandfather. Without Miss World to gee him up, he turned to poppers to pep up his sessions with young Maureen. If he wanted anything from sex it was an exaggerated sense of novelty. A vigorous snort and he was under the illusion that he was experiencing a woman's body anew. The interval between snorting and release was one of youthful immediacy. His circulation went crazy, he was overwhelmed by the need to keep going.

Drugs went down wholesale in the Taylor household. James was on the Mod scene and, at fourteen, was going out with a twenty-year-old model. They took purple hearts when they went to see the Who play in Wardour Street, Soho. A blue, triangular pill, the purple heart was the invention of Smith, Klein and French, who called their new amphetamine Drinamyl. It was integral to Pete Townsend's guitar-bashing and the crowd's frantic attitudinizing. And James's teeth-churning grin and gritty eyes suited his short-waisted Roman jacket and narrow trousers.

At seventeen, Victor was receiving an allowance that paid for trips to Paris to buy his clothes. He had the latest Jaguar E-type but speeding was not enough for him. So he signed up to Lady Frankau's Wimpole Street surgery. She was the junkies' doctor, providing one sixth of the heroin being taken in the UK.

Lady Frankau was a white-haired, elderly doctor who spent her weekends at Ickleton Grange, her country home near Saffron Walden, Essex. There she prepared Sunday lunch for her husband Sir Claude, a consulting surgeon at St George's Hospital. During the week, from her elegant consulting-rooms, she prescribed for a Bohemian circle of poets, writers, actors and musicians. She specialized in treating addiction.

In the United States and Canada prescribing heroin was banned, so when Lady Frankau went on a lecture tour, outlining her sympathetic treatment of addicts, a fan club of admiring users followed her back across the Atlantic for 'treatment'. They got lots of it.

But, unlike some of her more unscrupulous colleagues who made a brisk trade out of prescribing, she cared for those who saw her. Addicts who visited her surgery recall that she would often let patients off the consultation fee if they were caught short. The jazz musician Chet Baker paid her a visit in 1962 while filming *The Stolen Hours* with Susan Hayward.

'Lady Frankau,' he wrote in his journals, 'was about seventy-five years old ... and very businesslike. She simply asked my name, my address and how much cocaine and heroin I wanted per day.'

For the equivalent of £1.80 she wrote him a prescription for cocaine which would have cost him £300 in New York, and another for 10g of heroin.

'After that first day my scripts were all for 20g each and I was off and running,' he wrote. Once he had finished filming and his work permit had expired, Lady Frankau lied, claiming he was too sick to travel, to allow him to stay in England. After a month in prison on drugs charges he was deported to France.

■

Lady Frankau's life spanned an era of changing attitudes towards drug use. When she was a young girl Harrods sold laudanum. Opiate use was confined to the elegant boudoirs of ladies who dipped into Knightsbridge for their more exotic groceries, or for professionals seeking relief from the pressures of funding a large establishment. Addiction was a middle-class phenomenon confined to a large extent to the medical profession itself. Towards the end of Lady Frankau's career it was heroin that had become more widespread. During this period, addiction lost its bohemian gloss and drug addicts no longer had nice manners. What had once been an upper-middle-class pastime had become a socially infectious condition which needed to be controlled.

There were never more than about half a dozen doctors prescribing for Britain's addicts in the 1960s. Charlie and his boys knew them all, because they always needed extension work done to their surgeries. 'I'm off to Pill Island,' they'd joke when on their way to feed their habits. Quacks had been operating from fashionable and expensive Harley Street for years. But this generation of doctors helped to create Britain's heroin problem. They prescribed in such huge quantities that their patients were able to sell their excess supplies on the street.

Within a remarkably short time the number of heroin addicts in London had multiplied many times. And by the time the authorities stepped in the situation was perfect for smugglers: there were now enough addicts to make an illegal business venture worthwhile. By 1965 Home Office inspectors concluded: 'Well gentlemen, I think our problem can be summed up in two words – Lady Frankau.'

Both my uncles became addicted to heroin because neither of them had strong motivations in any other direction. Charlie had ensured they wanted for nothing, and Lily, in her fearfulness, had discouraged them from seeking a life outside the family. They were encouraged to be like their father, to seek instant gratification, to be childlike in their outlook. They lapsed into depression when life was not treating them well, and refused to assume responsibility. After all, they were young, good-looking, and wildly exciting to be with. You never knew what the Taylor boys would get up to next. They had the readies to buy the clothes, the drugs, the latest records and they hit the night-clubs. Girls lapped them up. But that got boring. There was nothing left to do. No one left to entertain them. And when they broke free from their stifling apathy their behaviour was excessive and violent. My uncles were capable of anything. That they were unusually intelligent and frustrated by their inability to make any headway in life, that they were disorganized, unruly and unable to cope with pressure and that they were, quite simply, over-demanding both of themselves and of society meant that heroin won by default. If they could not be their father, there was nothing else for them to do.

Black Fred kept his eye on them. Under orders from Charlie he followed Victor and James around the night-spots of Soho and Bayswater. From Ronnie Scott's, where Roland Kirk, the blind saxophonist, blew Victor's mind, to the Blue Hall on Edgware Road, where Lily had once danced in the Thirties, the drug count was being calculated by a watchful Fred. He was well placed to keep this particular accounts book, being a pimp and a pusher himself. It never occurred to the boys that their father kept strange company, or indeed their mother. Although Victor did wonder why Fred phoned Lily late at night knowing that Charlie would be out. Victor stopped to listen to his mother whispering and giggling while she hugged the telephone to her bosom. It did occur to him that she might be giving vent to her penchant for black men. It certainly wouldn't surprise him; nothing would.

He had more interesting things to think about. Nothing delighted Victor more than his own projection of himself. He knew that Charlie had his spies out, but he had no secrets from his father. He lived his life inside out just for Dad. The junk enhanced the performance that he was staging for an audience of one.

∎

The city of bombsites, peeling paint and broken windows was being replaced by machine-patterned glass skyscrapers, concrete piazzas, and pedestrian precincts. Against this dynamic backdrop Charlie was playing the part of the businessman. He was at his prime, self-consciously preoccupied with the affairs of his state. There was not only the casino in Windsor. He and Billy Hill were quick to follow the new trend in the building boom. That year they bought the demolition rights to the Army & Navy Stores in Victoria Street.

The Stores had been at 105 Victoria Street since 1871. Back then it was a Members Only establishment where orders were placed by country houses, at long intervals and in vast quantities. Four hundred men were engaged in packing grocery orders which were dispatched five times a day via Victoria Station.

The Army & Navy engraved their client's visiting cards and printed invitations to his wedding, for which they also catered. They found him a flat or house, furnished, decorated and repaired it. If he was adventurous the Stores would furnish him with suitable equipment for climbing Mount Everest or exploring the Arctic. He was supplied with rose-water for fingerbowls, as well as all his food and drink, the Stores being careful to decant his port and deliver it shortly before dinner, although this was possible in London only.

All this history was about to come crashing down and leave Charlie sitting triumphant on a dust-heap. Retail practices move on, and the clubbable Stores needed a facelift. The demolition of the Army & Navy's Victorian Gothic edifice constituted one of the most comprehensive redevelopment schemes of the Sixties. When it was completed, the half-mile stretch of Victoria Street stretching from Vauxhall Bridge Road to Abbey Orchard Street and encompassing Westminster Cathedral itself would be completely rebuilt.

The freeholders concerned were the Army & Navy Stores, the Crown Estates and the Church Commissioners. The contract for the old mansion blocks' demolition was given to two well-known villains. The building trade is as nepotistic as any other, and this was by no means extraordinary in being a family affair. The interior designer of the new Stores was Ephraim Israel, the son of Old Man Moses of Bayswater.

With investors buying into promises of scrap steel that always failed to materialize, Charlie was making double his profit. With the money he made from the Army & Navy – all that steel that had to be sold on the sly – he could have retired, like sensible Billy, to a villa in southern Spain. But he wasn't going to give up now. He had all the props in place: tailored suits, a chauffeur-driven Bentley with personalized numberplates, a discreetly expensive address and active bank accounts with the Banks of Bilbao and Cyprus and Allied Irish.

Foreign banks were useful since it took ten days for them to clear cheques. Which was useful since Charlie was running a chain of long-firms. And if one of his companies gave a cheque to another which then passed a cheque to yet another with the sum ending up back with the first one, he could time it so that each cheque was fed in at the time when the debit was coming through the account. No wonder he was addicted to barbiturates. Because there was one problem. Keeping Billy Hill sweet was a massive drain on his inner resources. One slip and Teddy Machin might turn on him.

Banks must be kept sweet too. A record of deposits and withdrawals going through an account could be used as authentication of business for the police. Which was why the Bank of Valletta had been so useful in providing good references for fraudulent concerns. Which was also why it did not last long.

15 · Leaders of Society

Originally the residence of Lord and Lady Leigham, the Leigham Court Estate was bought in 1819 by J. G. Fuller, a wine merchant and proprietor of Boodle's gaming club. The estate comprised a single, grand house set in extensive grounds with lakes and woodlands. Fuller used the estate in Streatham as a country retreat for his fashionably jaded club members. In 1965, Charlie opened an illegal casino in what had become the Leigham Court Hotel.

The original villa had gone, to be replaced by a Victorian mansion with pretensions to Italianate glamour. The great sweeping drive led the eye to a portico entrance balanced by two stately columns. Leigham Court had all the style of Inverness Gardens. It had space as well. Charlie was content enough, at first, to feel that there was no need for him to hurry himself as lord of this manor. Here, in this ancient – to him, at least – house, rooted in a quiet park, where the ivy had had time to mature, and the gnarled oaks stood deep in the moss of a hundred years; and where the sun-dial on the terrace had recorded time passing for the house and land, it now crept slowly for Charles Taylor. There was the additional bonus that in the secluded backwaters of Streatham he was far from his nagging wife and family.

When Charlie first sat in the bar of Leigham Court Hotel, Cyril Green, the leaseholder, was on trial at Marylebone Magistrates court on a charge of fraud. Charlie let it be known that he won the hotel on the turn of a card. In fact, he wrested the lease from Cyril by approaching the freeholder, Oscar Davis, and offering to double the rent. There was little that Cyril could do. He was in a particularly vulnerable position. His trial had been halted in order to allow him to give evidence against some former associates. Charlie was quick to exploit Cyril's fall from the Richardson brothers' grace.

In 1964 Cyril Green had been approached by the south London gangster Charles Richardson. Given Cyril's invaluable experience as manager of the Bank of Valletta, Richardson was keen to use him as a front for a long-firm he was running. Richardson had tried many varieties on the theme of the long-firm. In 1962 he had set fire to a warehouse that he claimed was full of silk stockings. This was his first attempt at arson and his enthusiasm got the better of him. He managed to burn down most of Mitre Court, one of the few streets in the City to survive the Great Fire of 1666. Before torching the place he organized a knock-down, come-and-get-it-while-it-lasts, sale of the stockings. He then claimed the insurance money for them, and told the manufacturers that their goods had gone up in flames. There was nothing they could do when he said that he was unable to pay them because he was uninsured. He made £250,000.

On the proceeds he bought into five scrap-metal yards, contracts with the Ministry of Works, a perlite mine in South Africa and the car-parking arrangements at Heathrow Airport.

He decided to rope in some conmen to help organize his string of long-firms.

'There is a little place round the corner I want you to look after for me,' he told Cyril, and took him to a small warehouse in Camberwell. Cyril was installed as the blower-man to use his expertise in defrauding creditors. His fusty old tweeds and pipe were excellent props for the act. More than ever, he looked what he might even have been – who knows; one of a generation of distressed gentlefolk down on his luck, and forced to make his way in grubby commerce. As he made his duplicitous phone-calls he could not help overhearing an awful lot of 'shouting and hollering' emanating from the office next to his. It rather gave the game away at the other end of the line. He feared that this wasn't going to be a straightforward firm like the ones he had fronted in the old days.

At one point he saw Jack 'The Rat' Duval shoot out like a cannonball through the glass doors of Richardson's office. He landed head first, having received a kick in the pants from George Cornell. Jack was also known as 'The Prince of Fraud'. He had escaped from Russia in 1919 and enjoyed a stint in the French Foreign Legion before joining the RAF in 1940. His speciality was importing silk stockings and biting the hand that fed him. He disappeared after being booted out of Richardson's office. His crime had been passing dud cheques through the company accounts. After Jack's rapid exit, Cyril went into the office. Blood was everywhere, chairs had been overturned, and Richardson was patting George Cornell on the back: 'Good boy,' he was saying.

The next man to pass through Richardson's office was Duval's associate, Lucien Harris. Another conman, Harris was also a crossword compiler, with, as Richardson described, 'an accent and manner to go with his shop-window-dummy appearance and his fancy name'. On this occasion, Cyril was a witness to his boss's techniques in torture.

'Where's Jack?' Richardson demanded of Harris.

To which the inevitable reply was, 'I don't know.'

Richardson was eating a dish of scampi fried in deep batter. He forced a particularly fat one into Lucien's eye socket. His brother, Eddie, asked: 'Is this going to take long? There's something I want to watch on the telly.'

Roy Hall, Richardson's minder, suggested, 'Shall I fetch the box?'

The box was slightly larger than a 12-volt car battery. It was a plain wooden electricity generator with a handle and copper wheel. Cyril watched in silence and some horror as Harris was told to remove his shoes and socks. Wires from the box were attached to his toes. The handle was turned and Harris screamed, convulsed and then vomited.

Neither conman was prepared to suffer this outrage upon their person. But for them, reprisals should remain strictly cerebral. So they joined forces in plotting their day in court. A plummy-voiced Harris told what became known as the Clerkenwell 'torture' hearing: 'The leads were attached to my legs, my penis, the anus, the chest, the nostrils and temples.' He was smeared with orange juice which Richardson conjectured would make the shocks more painful. He was also stabbed in the foot.

The jury heard that once the Richardsons had tired of their work Cyril was dispatched to buy a bottle of Scotch. Harris was cleaned up and sent on his way with £150 to assuage his pain. After a five-minute break for a glass of Scotch and a cigarette, another man was brought in to be questioned.

Cyril kept watch as more men were tortured, taking notes and biding his time. He was in an awkward and potentially perilous position but that did not stop him from siphoning money out of the Camberwell warehouse. Pipe-smoking Cyril had decided that a quiet life would be just the thing, and that he had better make preparations for his retirement. His plans went awry when he was visited by George Cornell. George was soon to be shot dead by Ronnie Kray for calling him a 'fat poof'. But he was in fine fettle that day. He tipped

Cyril upside down on his chair and hit him across the head with a pair of pliers.

'Then he started hitting me with chairs and ashtrays, kicking me and punching me,' Cyril told the magistrate.

A woman in the public gallery shouted: 'He is not here to defend himself. You beast. You rotten, stinking beast.' And, worst of all, 'I shall come back to haunt you, Georgie Green.' ('Cyril' was his pseudonym.)

After the ensuing mayhem, the court was cleared and Cyril continued to give evidence against Charles Richardson, his brother Edward, Roy Hall and Francis Fraser. He told the court that Roy had brought a pot of boiling tea into his office and poured the contents over his head. Roy then set about punching and kicking him. Once he had tired of this he asked Cornell to break Cyril's toes. Cyril knew the ropes, and dutifully removed his shoes and socks. He arranged himself on the wooden floor and thought of Sussex, where he had so recently been dreaming of growing roses. Cornell's first attempts were futile so he brought out his pliers, and snapped Cyril's toes in half, one by one.

At this point 'Mad' Frankie Fraser decided that enough was enough. He tore up the floorboards, laid Cyril down, then nailed the boards back in place with a wretched, bleeding conman underneath them. Cyril was left to repent his sins for two hours, during which time he could hear the screams of another man being 'obliged'.

Cyril was eventually released for his part in the fraud (Richardson was gaoled for twenty-five years), and my grandfather was good enough to drive him to his retirement home in Sussex. He even sent Brother Will round to decorate it. And Ray Rosa was called upon to mediate in an ownership dispute between Cyril and Nicholas Van Hoogstraten. Ray's reputation for homicidal mania was such that his presence was all that was required.

'Sorry, Ray, we didn't realize it had anything to do with you,' said Van Hoogstraten's heavies. Ray had turned up at Cyril's house just as they were about to reclaim it on their boss's behalf. Cyril could finally rest easy.

Richardson was naïve to trust conmen. They are a breed apart from the average villain and have a habit of destroying criminal empires. Just as Cyril was the Richardsons' nemesis, if it had not been for 'Payne the Brain' the Krays would have got away with it. Leonard Payne was the twins' business manager. All was going well in their long-firms under the cover of a legitimate company he had set up on their behalf. It even had an account with the Bank of Valletta. When Ronnie's behaviour started to make Payne nervous, he decided to talk his way out of trouble. Ronnie heard that Payne was jittery, and put a contract on his head. Payne moved up a gear and found an ambitious policeman to give him shelter.

Nipper Read of the Yard was Payne's confessor, and Marylebone police station his sanctuary. George Cornell had just been murdered and the whole of the East End was one zipped-up mouth. Payne used his notorious brain to work a deal of immunity for himself, and the Krays were put away on his evidence.

No one should ever place their trust in a conman. Their instinct for self-preservation is fiercer than any thug's lust for blood. Besides, the police are usually prepared to negotiate a deal with them in return for information. And the sentences they receive are far lighter for the 'victimless' crimes they commit. For conmen, it pays to talk.

·

The name 'Streatham' is of Saxon origin, meaning 'dwellings by the street'. For the Romans it was just that – a resting post on the route they were constructing from London to the Sussex coast. Until 1666, it was a small village consisting of 100 or so homesteads straggling the main road for a mile. Once London had gone up in flames, city merchants decided it was time to escape the smouldering alleys of burnt-out London. Edmund Tilney, Master of the Revels at Court, and John Bodley, Charles I's moneylender, built country residences, and a Spa was established on the Common.

Even in the 1970s, south London had a leafy appeal. The commons at Streatham, Clapham, Tooting Bec and Brockwell are reminders of its agrarian past. Wealthy merchants were quick to feel at their lordly ease, and then everyone else ploughed in to take the waters. It was, in fact, a ploughman who first discovered Streatham's spring. Despite the water's 'mawkish taste', it was hailed as having medicinal powers, and was declared to be good for worms and the eyes. By the eighteenth century business was booming. The Common and High Street 'became fashionable promenades where all the leaders of society might be met'.

The bulk of my childhood was spent in the green glades of Streatham because of Charlie's dealings with local propertyowner Oscar Davis. Like a sailor with a mistress in every port, Oscar installed a girlfriend in each of the houses he owned. They took in lodgers who paid him rent. He drove around Streatham in his Corsair 2000E collecting his dues. He was not the only entrepreneur flourishing south of the river. Madam Cynthia Payne dispensed sexual services from a suburban villa not far from Charlie's hotel. For criminals, Streatham was wide open.

Charlie moved himself and Mistress Maureen into his new hotel on Leigham Court Road, Streatham Hill. It soon became a convenient resting-post where all the leaders of London's underworld might be met.

Teddy Machin evicted Cyril's staff single-handedly. Unlike Cornell and company he preferred to work alone. His great height and matching breadth, sunken eyes and quiet menace were quite sufficient to put the frighteners on a bunch of caterers. When the police arrived after they had complained of being 'manhandled', one of their number was Detective Inspector John Bland. Charlie dealt with him.

He 'turned' Bland for £100, turned him, that is, from being a policeman who ignored corruption into a policeman who was immersed in it. Bland became a regular and favoured customer at Charlie's hotel and poker club. Gruff, shifty and rapacious, Bland took to his criminal counterpart from the start. They talked the same language, as they liked to say, and worked in the same line of business. Besides, Charlie's hotel offered everything that a middle-aged man who was bored, unimaginative and lonely could want. Charlie and his team of builders had worked wonders on the Leigham Court Hotel.

The games room was in the sunlit conservatory and the games were overseen by Ray Rosa, the psychopath from Elephant & Castle. Crime was deeply ingrained in Rosa's family. When his brother, Jackie, who had been disqualified, died at the wheel of a car in a road accident, his last words to the police were, 'It wasn't me who was driving.' Rosa was employed by Charlie to deal with irritants such as the drug-dealer to whom James owed money. James confided to his father that he had been threatened by an irate pusher. Charlie rang the police, asking them to take the big bully off the street. They admitted that they were aware of his activities, but had 'nothing on him'. As a last resort Charlie told Rosa to deal with the problem. No one knows what became of the irksome drug-dealer because he was never seen again.

·

Apart from the casino, the hotel was run as a legitimate business with Boyd Williamson at the helm. The Scottish playboy-cum-heir to a fortune was a broken man, divorced, friendless and dependent on booze. He had come back from Australia and turned up at the hotel selling towel dispensers for public lavatories. Charlie greeted him like the old friend Boyd thought he was. He would not allow Boyd to degrade himself in this manner. Since he still dressed and spoke smartly, Charlie put him behind the desk at Reception. With Ray Rosa's villainous friends arriving for poker games and DI Bland drinking at the hotel bar, he was sitting at the nexus of south London's criminal world.

Charlie was still playing at Crockford's, where in a single night in 1966 he won £50,000. He bought more cars for his sons: an Aston Martin for Edward, another E-type for Vic, and the latest model from Ford for James. Charlie was the universal provider. Edward was lucky in not taking after his father. Victor and James, though, suffered from boredom.

In 1967, the year Lady Frankau died, Victor was arrested for forging a prescription. He had changed the dates on a series of seven scripts that were supposed to be cashed in on successive days. He wanted them all in one day. The chemist noticed the forgery and contacted Doctor John Petro.

Dr Petro was an alcoholic and furthermore was addicted to poker. For a guinea a time he wrote prescriptions in the lobby of a Bayswater casino. Once he had acquired enough money for a stake, he would wave the queuing addicts away. If Vic got there in time he would receive his daily 'script' for heroin. From here, he would drive to the all-night pharmacy in Boots the Chemist at Piccadilly.

If this was not enough he knew he could find Dr Petro at his other impromptu surgery, located in a black taxi cab outside Queensway Underground Station. The queue was twenty junkies deep. They lined up on the pavement. One at a time, they entered the taxi through the door on the kerb-side. They sat on the fold-down chair, consulted the doctor, and left through the other door. Dr Petro's minder, a toothless Canadian addict, would be waiting in the road to be paid.

Not only did Petro write scripts for heroin and cocaine, he introduced London's addicts to Methedrine. This was a drug used by Japanese suicide pilots in order to instil a sense of paranoia. It was particularly suitable for listening to the sinister sounds of the Rolling Stones' latest output. Devils, mass murderers and satanic majesties, Brian Jones's floating corpse in a swimming-pool, all added up to a state of rotten-ness. The old social norms were bound to be compromised when politicians were photographed with gangsters and the police were out-foxed by runaway train robbers. Even the Beatles were no longer lovable; they had grown long, straggly beards and refused to appear in concert.

Once the chemist was satisfied that the prescription before him was a forgery, the police were called and Vic was arrested. That night Dr Petro appeared on the David Frost programme. They were debating the legalization of cannabis, and the audience was full of Petro's patients. Once he had left the studio he was arrested by Sergeant Patrick from the Drugs Squad.

Petro was charged not for over-prescribing ('That's my clinical judgement,' was his defence) but for not keeping records. Victor was also arrested by Sergeant Patrick. He was twenty, and already, Patrick told Charlie, dying. He told the anxious father that there was no point trying to bribe him. Victor needed prison to get clean. Even Black Fred agreed with him. Charlie gave in, and his beloved son received a sentence of three months, to be spent in a detention centre.

Patrick was rare in that he was not corruptible. Drug addicts hated him for it. He systematically stripped them of their drugs, threw them into the cells of his West End station, and ignored their cold-turkey screams. Graffiti could be seen,

'Kill Sgt Patrick', on the carriages of trains coming into Charing Cross Station.

Even in the 1980s, when Victor was years out of detox and determined to keep clean, he could not take a walk down Charing Cross Road. And I could see why from my perch on the third floor of Waterstone's the Booksellers, where I was aimlessly dusting the shelves of the History Department. I watched the junkies who congregated opposite Waterstone's on the corner of Charing Cross Road and Denmark Street. I often wondered if I would spot my uncle Victor. And then I wondered what I would do if I did.

All his old friends were there. Skinny, washed-out, super-annuated young people in faded hippie gear, hanging loose, waiting for the next fix from their pushers. They were part of the West End's Theatreland, so self-conscious were they of their chemical exuberance. They gathered outside Macari's, the musical instrument shop that specializes in amps, guitars and dreams of head-banging rockstardom. The men wore their hair unfashionably long and greasy. They slapped backs and high-fived for the world to see. 'Look at me, look at me,' was what these unappetizing leftovers from the Seventies seemed to be saying. Especially the women, who strutted past Macari's, their bare, scabby legs on show. My gaze bypassed the dreamy smiles and glazed eyes and zoomed in on the tell-tale veins. Filled with poison, they were lumpy and green.

After Victor was imprisoned, Charlie made a telephone call to the prison governor. 'If anything happens to my boy I shall hold you responsible.' The emphasis was heavily on the 'you'. To reinforce the point he asked Sergeant Patrick to ring him, as well as the family's solicitor. But Victor enjoyed his three months at the detention centre, where his energies were spent surviving a boot-camp regime.

He came out fit and well and went straight to the Dilly

where Dr Petro had opened a new surgery, pending his appeal. It took place in the Lyons' Corner House opposite the Statue of Eros. Victor found his doctor studying the form in the *Greyhound Express*. He had been struck off, and was himself addicted to Methedrine. He hardly knew what he was doing, only that he had to do some more of it. Money was his main objective, so he began employing his surgical skills in the toilets of Piccadilly Underground Station where he lanced junkies' abscesses for a small fee.

■

Following Petro's trial drug clinics were set up but they did not prescribe heroin. Two days after he was struck off, Triad gang members were selling powdered heroin on the streets. With Petro off the scene, Victor and the 300 other drug addicts he had been treating had a problem. They were all psyched up with nowhere to go but Chinatown. The drugs there were impure, and the results were frightening. Victor overdosed in a public toilet. Charlie leaned on his police friends again. This time he managed to organize a trip to the Bahamas. Victor was under police escort to ensure that he got through customs clean.

I was three years old when Victor was undergoing cold turkey in our poolside house. I was the only child I knew who understood the terrors of withdrawal. First he had the sweats, then aching bones. He curled up like a hedgehog on the floor, but he was moaning and shivering uncontrollably. Everything that touched his skin felt like sandpaper. The porterhouse steaks my father had imported direct from New York abattoirs smelt rotten. Victor was delirious and all through the night I heard him banging his brains against the walls of our living-through-dining-room. Then his stomach and bowels collapsed.

Once Victor had cleaned out his system and acquired a suntan, Charlie gave him a job at the hotel. James had had the bright idea of building up custom by shipping in nurses from a local hostel as well as student teachers. He sent a fleet of mini-cabs to pick them up and bring them to parties which were given every Thursday night. Penniless students and nurses were plied with drink, and mingled with cops and villains. If women were in short supply, Charlie would ring a labour exchange that dealt in catering staff.

'Send some girls round, would you, luvvie?' he would drawl in the effetely nuanced manner he had picked up from his gangster friends. It felt glorious not having to bark out his orders. These days he could just wave his diamond pinkie at underlings. He could even subvert his unquestioned masculinity by camping it up like the great stage actor he believed he was.

The girls arrived in the morning, and the ones who had slept with him by the afternoon were invited to the evening's party. He excelled in his role as master of ceremonies.

The hotel was happening and hip to the groove of bell-bottomed flares, maxi dresses and matching waistcoats. Beads and bangles jangled, all you needed was love, and the girls swayed dreamily, providing endless possibilities for sex. Charlie dressed in white tie and tails for these occasions. No one else did, but he had standards of decorum to maintain. He looked on approvingly, enthroned in the red velvet cushions and gilt frame of a chair from the 100-piece dining-room suite he had acquired from a dodgy friend.

He sucked his Cuban cigar. More impenetrable than ever, he sat, smoked, and mellowed. While he pursed his lips and pondered, new business relationships and sexual liaisons were being formed on the dance floor and at the tables around him. He dragged the last smoke from his cigar, and, with calloused thumb and forefinger, crushed the glowing end in the heavy onyx ashtray by his side. He had seen enough, taken note of who was in, and who was out, and was calibrating the information for future use.

▪

Charlie was never satisfied. Business was booming at the hotel; his sons were gainfully employed under his roof. Police and thieves were drinking their fill. But on Christmas Day 1968 he chose to stay at home in Kensington. The plane from Freeport, Grand Bahama, had been unable to land at Heathrow due to fog. After an hour of circling the skies, the pilot informed us that we would be landing in Manchester. It was Christmas Eve, and after the long transatlantic crossing my mother and I would have to endure a coach journey to London in adverse weather conditions. I took care not to whine or complain. I was my mother's pride and joy and as good as gold. We arrived in London in the dead of night and took a taxi to Kensington.

Fog again, and it was bitterly cold. Dolly had piled my bed high with blankets and put a hot-water bottle underneath them. I screamed with fright as my feet touched the scalding heat. I told my mother there was a hot, clammy monster in my bed.

On Christmas Day, my mother awoke to find no one at home. To her dismay, everybody except Charlie had gone to the hotel. She had come back because she longed for her mother, and here we were alone with her evil stepfather. He cooked us a turkey lunch with all the trimmings. He made a great fuss of me from a distance, admiring my sun-dappled hair and repeating that I was as good as gold. He showed my mother his new Magimix. He asked her if she had any washing, so keen was he to display the latest front-loading washing-machine. He had all the mod cons, but still could not gain her respect. He gave up, and joined the others at the hotel. It was just me and her now. I had my toys, and Tom Jones was on the telly, but she was in floods of tears, inconsolable.

16 · The Fixer

Each of Charlie's sons had their role to play in Leigham Court's success. Victor was the manager. Edward headed a team of builders, painters and carpenters who all lived in chalets they had built themselves in the hotel's grounds. Gregarious James was in charge of entertainments – he roped in Rod Stewart to play a gig there, before he became famous. He invited footballers from Crystal Palace FC to add to the aggressive male vigour of the proceedings.

Lily could not bear to be kept in the shadows. She needed to be near her husband – he was her lifeblood. Besides, she too wanted to rub shoulders with the sporting stars of the day. So keen was she to get in on the act, she helped out with catering. Despite the fact that Kathleen was in charge of buffets.

Everyone, even the chambermaids, lived on the premises. Presiding over them from a suite on the top floor was Charlie. Kathleen had gained recognition as his consort and was openly living with him. She was no longer just slim. The flesh had fallen from her bones as anorexia had taken its grip. James was called from the office where he was embroiled in a fist fight with Edward. Charlie needed his help in talking Kathleen out of throwing herself from the window ledge.

'Let her jump,' he said.

As ever, Charlie had the answer to suicidal tendencies. Nothing was too much trouble for my grandfather. He had been asked to stand bail for an alcoholic doctor about to stand trial on a drunk-driving charge. The charge was dropped but the doctor was struck off. Instead of taking a fee for standing bail, Charlie moved him into the hotel. His official job was to make sandwiches for salesmen's conferences, but he was really there to keep an eye on Kathleen.

·

While footballers and student nurses were cavorting in the ballroom, the hotel bar became a playground for the disaffected and infamous. Frankie Fraser had *carte blanche*, as did Charles Kray, Commander Ken Drury and Detective Inspector John Bland of the Flying Squad. The Kray twins' older brother propped up the bar, largely due to the presence behind it of a former Miss Margate. Everyone was enjoying their host's generosity.

Charlie loved an open house. With the seamless comings and goings of London's waifs, strays, addicts, criminals and losers, it was just like being back at Stonebridge. Victor's friends lived in the greenhouse in the garden, where Tula, a French Vietnamese soothsayer, developed his astrological theories. He was one of those addicts for whom drugs open the mind. He believed in UFOs and would follow London's ley lines all the way to Greenwich to watch the skies for omens. When he came back to Streatham he would share the messages he had received via the constellations. Victor filled the greenhouse with the wilting blooms he found languishing on the steps of the Statue of Eros. 'Come back to my place, it's a groovy pad.' So they did.

They slept, ate and took drugs under a glass canopy sitting amidst the swathes of green lawn and hydrangeas. It was a continental mix. There was the wiry, fidgety Gerard, a French Corsican, who brought his own lighting system to the greenhouse. The strobe effects in primary colours were as spasmodic as his jerking limbs when he danced and took acid to the Byrds. Wolfgang, a German junkie, and Françoise, his Belgian girlfriend, joined in. They watched the night skies, smoked the pipe of peace and deferred to Tula's ancient wisdom. They were too stoned to make the leap in faith he required. But since every other authority in the land had been debunked, his gnomic pronouncements meant he must be in touch.

So he told them about the instructions he had received from super-groovy intergalactic voyagers. He was one of the Selected Few, and when the time came he would be carted off with other members of the Selected Few to a special place he simply called 'There'. He didn't like to be questioned too deeply about 'There', and became nervous when asked for particulars. But this was not a time for scepticism.

Victor was also battling paranoid delusions. But, instead of aliens, his involved the police. Even Kathleen laughed when Victor babbled about a crack regiment of SAS soldiers bathing in the kiddies' paddling pool. It was best not to take him too seriously. He could flip; become violent, and frighten old ladies like my great-aunt Dolly. Who was so terrified to hear of his visions she started having her own.

Two gay Australian boys with dyed blond hair brought a more maternal vision to the greenhouse. They waited on tables in the restaurant, and fed the exotic menage with the day's specials. They had travelled all the way round the world and landed here, where the dregs of the world had travelled to be fed by them.

■

By day, Leigham Court Hotel was a conference centre for salesmen. They turned up for assertiveness training wearing navy blazers and regimental ties. Their assertions of self-belief could be heard as they chorused *en masse*: 'I feel good.

I am happy. I have a positive mental attitude.' By night, they joined the junkies in games of crazy golf. The garden was lit up with fairy lights. Meanwhile, the *Daily Mirror* reported that investigators had shown that of all the men who wore regimental ties, six in ten were impostors.

Charlie was enjoying this fantasy life. His insomnia was not a problem when there was a constant roll-call of staff to be called upon through the night. They were studiously respectful as Mr Taylor regaled them with his wartime exploits with the Royal Sussex Regiment. He was a captain, he declared.

'More likely a general,' scoffed Charlie Kray, 'a general bloody nuisance.'

Despite the fact that my parents and I were living within walking distance of the hotel, I went there only once. My mother did not want to contaminate me with Charlie's presence. As a baby, it had been an unspoken rule that he was not allowed to touch me. I remember my mother warning me about Charlie's 'delusions of grandeur'. I know what she meant now. It was not just that he believed his own lies, he was also convinced of his omnipotence. Greta and I forged a compact. I was her child in shining armour and together we mocked his vaulting ambitions. To him we must have seemed as dreadful as the Furies as we parried his every word with shafts of contempt.

In 1972 we deigned to visit the hotel. The occasion was my grandmother's birthday. I wore a fur coat casually draped around my shoulders. I had brushed my hair a hundred times to make it shine. Under my coat I wore jeans and a T-shirt, to show how careless I was of girls' fashions. My mother and I were wary of revealing our feminine charms. There were too many predators about.

As usual, I was made a fuss of. No one meant it. They

were being nice to the boss's grand-daughter. Like my mother, I was offhand and distant.

DI John Bland was bleary-eyed and slumped at the bar. He asked me how old I was. I told him I was seven. 'That's a good age to be,' he said, and turned back to his drink. Not before I noticed he had the battered face and lopsided ears of an old lag from my favourite sitcom, *Porridge*.

'We missed the bastard again,' I heard him tell the girl behind the bar. He was referring to the armed robber John McVicar, whom he had sworn to shoot on sight. So this was a leading light of the Flying Squad, I reflect in hindsight. He was London's answer to America's G-Men as he raced around town in the latest Rover. But in my eyes he was pissed and frazzled, and barely able to keep his seat.

Next up was a tour of the hotel's bedrooms. The gracious Kathleen took me by the hand and pointed out the tasteful furnishings: melamine fitted wardrobes, labour-saving Teasmades and modern antiques. I enjoyed the sensation of treading on soft carpets, of being cooed to by the lady of the house in her soft, lilting tones. She was so glamorous in her smart beige trouser suit. She told me it was from a boutique in Croydon and had cost £200. I noticed a Royal Doulton statuette of a shepherdess on the dressing-table of the honeymoon suite. I wanted the graceful lady in her hooped gown. The word was passed to my grandfather. I wanted him, like Kathleen, to shower me with kind words and affection, but he handed it over with a curt nod. I knew I could get these meaningless love tokens from him. I did not value them because what I wanted was not on offer. But I continued to blackmail him anyway – with what, I did not know. But it didn't matter because he did.

Everyone wanted something from Charlie. The trouble was he had nothing to give. The endless parties were a fantastic masquerade of familial bonding. The consumption was frantic, the talk was raucous, the unspoken resentment deafening. Charlie sat quietly smoking as we partied around him. His gaze was turned inwards and he seemed to be the only person not enjoying himself. I raided my grandmother's wardrobes and put on a long chiffon dress. It was in royal blue with pink roses, and I sang for him. 'I love you, Grand-dad' – his favourite song. I cannot have been very convincing because he barely raised a smile.

On one occasion, Uncle Edward dressed up in a gorilla suit as a surprise for me and my cousin. But my cousin did not see the joke and attacked him with a knife. Once he had calmed down, the gaiety resumed and my grandmother and I took to the dance floor. We danced solo, side by side, twisting ourselves into the ground as we insisted that 'Croco-dile Rock' be played endlessly. We would have danced all night if anyone had cared to notice.

·

For Charlie, the real fun had started four years previously.

It is February 1968 in the empty dining-hall of the Leigham Court Hotel. Two men are talking in hushed voices. They are Charles Taylor and the sergeant from Streatham police station. Taylor hands over £100 to release his son from a holding cell at the station.

The following day Victor is released. He had been arrested for leaving his E-type in the window of Radio Rentals' shop front on Streatham High Road.

Charlie was so adept at doing deals that he became a fixer. A fixer, as he had learnt from Johnny Miller, is the man who acts as a go-between for villains and the police. Most of them are regarded as 'dirt' in the classification system 'dirt' to 'well-respected'. But the more crooks a Flying Squad man knows, the more valuable is his contribution to crime detection. Charlie became a very important man.

If you were a criminal with a record and you got arrested, you gave my grandfather £28,000. He kept £8,000 and gave the rest to his police friends. They dropped the charge. If your house was busted and the police took your colour television he would ring up the station and speak to his contact. He would tell him there would be trouble if the television was not returned. By the time you got home, the television would be sitting on your front lawn.

So confident was Charlie of his hold over the Flying Squad that he was unable to see them coming. Over drinks one night in 1972, Chief Inspector Reginald Davies and a man called 'Roberts' asked Charlie to invest £3,000 in a fraudulent flooring company they were running. He agreed, and a few months later got his money back with £1,000 interest. Later that year, the two men approached him again. This time they told him that a long-firm was to be set up in Stratford, east London. If he invested £30,000 he would get double his money back.

Charlie went to see a friendly bank manager in Streatham. He asked him for a loan of £30,000, and offered as surety a bag of diamonds. They were, in fact, Zircon, a new stone that was being advertised in Sunday supplements as being as near as dammit to the real thing. To convince the bank manager they were genuine, Teddy Machin was sent to a Hatton Garden jeweller to buy an eye-piece. He then turned up at the bank in the guise of a Jewish diamond merchant. He examined the gems through his eye-piece, and declared them kosher. The bank manager arranged the loan.

Charlie handed his 'hard-earned' money, as he called it, to Machin, who took it to Roberts. Charlie never saw the money again. Roberts claimed he 'lost [it] over the side of a boat'. Charlie was devastated by this piece of insolence. He knew Roberts had a boat but he also knew he had been conned. What was worse, they did not even bother to give him a plausible excuse.

'Of course I didn't believe it,' he later told an investigative journalist. 'But in the beginning I didn't think the police had anything to do with it and that [Roberts] had nicked it himself. It was only when I tried to get my police friends to help me, and after they told me that "things might get nasty and involve us all" that I realized they'd shared it between them.'

It was equally possible that his faithful minder, Teddy Machin, was involved in the con trick. By this time Teddy was a frightened man, and constantly on the move. His own family, the Tibbses who hailed from Poplar, east London, were engaged in a turf war with the Nichollses, sons of Stepney. The conflagration had its origins in the Nichollses' use of the word 'pikey'. Etymologically the word is relatively harmless, it means a user of turnpikes, but since the middle of the twentieth century it has taken on the more pejorative meaning of 'gypsy'. When a member of the Nicholls clan called the Tibbses 'a bunch of pikeys', sensibilities were outraged.

In 1973 'Old Man Tibbs', his three sons and Teddy's nephew, Michael Machin, were convicted of a variety of offences. They included conspiracy to pervert the course of justice, possession of 600 rounds of ammunition, conspiracy to blackmail, wounding, attempted murder and assault on a police officer. They were gaoled for a total of fifty-eight years.

At around the same time a masked gunman shot at Teddy through the bedroom window of his flat in Streatham. The gunman smashed the window with a milk bottle and fired blind through the heavy curtain. One shot hit the wall just above Teddy's chest. Another volley got him in the leg and buttocks. The gunman ran off leaving a double-barrelled, sawn-off shotgun behind him. A police spokesman said: 'It doesn't appear that robbery was the motive.'

Ted was shot dead in the street in 1974 by the nephew of his married lover. When the police searched his flat they found cash wrappers that Charlie claimed came from his wad of £30,000. Chief Inspector Reg Davies arranged to give them back to him so that he would not be implicated in the murder. The police also found a small black book in which Teddy had kept meticulous records of information he believed could be used 'to protect him'.

'I saw that book once,' Charlie said. 'It was on the desk one morning and I picked it up. There were things in there – initials of police officers – which could have implicated a lot of people. He'd put phone numbers in backwards. The book listed payments I'd made to police officers and other people: loans . . . that sort of thing.'

The book disappeared, but Charlie's relationship with Chief Inspector Reg Davies went from strength to strength. Ted was not dead yet, and in 1973 Charlie was still on the up and up. He paid for Davies and his wife to accompany him on a trip to Ireland. Black Fred, who was not allowed to visit the hotel because the police did not like his colour, chauffeured the Rolls-Royce Phantom. It had been acquired specially for the occasion. Charlie and Reg toured Cork, including the grounds of the Marchioness's estate. They kissed the Blarney Stone, too. Charlie paid for everything, the entertainment and hotel accommodation. He was in his element.

When Reg was promoted to second in command of the Flying Squad, Charlie was invited to the celebration dinner at the Dorchester Hotel. He was photographed sitting at the same table with Deputy Commissioner Jock Wilson. He was photographed chatting and laughing with Sir Robert Mark. Maureen was with him, so was Victor, who smoked a joint in the toilet. Charlie didn't care. He was beyond caring. He was triumphant: this was his reward for being cheated of £30,000.

•

Like other leading criminals, Charlie's close relationship with a number of officers went far beyond what could possibly be regarded as legitimate for the police. At first, he used his police contacts to get special attention for his sons. As far as he was concerned, their drug addiction was something that could be fixed by bribing representatives of the Law. Sometimes he wielded his influence wisely. James's habit was becoming so bad that Charlie arranged for him to be arrested just to get him into a police cold-turkey unit at Ashford Remand Centre. As for Victor, his father's name gave him immunity from police action throughout London.

Victor cruised the streets in his Jag, high on drugs. One night he had been taking speed with some friends when they took his clothes. He broke down on a zebra crossing. He was naked and the car would not move. James got a phone call from a patrolman to come to the aid of his brother. When he got there, the patrolman tactfully sped away on his motor-cycle. There were no charges levelled against Victor.

James was stopped many times for speeding. When the police asked his name they let him go. On one occasion he was racing Wolfgang. His name and address were taken. James's were not. Instead, the officer said he would tell James's father. If Charlie was the king of Streatham, his two younger sons were its wilful princelings.

•

What can you do? My mother had decided that it would be a nice treat to take me to visit my grandmother. It was the last blazing hot day of the summer term and we made for

Kensington, our mecca. I was eight years old and wearing the summer uniform of Streatham Hill and Clapham High School for Girls. It consisted of a green felt hat shaped like a policeman's with a tartan braid round the rim, a cotton dress in green and white gingham, and knee-high white socks and brown sandals. I looked pristine and sweet, and I knew it.

We climbed up the steps, hand in hand, and my mother let fall the brass knocker. After an age, Great-aunt Dolly opened the door. She sighed. I could hear music coming from the front room. Dolly took my mother to one side, and I sallied forth expecting a hug and a present from my loving grandmother. But I was greeted by a scene of confusion. Uncle Victor was dancing a strange, cavorting waltz with his mother. The volume was turned up full on the record player, and a mess of guitars strummed and shrieked behind a flat, rambling voice. It was Eric Clapton, Victor's new friend.

Lily was proud of her family's connections with celebrity. It made her feel part of a scene. All she wanted from life was to dance, flirt and giggle. She could not understand why her sons were so bent on self-destruction. They had felt the soft edge of so many advantages. She had coddled them so that they would never have to experience fear.

I heard her tell my mother that only that morning Victor had threatened to cut his arm off – the arm that was riddled with track marks. He had taken a carving knife to his shoulder in a bid to stop Charlie hitting his mother. One fix later, and his despair had turned to fake elation.

Lily's sheer nylon tights did not hide the bruises on her shins that told where Charlie had kicked her. When I think of my grandmother her legs are bloated and blue, with red veins in jagged relief. But for now she was happy to be gyrating to the sound of Derek and the Dominoes.

She gushed as she told me that Vic had met Eric in a

drying-out clinic. That he had even been round to the house. Eric had dried out, Vic clearly hadn't. The friendship, unsurprisingly, was short-lived.

But Lily was thrilled by this brush with a rock supremo and rushed out to buy his latest record. 'Layla' was the song that was playing. The story of Eric's love for a Beatle's wife had induced in Victor a trance-like state. He, too, was a victim of the Woodstock generation. To prove it, he wafted around the room, raising his arms to the ceiling and treading his bare feet on the blue carpet in slow, ceremonial step to the churning guitars.

I was puzzled. My uncle was wearing a red kimono with silver dragons on his back. Though I did not realize it at the time, this was Mick Jagger's influence. Vic had been to the Hyde Park concert, and mourned Brian Jones's death. He even spoke like Jagger – a whining, Cockney drawl like that of a fishwife stoned on Valium. After Hyde Park he had put away his loon pants and adopted the androgynous look. But the winged sleeves of his kimono made him look sinister, like a bat. I watched as my grandmother struggled to pin his arms to her waist, and he fluttered free.

He noticed me standing in the corner. He fixed me with his bombed-out eyes, ringed in kohl. Something about me amused him. Then I realized he was wearing bottle-green varnish on his toe and finger nails. He was riveted by my uniform.

'Come here,' he demanded, and took me into his mother's bedroom. I sat by his side on the stool at her dressing-table. The sun was streaming through the gently rustling net curtains. This beautiful, breezy day was the beginning of my summer holiday. All the grace and elegance of centuries of wealth had aligned themselves in the stucco fronts facing the window. I longed to roll down the slopes of Kensington Gardens and pretend I was a fun-loving child. I wanted to hear Dolly's story about Timmy the poodle jumping over the railings of Kensington Palace. I longed, more than anything, to be a member of respectable society, and not worry that I was betraying my lack of class.

Victor took the felt hat from my head and twirled it on his finger round and round. I was worried that he might bend it out of shape. My mother repeatedly steamed it over a kettle to achieve the perfect policeman's mound. I made a feeble lunge, but he was faster. He put my hat on his head, and giggled. He was just like my grandmother, who was just like me. He wanted to be like me, too; he had long since abandoned hope of being a man. I tried to giggle alongside him but caught sight of myself in the mirror.

I was frightened. My hat was tiny and irrelevant, perched on his greasy, permed curls. I was worried that since he was so bad and dangerous he might make it dirty. He was contagious, but what could I do?

'Come on, Lily.' That was my mother, brusque and resentful. The family she needed so badly had let her down. I asked for my hat back. My mother snatched my hand and marched me out. We sat in silence – hers was fraught, mine complicit – throughout the long bus ride home.

17 · Frankie and Dino

If only Charlie had learnt the economic value of truth. He boasted; being 'big' is essential in the underworld. He lent vast sums of money in order to impress. Junior policemen wanted to associate with him as a means of networking with the higher-up. He found it consoling to boast of his prowess at fixing things with the police, of his money bags, and his friendships with notorious villains, high-class society types and well-placed cops. It was talk, talk and still more talk, and with all the substance and bravura of a blustering infant.

Just like Lord Colwyn, Charlie sat up till the small hours holding court over his retinue of chambermaids, waitresses and carpenters. He preferred the company of his employees these days. The aristocracy had let him down when Colwyn had failed to return monies owed. A real gentleman would not do that, he figured. So his staff listened as his disquisitions on history grew more elaborate. His speciality subjects were General Custer, English rule and the North African campaign of General Wavell. He sat with a little glass of anisette in his hand, thinking it was a *mafioso*'s drink. He had just finished the latest biography of Frank Sinatra. He identified with the skinny kid from a broken home who had made it big and was a wise guy. And hadn't his sister Nell been a grand singer?

'In the pub!' snorted my grandmother.

At the same time as Charlie began to think he was doing

it His Way, my father was kidding himself he was Dean Martin. He was back from *la terra promessa* of the Bahamas. The dream, like life itself, was a racket, he had decided. In their turn, the Bahamian government had decided that its indigenous population was entitled to employment in the island's casinos and golf clubs. Along with the other ex-pats, my father's work permit was not renewed. So I watched him stagnate on Streatham Hill. Our block of flats was down the road from where a gibbet had once been. Brixton Prison now stood in its place.

Our street was built up with sullen housing estates and menacing boys gathered in informal clumps. Inside Number 73 Cameford Court, the claustrophobia was intense. I knew that we were living in one of my grandfather's leftover flats because, despite its compactness, there was a telephone in each of its tiny rooms. Even the bathroom had one. Dolly said that it was because Teddy Machin had been so frightened he could not bear to be without a lifeline. So there was a telephone in every room but there was no room to hide from the demands of highly-strung individuals at war with each other. My mother told me that my father had a mistress back in Freeport. If he seemed sad it was because he was missing her badly. I tried not to digest what she was saying, and concentrated on playing with my Barbie dolls.

My father interrupted Ken and Barbie making love in their Mattel beach-house with an offer to teach me poker. I reluctantly left my bedroom – the room in which Teddy Machin was nearly shot dead – to join my lonely father in his game. He showed me how to shuffle a pack on the chessboard pattern of our glass coffee-table. I admired his fluttering hands but he recited the rules too quickly. I was too flustered to memorize the sequences so I disappointed him once again. He let me have the pack anyway. It was a full set of hand-painted Viennese playing-cards with pictures of graceful kings and queens. I would lay them out on my bedroom floor and gaze at their rosy-cheeked faces for hours.

Pino (it even rhymed with Dino) was frustrated. Okay, he had a big, shiny motor – an American Dodge, as a matter of fact, which the LAPD had just adopted as their squad car. And oh, how my father yearned for America, how he longed to take to its roads. To exchange admiring glances with other drivers who would appreciate his smooth control over this gleaming machine. But it was a white elephant on Streatham's sedate Avenues and Rises. There were no free-ways here, and I felt foolish when he picked me up from school. It was a girls' school, and we were not susceptible to the charms of a four-door sedan with hideaway headlights. Poor Pino was eager to impress but my mother and I were no substitute for a Rat Pack.

We did not see much of Charlie then. My mother thought it was best that way: one fantasist was enough for any woman and her growing child.

▪

Despite his increasingly feeble hold on reality, my grand-father still had his uses for the police. In 1972 a photograph of Commander Ken Drury appeared in the *Sunday People*. It showed him relaxing on holiday in Cyprus with Jimmy and Rusty Humphries, famous Soho pornographers. No one believed Drury's excuse that he was attempting to find Ronnie Biggs, the escaped Great Train Robber. A squad was set up to investigate him.

Later that year, Peter 'Pookey' Garfarth, a hotel thief and conman, was attacked in the toilet of the Dauphin Club in Mayfair. He accused Jimmy Humphries of giving him a severe slashing around the face as punishment for having an affair with Rusty. She was a striking woman who had once been a stripper, and half the Soho Vice Squad was in love with her. Humphries was arrested. He denied the attack on Garfarth, claiming that he had been framed in revenge for Drury's suspension. He accused Detective Inspector Bland of organizing the frame-up and named Charles Taylor as his principal aide and abetter.

Garfarth was placed on police protection in a room at the Leigham Court Hotel. His evidence caused Humphries to be gaoled for eight years. He was released after six with a royal pardon for his part in rooting out police corruption. He and Rusty opened a nightclub in Surrey. Ken Drury resigned. Peter Garfarth committed suicide. Strikers were hitting the streets, corruption in high places was about to be exposed.

Charlie was finding it hard to keep the good times going and Victor was losing interest in the hotel. Wolfgang and Tula had been caught in crossfire during a drug deal gone wrong in the French port of Antibes. Then Kathleen bailed out.

Charlie was in a business meeting with a Heathrow Airport employee called Larry Hawkins, who specialized in exploiting Thief Row Airport's lacklustre security arrangements. Larry looked very smart in his gold-braid security guard's uniform, which provided the perfect front for his activities as a 'middle man'. He could locate the weak points in the security surrounding shipments of gold bullion. These coins were called krugerrands and they were arriving in large batches once a month.

The South African krugerrand had just started being mass-produced. Each coin contained an ounce of pure gold. The idea of striking a coin containing one ounce of gold without a face value, the price of which would move in accord with the daily gold price on world markets, was a new one, and my grandfather was quick to seize his share.

So Charlie and his new friend Larry – 'new' because he had not needed him before and 'friend' in the loosest sense – were not to be disturbed. Kathleen took her chance and stole two antique French clocks from the hotel and took the keys to her lover's old Alvis. She emptied his bank account and with one of Charlie's camp followers, boarded a plane to South Africa.

Alarms started ringing in Charlie's head. He had grown dependent on Kathleen's unflagging devotion to him. A woman's unreasoning passion shored up his mental defences as evidence of his all-conquering power. The fact that she had gone was an omen that his sphere of influence might be waning.

He got the police to track the car. Larry Hawkins found her name on the passenger list at the airport. Perhaps Charlie's ability to track Kathleen's every move was consolation for his inability to stop her leaving him.

His newly discovered sense of powerlessness extended to his own family. He was dismayed when Victor went absent without leave from the hotel. At twenty-four years old he had had enough and checked himself into Ward 13B of Tooting Bec mental hospital. The reason? He had been injecting himself with a mixture of heroin and barbiturates in order to come down from an extended run of methamphetamine abuse. The mixture induced a pleasurable high but was a hazardous practice. Both drugs depress respiratory control centres in the brain.

It was to everyone's surprise that Victor had lived long enough to become addicted to barbiturates. But if they had not killed him, and he had had an overdose or two, they had done the next best thing. Life becomes sheer misery, and then withdrawal can kill you, too. In addition to the common-or-garden variety of symptoms – chills, cramps and insomnia – barb detox can cause delirium, hallucinations, seizures and coronary arrest. Charlie had wanted Victor to invest all his energies in taking over his empire and in keeping the family together. Instead he had fallen apart.

18 · Sheffield Mata Hari

In 1974 Charlie was laid low with a strange and fearful lethargy. His delight in schemes and games had become paranoid obsession. His judgement and memory were impaired. He was tired. He lay in bed for what seemed the entire year watching endlessly flickering images on the biggest television set money could buy. The sound was turned off. He did not want to hear the disturbing news from the outside world.

It was as though the Thirties had come back to haunt him. In response to the Yom Kippur war, OPEC had quadrupled the world price of oil, ending the affluence of the happy-go-lucky Sixties. Upward social mobility was over. A worsening economy, electricity cuts and terrorist bombs were taking their toll on public morale.

England was in desperate straits, and Charlie was too frightened to leave his hotel. Teddy Machin, his lieutenant and minder, stood watch at the foot of his bed. His brooding figure circled Charlie's waxen heap like a vulture waiting for meltdown. He was supposed to be protection, because Charlie was afraid. But then he went and got himself shot.

Charlie had no friends left. The Paddington Circle had broken apart. Black Fred died of a heart attack during a cabaret tour of West Germany. Davey Perkins had tired of pandering to the sick and famous, and escaped to Cornwall. The laughs they had shared in the parlour of Number 1 were over. As for Billy Hill, he was too astute to want to know. Charlie had outlived his usefulness.

For the first time in his life, my grandfather lost interest in his appearance. It was as though there was no one left to impress. His muscle had collapsed into clammy, grey folds. The striped polyester of his pyjamas stuck to his skin. He began to smell because he could not hold himself in. His speech was blurred, his breathing was shallow, his eyes were unfocused. The air was thick with the fug of his sweat and fear. From deep within the gloom of his bed the only colours to be seen belonged to the shiny capsules he lodged in his mouth. Amytal were the Blue Heavens he did not believe in, Nembutal were the Yellow Jackets he once had worn, Seconal were the Red Devils he rode till he made it over the Tuinal Rainbow. Finally, he evinced a profound and blissful lack of concern as the powerful depressants slowed down his mind and nervous system, turning what was left of his muscles to mush. He dissolved into his feathered pillow and was awash with lurid dreams.

On the back of his failing powers, his friends in the Flying Squad gained the upper hand. Because if you organize long-firms for any length of time the police will eventually latch on to them. They are duty bound to investigate complaints from the public, and Charlie had a lot of explaining to do, and it had taken a lot of money to make it all right. He had to persuade the officer to go back to the complainant with a story. So the sergeant might say to the credulous creditor: 'No, it's legit. But it's the kind of business that takes a long time to make money.' Or, if that was not plausible: 'It's vanished. Be more careful next time.'

People who had befriended Charlie were getting wise to the dangers of associating with such a man. His new business associates were far more ruthless and cunning than anyone he had come up against before. He could not manipulate these guys as he had the trusting sons of Scottish noblemen, or the relics of an *ancien régime*. They were young up-and-coming villains who knew how to work a man.

Charlie received his visitors with magnificent disregard to the dishevelled state of his bed. If he had to get out of it – to stand bail in court, say, for the friend of a friend – it was never for less than five grand. Gradually he began to drift into another role for which he was ideally equipped. He had been dealing for so many years with leading criminals and their equivalent in the police force that he decided to put the two together. As he had lain in bed all year his mind had been slowly working.

It could have been the barbiturates. Perhaps they released my grandfather's innate deviance from any moral restraints that might have been loitering at the back of his mind. Barbs are known to be powerful disinhibitors. But the source of Charlie's arrogant disregard for reality lay in his own inflated sense of power. He knew that if a chap wanted to get off a charge or have it reduced to a lesser charge, or if he wanted to get something good said about him in court, or to get evidence dropped, or some mishap to occur whereby evidence was lost or a witness failed to show up, he could arrange this. All he had to do was to speak with certain police officers. No matter where they were, it could be arranged through Scotland Yard.

Given the level of control he possessed, he had it in him to be a dangerously duplicitous man. So his next move was to organize major crimes, then go to his police friends and say that he had heard on the grapevine that such and such a job was going to take place. They would be pleased with the tip-off, and things would happen at their end. Finally, he would go back to his colleagues in crime and say, 'I've been talking to a friend of mine in the force. He knows all about what's going on, what we're doing, but I can square it with them for x amount of pounds.' Of course they would be delighted and chip in their share. He would keep it.

'Leave it to me, luvvie,' he sighed as he picked up the phone. Then that day's supplicant would be treated to a gala performance as Charlie bellowed, cajoled and finally cooed down the line. He received £7,000 for one such gig. This one involved interceding with the Fraud Squad on behalf of a Mafia 'paperhanger' turned supergrass called Mike Sylvester. Mike had originally made a living by selling bonds for New York bosses, but he turned on his masters and arrived in London on the witness-protection programme. He had jumped bail, gone to ground, and now wanted to return to England.

Mike turned to the crime world's favourite travel agent, Larry Hawkins, for assistance. The only place for that kind of help was in Streatham. Charlie did his act – Larry could not know that the camp old rogue was petitioning the speaking clock to do his bidding, and told Mike it was safe to return. In the meantime, Charlie told his friend at the Fraud Squad that he had lured Mike back to Blighty and Mike was arrested as he got off the plane at Heathrow Airport. He received seven years, and my grandfather's friends started to wonder.

Charlie was doubly blessed because, as an informer, his rewards consisted of 'dead men's wages'. The term keeps creeping up on him. But this was not the old National Insurance scam that he had worked with Johnny Miller. These wages consisted of the money policemen reserve for their snouts. Charlie had moved from being an outsider who exploits a system to being an insider who is in its pay.

His last performances would take place in the witness-box on behalf of men like Larry Hawkins. His latest accomplices were bent solicitors. But Charlie was disregarding the first rule of crime. When he turned up at court,

'He looked like an old tramp,' said Larry. He had tried to look like a mug once before. Now, at fifty-eight, he was a doddery old man. Since Lily still liked to dress up, and was a well-established performer, criminals often turned to her, for a price, to act as their character witness. My grandparents had a nice little family business going, and it kept them at the forefront of London's underworld.

·

The man whom I know only as 'Roberts' made two introductions to Charlie that year. One was to 'Tricky Dicky' Sullivan, 'King of the smugglers', money-getter, frightener, et cetera, of London. The other was to Leonard Ash, conman, 'supergrass' and panel-beater, of Lincolnshire. In theory, with his steely blue eyes that refused to twinkle and the build to back them up, Tricky Dicky was the one to be wary of. In practice it was Leonard Ash.

He was thirty-seven, a slight, fair-haired man with a retroussé nose and an ingratiating manner. He came into Charlie's life at just the right time. Since Victor was still in ward 13B of Tooting Bec Hospital, Charlie roused himself in order to sell the hotel. It was an act of petulance. 'If my son doesn't care, why should I?' he asked himself. The dream of a family business had shattered with Victor's unceasing experimentation with drugs. It was apparent that James was going the same way. Charlie could not understand. How could his sons not be straight after all he had said and done for them? He should have heeded the lyrics of the records they played so loudly. Perhaps they played them for his benefit. Jim Morrison, John Lennon and Old Rubber Lips articulated what his sons were unable to say themselves. It seems that only I took note of their special way of pleading.

As for Charlie, he was stuck with confusion, dismay and disappointment. Edward, at least, was pursuing the old

Taylor trade of navvying. He worked day and night with a
zeal that had not been seen since the days of George James.
That way, he didn't have to spend much time with his family.
But Charlie's eldest son was boringly straight, and out of the
mess of emotions Charlie felt, boredom trumped them all.
He bestirred himself. His astonishingly quick recovery from
what should have been his deathbed exposed him as emotion-
ally bankrupt. Charlie was in the market for new business
interests.

'I liked Ash straight away,' he told his last friend, an
investigative journalist, in 1978. 'I thought he was an honest
man and before long I'd have trusted him with my life. I
misjudged the man, I see that now.'

When Leonard Ash came to visit at Kensington he showed
great interest in the photographs on the mantelpiece.
Especially the ones that showed Charlie socializing with well-
known members of the police force. Charlie was only too
happy to tell him everything. At last he had found a young
man who wanted to listen and learn from the master. Or, as
Charlie put it: 'He was an inquisitive sort of bloke.'

The last two years of my grandfather's life resemble his
early childhood inasmuch as they are documented in the law
reports of various newspapers. But whereas his formative
years were covered by the *Willesden Chronicle* and *Wembley
News*, his dotage was featured in *The Times*. The main
ingredients of their reports consist of gold krugerrands,
counterfeit sovereigns and dodgy dollars. What resounds
most tellingly is the flavour of betrayal. Charlie was
informing on someone who was informing on him. And that
was not all. A third person was informing on them both.

·

Number 1 Inverness Gardens was turning into a madhouse.
For me, it was an asylum from the tense relations between

my own parents. Far better to seek the clues of their mutual loathing in a more spacious and sumptuous setting. There was room to hide in this house, and lots to observe. If my parents' home was a miserable swamp, my grandparents' was one of its tributaries.

When the adults were discussing private matters – things usually to do with drugs or crime – my grandmother would sit me down in front of the telly in the shabby parlour. It was here while I was nuzzling a family-sized packet of crisps that Major Stoop made an appearance.

The newscaster told us that it was to Stoop that Lord Lucan wrote his third letter after the murder of his children's nanny. And it was Stoop's Ford Corsair that he had borrowed before the murder. Stoop didn't ask Lucan why he wanted the Corsair, rather than his Mercedes. He assumed it was in order to drive around town without being recognized by his wife. That's what he said, anyway. The detectives investigating the murder of Sandra Rivett were of a different opinion. They suspected that Lucan wanted it because it had a boot big enough to contain a woman's body. But Stoopie stuck by his old friend and, under the aegis of the Clermont set, led by John Aspinall and James Goldsmith, declared his old playmate to be dead.

A gentleman's word is his pledge, and Charlie was dead impressed.

∎

Timmy the poodle licked the salt from my fingers, and Dolly and I took him for walks. We ambled down Kensington Church Street, past St Mary Abbots and into the recherché hippie wilderness of Kensington Market. The scent of incense was overwhelming. Hell's Angels crowded into the tattooist's stall and I stole my share of long, flowing beads and the latest in tank tops and bogart trousers.

Charlie was hardly ever *en famille*. He could not contain our several bids for self-destruction. I was a particular thorn in his side because I liked to remind him of his lack of moral authority. I was determined to vocalize what no one else dared to acknowledge: that he was incapable of setting the boundaries of good and bad behaviour. Although the language I chose was more precociously upfront: 'How dare you speak to me like that?' I challenged him, my eyes blazing with indignation that this fat old man should have the cheek to order silence.

He was bemused by my arrogance, and incapable of checking it. I only kept my peace once he handed over some money. I would take it and run to the bookshop at Notting Hill. Shivers of pleasure ran through me as I filled my satchel with Enid Blytons and a set of Caran D'Ache coloured pencils. I never drew anything with them – I just liked to look at the colours at my disposal. I stole because I wanted my blood money as well as the goods. If the worst should happen I figured I could talk my way out of apprehension. If I considered that eventuality at all. And if I didn't, it is because I considered myself to be invisible. I was apart from the rest of the world – its governing forces had no control over me. So I walked past the till with an air of guiltless insouciance. This series of little thrills was addictive. I wanted to be like Charlie. I wanted something for nothing.

On the whole, Charlie liked children. He encouraged us to stay one step ahead of the average punter. He would regularly give my cousin ten pounds to go into the front room and kick my father. Once Charlie heard the shout of pain, he would appear in the doorway and silently challenge Pino to retaliate. He knew that if my father had his way he would smack the unruly child. But with Charlie fixing him with his blacked-out gaze, my father pretended to laugh. He even ruffled the boy's hair with an unconvincing show of affection.

My cousin, Edward's boy, was Charlie's favourite child. He admired his grandson's hysterical precocity, and let him sit in on meetings with his gangster associates. Donald would straddle Charlie's knee uncomprehending but pretending to be wise to what he was hearing. Whereas I was, as a rule, studiously polite, Donald was voluble and arrogant. He wanted to talk politics and history like Charlie; to be respected by his elders. Although he was my age, his unformed opinions on the day's issues were mutely accepted. It was best not to argue with him. The screams and flailing limbs of his tantrums were awful to behold. When they occurred at school and his teacher slapped him, Teddy the hitman was sent to warn her against ever touching or reprimanding him again.

More often than not, I provoked the tantrums. Like my mother and grandmother before me, I knew how to provoke men to violence. I taunted him, and worked on his weak points. If he struck out, I knew he would get into trouble. And I wanted trouble. I wanted to disrupt the surface calm. Besides, I was jealous of my grandparents' favouritism. Lily always gave the largest portions to her menfolk, and like an Arabian harem, my mother and I were served last and least. Poor Dolly did not even make it to the table. I was amazed at my mother's mute resentment. She could wear a man down in several of the Romance languages at Number 73 Cameford Court. Faced with her family, she buttoned up her resistance. I have never seen lips so tightly clamped together.

At this point my mother started weaning me off visits to Kensington. I thought it was because she did not like the insistent, hoarse imprecations of Rod Stewart. And Eric Clapton was still whining about lost love. But neither of these sounds could disguise the constant quarrelling. Charlie had lost his power. Lily was in the ascendant. She could smell when a man was down on his luck. Her senses were so finely tuned that she had picked up on Charlie's loss of form. Once his powers of persuasion and infinite charm had withered to nothing but a plaintive and gullible, prematurely aged, foolish old man, she lost interest.

He was too uptight to notice. Even my Uncle James was distracted, and would not play with me. I followed him up to his bedroom but he shut the door in my face. He did not want me to see him shooting up.

·

Some time after my twelfth birthday my mother told me that Charlie was involved in a massive fraud involving the Bank of England. She told me because she did not want me hearing about it from someone else. Be prepared.

I have since read in the back issues of old newspapers that in February 1976, 'a detective called Bland' told Charlie that a fraud was being perpetrated in Lincolnshire. He mentioned several names. A few days later a detective chief inspector from the Yard asked Charlie to 'watch' Leonard Ash. He then told my grandfather to go to the fraud squad offices in Holborn, sign in under the name of Trainer, and collect £500. Charlie was beginning to resemble a counter on the Monopoly Board as he circled the city limits. He passed Go several times on his way to Gaol but somehow he always managed to pay his way out. He sent other men to gaol, and several others were released on his word. But if he thought he was in control of his destiny, he was deluding himself.

The last years of my grandfather's life are as muddied and indistinct as his first. It seems that in watching Leonard Ash, Charlie became enmeshed in a fraud of gigantic pro- portions. In Westminster Reference Library I read that in the spring of 1976 information reached the Treasury that 'certain persons were planning to carry out a substantial fraud by using the dollar premium system', and that a member of the staff at the Bank of England was involved. Never mind Lincolnshire, this was truly global.

Charlie told his friend Detective Chief Inspector Bland that the 'matter' concerning the Bank of England was 'a fiddle'. The dollar premium scam was the latest in international fraud. Under the new Exchange Control Act, a rebate was paid by the Bank of England on cash brought back to this country after the sale of foreign investments. It was very simple, really. Charlie's latest gang was busy borrowing vast sums of money from foreign banks. They then presented the money as proceeds from the sale of securities on which they could claim the dollar premium.

Meanwhile Leonard heard that the police were interested in his fraudulent company in Lincoln. He asked Charlie to use his contacts to find out more. Charlie told him that he had discovered from his friends at the Yard that the company was under suspicion as a long-firm.

But Leonard had made another friend since arriving in London from the sticks. Her name was Mariella Novotny.

•

It was Lord Denning who called Mariella's December 1961 orgy the Man in the Mask Party. She preferred to call it the Feast of the Peacocks. It had taken place in Hyde Park Square, where Lily and Charlie had been billeted two years previously by Paddington Council. But Mariella's mansion apartment was a much grander affair than their attic room. Mandy Rice-Davies and Christine Keeler arrived fashionably late in the evening. They were greeted at the door by their mentor, the society osteopath Stephen Ward. He was dressed in a sock.

Everyone else was naked. Apart from Mariella, who was in bed with six men. She was wearing a black corset and was wielding a whip. Alongside her, Mandy spotted some well-known actors, a Conservative Member of Parliament, and a barrister. Stephen Ward told her that the man in the black mask with slits for eyes and laces up the back was the Minister for Transport, Ernest Marples. He was strapped between two pillars, and, as well as his mask, was wearing a lace apron such as my grandmother had worn when serving tea at the Cumberland Hotel. As each guest arrived they were invited to flay his naked body. Mariella joked that she was the Government Chief Whip.

Denning was coy when it came to naming names. So the general public and conspiracy theorists were free to speculate as to the man's identity. Some said it was not Ernest Marples but Anthony Asquith, the son of the Liberal Prime Minister. Others that it was Harold Macmillan or even the Duke of Edinburgh. Charlie was convinced it was the Duke – he had seen him at the chemmy table in Windsor, and thought he recognized a man after his own heart.

Whatever Denning's report achieved, it could not alter the impression that his peers – Members of Parliament and high society – were leading private lives that made a mockery of their public roles as upholders of decency and the common good. Their decadence was irresistible.

'I cooked a pair of young peacocks for the main dish,' Mariella revealed in her diaries. Like Teddy Machin's disappearing little black book, they were written with an eye for posterity. She went on to describe her peacocks: 'I skewered their necks and heads in position, and added the colourful tail feathers of older birds. When they were carried to the table, a girl became hysterical and screamed that they signified death. She created havoc and had to be sent home, before she ruined the party . . . Badgers were another unusual animal I cooked.'

Mariella was sharp. For her, women's liberation meant that men got sex for free. This was bad news, since, according to her, if you weren't Germaine Greer or Barbara Castle, all women had going for them was their sex. And she was sexy.

She had made her London début in 1958 as a topless dancer in Soho. It had been her mother's idea. Two years later she married Horace 'Hod' Dibben, a sado-masochist and friend of Stephen Ward. David Bailey took the wedding photos.

Hod dealt in antiques and official secrets. He ran nightclubs in Shepherd Market and Mayfair where he played host to Anthony Armstrong-Jones, the Duke of Kent, Lord Astor and the Kray twins. He held dinner parties, with his lovely wife as the table ornament, for Earl Spencer. Hod was fifty-six. Mariella was eighteen, and already a veteran.

She could tap directly into men's sexual peccadilloes. She egged them on, encouraged their flights of bizarre fancy. She was like Charlie. In manipulating men's weaknesses she gained control because sometimes men were shocked at just how far they could go.

Mariella met Harry Towers, a middle-aged show-biz whizz kid, at one of Stephen Ward's sex parties. He was on the look-out for likely girls. He said he would get her a modelling contract in New York. What he meant was that he would set her to work as a prostitute. In May 1961 Mariella escaped from a hotel in New York where she had been restricted by a probation order as a minor on vice charges. She arrived back in England on the *Queen Mary*, and sold her story straight away to the *News of the World*. It was a good one. She told the senior crime reporter that she was the niece of the former Czech president, Antonin Novotny. And that, as a child, she had spent four years in a

Soviet Stateless Persons Camp. She even had the heavy accent to back it up.

Another fact that Denning did not lay bare in his report was the international impact of the Profumo scandal. It was not Christine or Mandy or even Stephen Ward who excited the interest of the FBI. It was Mariella. Whilst in New York she had taken part in a game of group sex with President-Elect John F. Kennedy. On that occasion she had worn a nurse's uniform. So had her Chinese colleague, the notorious top-class call-girl Suzy Chang. The women were hospital staff, and JFK was their prone but able patient.

So it is not surprising that no less a person than the President himself should express concern over the findings in Denning's report. It was bad enough that one of the nurses was Chinese, but the other was a runaway Commie from Czechoslovakia. Robert MacNamara, the US Defence Secretary, told a senior FBI agent that he 'felt like he was sitting on a bomb' as headline after headline in British newspapers opened the lid on the Profumo affair. Even Robert Kennedy, it emerged, was caught up in this sex and spy ring. Lord Denning decided not to name 'the Czech madam' as one of his principal witnesses.

Mariella Novotny was, in fact, Stella Marie Capes, the daughter of a shorthand typist. She was born in Sheffield in 1942 and could have been the result of her mother's brief affair with a Czech pilot. Her MI5 codename was 'Henry', and she swore that she was part of an FBI smear campaign that had President-Elect Kennedy in its sights. Her escape had been arranged by secret agents in return for her address book.

Little Leonard Ash, fresh from Lincolnshire, was dazzled by the glamour and distinction of his new girlfriend. By this time she was calling herself Henrietta Chapman. She led him to believe she was twenty-one years old (she was actually thirty-four but heavily masked in pancake make-up, prune eyeshadow and spidery eyelashes). She told Leonard that she was unmarried and had been an undergraduate at Girton College, Cambridge. She passed off her seventy-three-year-old husband as her father and her eleven-year-old daughter as her sister.

■

The Seventies had not been kind to Mariella. She could no longer trade on her jailbait youth, and heroine addiction had ravaged her shiny, plump face. In 1971 she put her extensive experience of the demi-monde to literary use. The result, *King's Road*, was plugged as '*the* novel of Britain's Permissive Society'. It told of the turned-on and elegant Tricesta St Regis and her involvement with incest, the Black Power Movement, vaginal piercings and kinky MPs. It bombed.

Her gift for fabrication was wasted on the British public, so she told Leonard that her family was influential in the Foreign Office, the Treasury and the MOD. Furthermore, that her uncle had at one time controlled the military and naval intelligence of this country. She also maintained that she worked actively for MI5. More to the point, she was sympathetic to the troubles Leonard was having with Charlie.

He told her that he did not know what to do or where to turn because whenever he complained Charlie applied more and more pressure. Pressure to do a little something for him here, to go and see someone there, to get that little bit more involved in whatever Charlie was doing. He told her that my grandfather was totally unscrupulous.

They arranged to meet for drinks at Brown's Hotel in Mayfair. It was all very plush and Establishment, and man-eating Mariella was wearing her leopardskin catsuit. She divulged that she knew all about Leonard's 'problem at

Lincoln'. How? he asked. Darling, she drawled, it's like this. And she told him that Charlie was giving the police detailed information about his activities. She said that her family had been interested in Charlie for a long time, and that she would appreciate any information he could provide. Understandably, Ash was sceptical until, in his words, 'She produced statements purporting to be from Taylor to the police, the contents of which assured me that what she was saying was authentic.'

Mariella was impressive, and Leonard was hooked. They decided that she should go to her 'people', explain the situation, make inquiries and have it all checked out. She was sorry but she could not be more specific. She was in fact mysterious to the last: 'When I say my people I mean my people. The people who I work for.'

If her brief in 1961 was, as she claimed, to 'get' President Kennedy, by 1976 she had come down in the world. Her target was my grandfather, who was being stalked in an investigation that would expose corrupt policemen. It was called Operation Countryman.

·

The summer of 1976 was viciously hot. Victor had moved back into the family home, where he was shooting up cocaine and experiencing yet more waves of paranoia. He saw policemen in the most bizarre places. He would be in his car on Notting Hill Gate having just picked up from the chemist. After shooting up he would see them in bullet-proof vests and balaclavas creeping along the side of the pavement, hiding behind cars, bearing down on him, ready to shoot. He was terrified, and when the cocaine wore off he had another fix and the action recommenced.

He was in love with a girl called Emma who wore straw hats and flowered dresses. Emma had previously been James's girlfriend, but the two brothers did not mind sharing girls and drugs. As well as introducing her to Victor, James had turned Emma on to drugs. Dolly told me she had cleaned up the vomit in the bathroom. Heroin always makes you vomit the first time, she explained.

Emma was as pretty as a box of chocolates but so was Victor. I was fascinated by the mirror image they presented. They liked being watched as they danced to Rod Stewart on the record player. 'Killing of Georgie' was their favourite track. 'How could his son not be straight,' sang Rod, 'after all he had said and done for him?' It was as though Rod, who had been a Mod when Victor was prince of Streatham, was asking the questions his father had tired of.

■

Leonard told Mariella that Charlie had set him up as the mastermind of the Lincoln long-firm. When all along, and this was the killer, it had been Charlie himself. Leonard was even more angry when he was charged with the fraud while Charlie was left at large in the community. True, Charlie stood Leonard bail for £30,000, but this only made him more resentful. Charlie could withdraw bail at any time and put Leonard back in prison.

Generous as ever, Charlie moved his scheming friend into a room in Inverness Gardens. He was still dangling the £30,000 bail in front of him. Leonard was useful – if he kept pinning things on him, who knows what he himself could get away with? But he was strangely unmindful of the fact that photographs and documents had started to disappear from the house. He was growing careless.

Mariella convinced Leonard she had intelligence connections. But the connections which came into play were not the ones he had bargained for. His information was going to PC Pulley of the Special Branch. Perhaps Mariella was reluctant to admit the true identity of 'her people' because a PC was too lowly a contact for the girl who had pleasured JFK. But she needn't have been ashamed of her descent down the espionage ladder. Mr Pulley was also a famous man, at least amongst the prisoners in his care. Allegedly they had a saying about him: 'The proof of the Pulley is in the beating.' But all that was behind him now that he had Mariella whispering sweet nothings in his ear. The Special Branch was delighted with her convoluted story.

Charlie's double bluffs had placed him in a precarious position in the underworld. He would never admit it, but the intrigue with which he surrounded himself had dwindled to this: he was a pawn in the frantic politicking of the two main departments of the greatest police force in the world.

Tempers had reached such a pitch that London's uniformed plods and the detectives from CID were not talking to each other. Their mutual dislike was intense. Charlie's problem was that his friends were detectives who flounced around town in cheap suits and expensive cars. They were blatantly taking backhanders. Attempts by the Home Office to root out corruption had so far been unsuccessful. What was worse for Charlie was that the officers to whom Mariella was talking were from the uniformed branch.

John Bland and Reg Davies were by now numbers two and three in the Flying Squad, and still in cahoots with Charlie. They warned him that they were under investigation. Someone was selling their story.

He was furious. James was at home when Charlie came back from a meeting. He said he had heard something about Mr Ash that did not please him very much. James knew that he looked upon Lennie as 'a second son'. For Charlie's purposes his three useless boys had been rolled into one. When the prodigal eventually did turn up Charlie locked all the doors and said, 'I want to talk to you.'

James listened at the door as Charlie fumbled to get to the truth behind the rumours he had heard.

'Do you know a lady by the name of Marietta?'

'No.'

'How about Marella?'

'No.'

'Henrietta?'

'No.'

Two hours later, the doors were unlocked and Leonard and Charlie were the best of friends. My grandfather had done the unthinkable and turned soft. He was finally being taken for a mug. Just like Johnny Miller, he was unwilling to believe his second son could betray him. So he fell for an even bigger sucker punch.

Leonard managed to persuade Charlie to become involved in selling gold half-sovereigns ostensibly as pendants or on rings. Some days later James watched as a gold-sovereign printing machine with a 410-volt supply was carried up the stairs of Number 1. He was puzzled that his father would not allow him to touch it. He should not have been. Charlie did not want his family near that machine because of the danger of their leaving fingerprints on it. James was even more puzzled when his newly invigorated father went on holiday to South Africa. He did not know that when Charlie came back he had a client ready to buy counterfeit krugerrands.

That month Billy Hill and Gypsy visited Frankie Fraser in prison, where Cyril Green had put him. Mad Frank asked after Charlie.

Billy Hill said, 'He's getting a bit warm.'

•

Charlie was enjoying himself. He was at the centre of things again. His new friends needed him, and he could afford to play games. But, like all men of a criminal disposition, he was fatally short-sighted.

So much hard work and mental effort is put in before the crime that there is hardly any thought as to disposal or care afterwards. For Charlie, the excitement of the plotting was an end in itself. It was an interminable crescendo that was addictive because it obliterated the descent to the banalities of everyday life. He could not bear reality. Neither could I.

·

When, years later, I could no longer spend my summer holidays rejoicing in the luxury of Kensington, I would spend every day in front of the television. I rose at noon in time for the love boat, and shaded my eyes from the sun baking the grass on the lawn outside our block. The galloping gourmet and panting horses all passed me by as I sprawled on the living-room sofa. It was absorption by osmosis, and it lasted for months on end. It did not matter what form the stimulants that seeped through my pores took, as long as they did not cease. At thirteen, I lost interest in my appearance. Like my grandfather I did not bother with bathing, or washing and brushing my hair. He felt it was hardly worth the effort. I wanted to obliterate distinguishing features.

I was no longer my mother's good little girl. The English teacher at Streatham Hill and Clapham High School had told her I was amoral, and would end up like a train robber, but in prison. My mother told me that at this point in the parents' evening she had fainted.

·

At least Charlie had thought sufficiently far ahead to line up a fence for his snide krugerrands. That is one point in his favour. He was busy, too. There were so many solicitors and villains to arrange deals with. Quite often, they were almost indistinguishable. On 5 July his friend in the gold braid uniform, Larry Hawkins appeared in court. He had been arrested for his part in a Heathrow Airport robbery involving a quarter of a million pounds' worth of krugerrands. Charlie had tried to help. He had got in touch with John Bland who said he would contact the officer in charge of the case and that help would cost £5,000. Larry handed over the money. But it seemed that Charlie's influence had waned. He managed to get Larry's sentence reduced to two years but that was small fry compared to the old days. You do not dally with a criminal's liberty and remain unscathed. But Charlie did not know that yet. He thought he was still playing with dice. John Bland, Reg Davies and the rest of the top brass at the Flying Squad did not realize it, but they were under covert investigation. Larry, Tricky Dicky and Leonard were most bemused.

That Leonard was informing on Charlie is certain. That Charlie was informing on Leonard is equally certain. That Charlie was informing on Larry and Tricky Dicky is highly probable. No one person is responsible for the ensuing confusion. Though Charlie is the fulcrum, they all corrupted and diseased each other. That Charlie got what was coming to him was inevitable.

19 · Gangbuster

'Ash took the photographs,' Charlie told his friendly reporter, who was the last friend he ever had. 'I don't know if there was some form of deal but it was the only way anyone could have got hold of them. Ash knew all about me and the moment he was collared for the Lincoln fraud he decided to get himself off the hook by telling the police everything he knew.'

Charlie was not to see these mementoes of the good times again until they emerged as photographic evidence in the 1,800-page Pain Report into police corruption. The team behind it was so thorough they even managed to track down Lady Colwyn. His Lordship had died in 1966 on his beloved island of Ischia, at which point Charlie's faith in the aristocracy had been briefly rekindled. Colwyn's solicitors had tracked him down to repay the old loan from his days as my lord and lady's builder on Connaught Square.

By the time investigators had caught up with Lady Colwyn she had married again – to Sir George Taylor, director of Kew Gardens. But this was not the time for nostalgic reunions. The former Lady Colwyn was not best pleased to be reminded of her odd-job man, especially one who entertained the idea that he was a major *mafioso*.

He was being minded by corrupt police officers, therefore he was untouchable. But he had not factored in Leonard, his faithful underling. Still on bail, he had nothing to lose by telling the police everything he knew about Charlie, his junkie sons, and his police friends.

As a result of Ash's allegations, Gilbert Kelland, head of CID, arranged for Commander Bert Wickstead to lead an investigation. Wickstead's findings led to Barry Pain, Chief Constable of Kent, being called upon to head a top-level inquiry into the involvement of Charles Taylor with senior detectives. The fact that an outside chief constable was heading the rout was a measure of the seriousness with which Scotland Yard took the complaints. And of the seniority of the officers implicated. My grandfather's status as a leading member of the criminal fraternity was confirmed, as it were, in writing. But what must have been more gratifying to the son of a Stonebridge slattern was that finally he was the centre of attention. The fact that it took more than stealing his mother's milk to get there is almost irrelevant.

■

Bert Wickstead was one of Scotland Yard's finest detectives. He had broken the spell of the Tibbses and the Dixons over the East End, and had investigated the affairs of prostitute Norma Levy which led to the public humiliation of the Conservative minister Lord Lambton. One of his cases has since proved somewhat controversial, however. This was the investigation of the so-called Torso Murders in 1977. It ended with the jailing of two men who claimed Wickstead, or 'Gangbuster' as he liked to be known, had fabricated the evidence against them. For twenty-three years they have complained of a miscarriage of justice. But Wickstead was only interested in making arrests. He ensured that Leonard was wired up. He had his eye on the top job at the Flying Squad. And, as every ambitious young officer knew, he had to network with all kinds of people to get to the top.

.

There was an air of gathering crisis about Number 1 that made it very difficult to be there. The old house was tired. It was time to lift the lid on its inhabitants. As Victor was injecting large amounts of amphetamine sulphate in the front bedroom, he was convinced he could see policemen standing on the corner by the post-box. They were watching the house and taking notes.

It was not so much Rod Stewart, as Charlie's new friends, that deterred my mother from visiting her family. She did not like their probing questions or solicitous concern for Lily's asthma and the boys' drug intake. She could not understand why smarmy, sweaty Leonard wore a raincoat on relentlessly sunny days. Even once inside the house, he kept his coat on. Of course, we all know why now: underneath the gaberdine, he was hiding a tape recorder. On the morning of 17 November 1976, Tricky Dicky dropped by to discuss that day's business with Charlie. At 10.30 a.m. Lennie arrived with Jimmy the Jew, a man so reluctant to reveal his true identity that I doubt if he was even Jewish. As for his part in the following proceedings they remain as enigmatic as his moniker. But what is certain is that as Lily was brewing a fresh pot of tea and Charlie was dispensing wisdom from his four-poster, Lennie planted dies for making gold sovereigns in the drawer of his bedside cabinet. What is less certain is that Jimmy the Jew, awaiting his audience with Charlie in an antechamber, hid $7,000 in counterfeit notes under the cushion of his chair. It could have been him, but then it could have been any of my grandparents' visitors that day.

Major Porter, an elderly ex-Para and a mug in the mould of Wing-Co Eaves, was the next gentleman caller. This damp

November morning had stirred the old war wound in his chest. He was aching and frail, but needs must. The night before he had lost a couple of thousand in a poker game with Charlie. He had come to borrow it back.

The house was filling up, so Leonard and Jimmy the Jew said their goodbyes. Surprisingly, they asked Tricky Dicky to join them. In fact, they were rather pointed in their request for his company. But Charlie shooed them away with an imperious wave. 'We've got business to discuss,' he said grandly. Like a pallid, fat slug in flannel pyjamas he slithered back under the blankets. The day was shaping up nicely.

Lennie and Jimmy climbed into their car as an attractive young woman came to the door of Number 1. She said her name was Eileen and asked Lily if she could speak privately with Charlie. Lily told her philandering husband about the mysterious redhead who insisted on waiting on the steps outside. She was standing on the very step I used to sit on when I was little. It was as though I was advertising my presence outside this magical, mysterious house.

Intrigued, and with the flush of early morning still upon him, Charlie roused himself from his crumpled bed and, trailing his dressing-gown cord behind him, went to investigate. Eileen engaged my grandfather in conversation. Then the police raided the house.

WPC Eileen Randall brought up the rear as PC Pulley, Sergeant Evans and Detective Chief Inspector Michael Taylor stormed Number 1 Inverness Gardens. Charlie was escorted into the front room. 'What do you want, boys?' he asked, somewhat bemused by their sense of urgency. But PC Pulley – Mariella's special friend from the Special Branch – went straight to Charlie's bedside table. Of course, he got what he wanted. And, as Sergeant Evans lowered himself onto an armchair, he reached under the cushion and waved $7,000 in counterfeit notes in my grandfather's face.

'Who's in charge here?' Charlie demanded, for the last time asserting his authority. The policemen exchanged glances, momentarily confused, until PC Pulley, the lowest-ranking male, said he was. Which seemed strange to Charlie, but then he wasn't to know that Pulley was the man who had been primed by undercover agent Henry aka Mariella Novotny aka Henrietta Chapman aka Stella Marie Capes.

Anyway, there was no time to dwell on the incongruity of the situation because Major Porter chose that moment to have a heart attack. The old man lay writhing on the floor but PC Pulley raised a sceptical eyebrow. He and his colleagues refused to believe that the sick man wasn't in fact a kingpin of the criminal underworld. They had seen his play-acting type before. Despite the major's cries of distress they carted him off to a police station in Essex along with Charlie and Tricky Dicky.

There was a big crowd of policemen waiting to cheer my notorious grandfather's arrival in the car park outside the police station. I don't think he took a bow.

In the course of his arrest, Charlie was told that Larry Hawkins had also been arrested that morning. And that a team of fraud squad officers had been on surveillance duty outside Number 1 for the preceding six months, which news brought some comfort at least to Uncle Victor, who was able finally to refute that particular charge of paranoia.

Charlie was arrested in a police raid which, said the *Evening News*, smashed 'a forgery plot which could have threatened the world's gold market by flooding it with fake half sovereigns'. After the information Leonard had given on police corruption the raid was inevitable. Any immunity or influence Charlie had once had dried up immediately. Police found dies which they alleged were to be used for manufacturing sovereigns. They also found forged dollar bills which became the main exhibit in further charges. The attractive young woman had been a plant because they knew the sight of her would distract my grandfather as they rallied to bring him down. During the raid the photo of Charlie with Jock Wilson disappeared.

On his first night in Loughton police station Leonard brought Lily to visit Charlie. She saw Leonard in conversation with Bert Wickstead. She told Charlie, who made much of this fact. As have others. If, as some say, he did plant Leonard on Charlie it was because he wanted Jock Wilson's job. The only way he could get rid of the Commander-in-Chief of the Flying Squad was by exposing Charlie. But Bert had other reasons, too. He had a genuine hatred of power-crazy policemen's snouts and hated Charlie for corrupting the upper echelons of the Flying Squad.

∎

In the cells of Loughton Police Station, Essex. My grandfather is banged up all day, and brought out at night for questioning. Commander Bert Wickstead of the Serious Crimes Squad orders him to his feet.

'You know who I am? I'm Wickstead, the Old Grey Fox [his other *nom de plume*]. You'll never come out of here again, do you know that? Your cover's blown and your police friends, too.'

Charlie smiles.

'Knock that fucking grin off your face.'

Bert rattles off the names of three policemen.

'You know them, don't you? Of course you do. We know what's been happening. Just think it over and I'll see you later.' He turns to another officer.

'Shut the door on the cunt.'

Charlie was frightened of Wickstead, who had already written a book about his exploits. It was called *Gangbuster*. He said about Bert: 'He interviewed me three or four times about the sovereigns, but he was never really concerned with the case. All he was interested in was the police I'd known, especially Reg Davies, who was second in command at the Flying Squad.'

Charlie felt let down and betrayed. He had had enough. He thought he would be saved by his friends. They could get him off anything. But the doctor who had made sandwiches in Streatham came to visit. He said, 'I told you all along, Charles, they'd never help you when you needed it.'

Charlie denied his guilt in the sovereign charges and implicated Leonard as the informant in what he claimed was a fit-up. Just as, all those years ago, he had sought to turn the table on the Springers, turf accountants of Wembley, his efforts came to naught. He was denied bail and taken to Bedford Prison. He was there for six weeks before being transferred to Lincoln Prison. Here he stood trial for perverting the course of justice in Boston, Lincolnshire. Leonard was vindicated. Charlie was cornered, and there was not even room for his delusions.

He had entangled himself so inextricably in his own deceptions that he could not find his way out. What was worse for the great escape artist was that the prosecution case against him was deeply flawed. Based, as it was, on the word of a disreputable and dastardly Leonard Ash, there must be some hole through which he could wriggle out. But what was the point? Its basic tenet, and Charlie must have known this, was irrefutable. He'd been found out, and the powers-that-be knew he was up to no good.

·

By 1977 life was vain and empty for Charlie. Not because of the harshness of childhood poverty or the lack of maternal care, but because he had not given himself, nor anyone else for that matter, the chance to experience it in the round. His caricatures, his sleights of hand, and sly disguises – what had come of them? That reminds him, there was once an old man. Who is he? He can't get him off his mind. He knows he did something to him. He knows it was bad, and it involves letting lying dogs die. One day in court Charlie collapsed. James was sitting next to him watching in disbelief as his father popped pill after pill as though they were Barker & Dobson's boiled sweets. Oh yes, Johnny Miller. Perhaps he should have tried to help him. Perhaps he shouldn't have given him all those pills. But now he knew what it was to want to die.

·

On 20 November 1976 Charlie, Larry and Tricky Dicky appeared at Epping Magistrates' Court accused of conspiracy to forge gold coins and currency. But that was nothing.

One month later six men appeared at Bow Street Magistrates' Court charged with 'conspiracy to defraud specified banks of cash by falsely pretending that foreign currency which they intended to sell was the proceeds of the sale of foreign securities which attracted a premium'. Amongst these men was Alfred Taylor. My grandfather had always been Charlie to me, to his children and to everyone who knew him. Even those who had known him as Alfred went along with the change in name and all that it entailed. If they didn't they fell by the wayside. But he was no longer Charles, not even Charlie, and George and Katie had neglected to bestow a middle name to cushion their youngest son's fall.

Leonard Ash stood in the dock with him. As did the Taylors' family solicitor, Brian Wooding, who had proved very useful over the years as a conman's fool. Charlie had worked on his flexibility over legal niceties and ensured him that the venture was as safe as houses. How could it not be? Their man at the Bank of England was John Wales, who worked in the Exchange Control Department. He would never even have to meet with his co-conspirators, because eager-beaver Lennie Ash was the go-between. That boy was into everything.

Treasury investigators had kept watch on the men as they gathered in the bar of the Waldorf Hotel. Over cocktails and cigars, they engaged in lengthy conspiratorial meetings. Wales, the plotter's safety net, had been present. He was most impressed with their debonair approach to international commerce. Charlie had kept his distance from the plotters, but kept himself abreast so as to inform his police friends.

A file recovered from John Wales's office at the bank contained a letter giving blank authorization for the claiming of the premium. It was signed by him on behalf of the Bank of England and confirmed that his friends qualified for the premium. It was a licence to print money, prosecution said.

Charlie's bail was set at £30,000. No one came forward to offer the surety. Lily was distraught. The house in Kensington had to be sold. There was no one to turn to and nowhere to go. She tried Number 4 Moscow Road, where Charlie's old friend Billy Hill was still living. She turned on the tears to no avail. He pleaded poverty but, in truth, he wanted nothing to do with her. A Nigerian carpenter who had worked at the Leigham Court and whom Charlie had helped buy a house came to visit. He was distressed to hear the calamitous news. He offered to help. Edward stumped up the rest.

Charlie told the judge: 'I have no friends, my lord, except for a black man.'

20 ▪ Waterloo Sunset

It is said that certain areas of London defy redemption. Mortlake is one of them. The last two years of Charlie's life were passed in a squat, two-bedroom cottage in a dead-end street which had long been associated with plague pits. Each morning he steeled himself for his journey into town after a night spent contemplating imminent imprisonment. From East Sheen, he took the train to Waterloo. If he was lucky, Tricky Dicky, one of his co-defendants, would meet him there to give him a lift to court. Charlie had a lot on his mind. First, he had to clear up the bank fraud, then there was the little matter of Lincoln, and last but not least, the mysterious machinations of the printing press. My mother and I tiptoed across the railway sidings to reach my grandparents' new house.

Lily sat slumped in a chair, an inhaler hanging from her mouth. She had sold her jewels to her sister Irene. Dolly had stepped in to buy one of her rings. She kept it in the zipped compartment of her shopping trolley. It was an unlucky opal as delicately nuanced and unstable as a London sky. She gave it to me in a fit of sadness. 'It was your grandmother's.' When I noticed that it rattled around in its gold surround, and that some gems were clearly missing, she had to improvise another little white lie. 'The diamonds fell out when Lily knocked her hand against the hospital bed frame. They disappeared on the floor of the ward.'

It wasn't one of her best fabrications: it lacked the poignancy of poetic justice, the neatness of retribution, which she liked to bring to her elaborate stories. But she did not want to tell me the grubby truth. Charlie had prised the diamonds from their setting and taken them to his pawnbroker's on Edgware Road, along with Lily's silk frocks and furs. Somehow, the opal was spared, and I was left with a stone so opaque as to reflect my family's history.

But not even Dolly could hide from me the fact that Nana's oval, diamanté-studded spectacles had been replaced with NHS plastic. Or that her lank grey hair was not receiving its weekly primp and rinse at her favourite Kensington salon. She had nothing to give me but an old tea-cosy. I went home, bemused and disappointed. Poor Lily, such were her feelings of inadequacy, such was her inability to express love, she had to give me something I could hold on to. Unfortunately, her generous impulses helped instil in me a furious greed for goodies. I could never have enough pretty things.

I did not like going to Mortlake. Everyone was miserable. There was no music playing – just silence interrupted by Lily's whimpers. She's gone doolally, whispered Dolly, who should know. The walls were stained with various attempts at decoration. Whilst on remand, Charlie painted them a different colour every day just to distract himself. His enforced presence introduced a surprising new aspect of his personality to the family. He discovered feelings of tenderness for his wife. She was stricken with asthma, so he would not let anyone – not even his new friend the investigative journalist – smoke in her presence. I was not there to witness the new Charlie, but I can imagine that just as Lily should desist in her blind passion, Charlie's devotion should, just as suddenly, awaken.

All I could see were the rococo chairs from his hotel and

a faded, filthy carpet. Uncle James was not my fun-loving, wicked uncle any more but a seedy and feverish stranger.

▪

That Christmas Eve, Lily, the skivvy who thought she was Ginger Rogers, had a stroke. The clots that had massed in her shapely legs travelled upstream to her brain. It was touch and go, Charlie said, as my mother and I joined him at her bedside. Although she lay in a coma, her fingers were working the hospital blanket. They would not lie still in their desperation to hold on to something.

'Have you forgiven me?' Charlie asked my mother on the steps of Charing Cross Hospital. She almost felt sorry for him. He looked terrible. Before leaving the great house at Kensington he had fallen down the slippery steps and lost the caps on his front teeth.

'Of course,' she said. But she hadn't.

Charlie was her ogre. He had looked for nothing in life except his own well-being. Delusions of grandeur, the sense of his own apartness, both moral and legal, had destroyed him. If that was not bad enough, he had brought down others with him. My mother would never forgive him for offloading his disgust at himself on to her. Thus immovable in her loathing of him, he had banished her from hope and happiness.

My grandfather thought he could purge himself without retribution. Alfred the monkey thought that changing his name, and protecting himself from exposure, would do the trick. Charlie the spiv thought he could hide behind the dazzling effect of his virility and mental vigour. Charles the husband and hotelier was a bully who never grew up; criticizing and judging others in order to detract from his own sense of worthlessness. But we loved him. We couldn't help it. The reason he tried to bring us all down to his level was because he could not bear to be there by himself. He almost succeeded. But, ultimately, nothing worked out as he had planned.

On the few occasions that I caught my step-grandfather looking at me, I was puzzled by the look in his eyes. I know now that when he looked at me he saw himself. The lack of pity overwhelmed him. It stopped him keeping his eye on the main chance. Greta, too, was a constant source of reproach. He saw the cold glitter of contempt in her eyes. She thought she was helpless. What she did not realize was that Charlie was frightened of her.

With Lily immobile and uncaring, his police friends gone, his sons on another planet, he was isolated in a funk of doubt and apprehension. Still he persevered in the art of making a quick buck. He had to, all his money had gone on lawyers' fees.

•

One day in 1977 Victor found himself handing out leaflets on the concourse of Waterloo Station. There he was teetering above the rushing commuters in his *démodé* red platform boots with two-inch soles and five-inch heels. The passers-by were so busy, it made him feel dizzy. Like 'Waterloo Sunset'. It's funny how life echoes our favourite songs.

Victor did not know if he was hallucinating or if this crazy jive was for real. He looked down at the leaflets in his hand. They advertised a solar-heating company based in Mortlake. The scam had been Jimmy the Jew's idea and he passed it on to my grandfather. Maybe it was out of pity or some sense of guilt. Probably not, since Charlie had to part with serious cash for it. It was Charlie's last long-firm. The plan was to take deposits from punters, install the latest development in heating technology – which, in this instance, was solar panels – and disappear. Victor turned to his father and laughed. How the mighty had toppled.

When the firm was featured on *That's Life*, Esther Rantzen softened the blow to Charlie's pride by saying: 'At least they installed the panels.'

■

Charlie picked the very expensive and top-of-the-range Victor Durand QC to defend him at the Old Bailey. He paid for Mr Durand's services by selling the lease of Number 1 Inverness Gardens (which he no longer owned – if, indeed he ever had) for £20,000 to a Nigerian chief of police. He instructed his smart new barrister to deny the various charges against him. He had nothing to lose and was ready to proclaim to the world that he had been acting as a police informer.

'My client was running with the hares and hunting with the hounds,' pronounced Durand. 'He hoped to get a large reward from the Treasury for the tip-off.'

It did not work. The defendants were charged with conspiring to obtain money from unsuspecting dealers in investment currency by pretending they had currency for sale which would attract the dollar premium. When prosecuting counsel David Tudor Price said that the amount the conspirators planned to pass through the system was as much as £20 million, they were done for.

■

This was the Seventies, when a million pounds really was a million pounds, and out of reach to almost everyone. If it did come within reach, I remember my father complaining, the taxman grabbed hold of it first. He did not like England, he had decided. He did not like our shabby flat in an anonymous Thirties block in Streatham. He did not like the fact that Dolly and Timmy the poodle had taken up residence in our living-room along with other remnants of the Kensington house. He did not like the weather. Or my mother. And he certainly did not like it when in December 1977 I was arrested in Boots the Chemist on Streatham High Road for shoplifting.

The store detective, a slim woman with a shaggy blonde perm, but otherwise nondescript, placed her hand on my shoulder. She wheeled me round and marched me back to the manager's office. I walked through the shop, head held high, and watched the girls behind the counter watching me. My captor emptied my bag on the manager's desk, to reveal a strawberry-flavoured lip gloss and some blank cassettes from W. H. Smith, which was next door. I had intended making a tape of my favourite Beatles songs. 'A Hard Day's Night' was going to segue into 'Let It Be' because I didn't have time for the music in between.

I had a fabulous record collection. I selected one a week from the Freeman's ('where Lulu buys her clothes') catalogue, and Dolly paid for them on a weekly basis. Though we could not see why she should have to – life was bad enough as it was. We must be able to get something out of it.

'It's not fair / My brown hair,' was Dolly's favourite refrain. She stole, too. But she stole tinned goods from Safeway, which was on the other side of Boots from W. H. Smith. She left parcels of food on the doorsteps of people's houses. When the police arrested her, she protested, 'But they're poor.' It was not long before another member of my family was admitted to Tooting Bec Hospital.

We went to visit her and I resented my mother for lying unconvincingly through her good cheer. I knew she was waiting for me to crack, but I wasn't going to make her day. Dolly was propped up on a narrow bed, bereft of lipstick. All around her toothless old women were wailing. Her eyes were telling me that she was scared. She smelt strange, too. A clean, sharp smell that made me keep my distance. Was it the smell of madness, I asked myself?

When the store detective found that I had a twenty-pound note on my person, she asked me why I needed to steal. I could not come up with a good reason.

I was taken to Streatham police station, where my grandfather had once had the sergeant in his pocket. He had even sent him to White City Stadium to place bets for him on the dogs. But the sergeant had been sacked for receiving a wedding present from a certain Charles Taylor.

On being charged, I was taken to a cell where my shoelaces and the ribbons in my hair were removed. A statuesque WPC walked past the door. She had once been the girlfriend of my uncle James. I had seen her towering over him at parties. I knew her name and I knew that she had also slept with my grandfather. She shook her head dolefully at the youngest member of this recidivist family, and said, 'You do realize I can't help you?'

·

My father split this tawdry scene and went to work in a new casino in Africa. It was *la terra incognita* for him – wide open, somewhere he could start all over again and get his thrills. And he wanted them now. He needed them to blot out the fact that he had married a resolutely unhappy woman, given rise to a kleptomaniac daughter and become involved with their out-of-control family.

We accompanied him to the airport. The Dodge had been sold so we used public transport. It felt strange to see my haughty father surrounded by punk rockers and blue-rinsed pensioners on a bus. But I refused to show any sign of emotion concerning his impending departure. All I could admit, even to myself, was a profound sense of relief that at least one load had been lifted from my twelve-year-old shoulders. I let my eyes glide over the chiaroscuro planes of his face, and assumed the smiling position. I felt a trickle of heat run down my thigh. A spot of blood had seeped through the denim of my skirt.

■

That night, and six years later, on the night of Dolly's death, I read till morning. During periods of intense activity within the family, television did not suffice. I needed answers. So did my mother. We surrounded ourselves with the texts of radical separatist feminists. We joked that we would send Charlie a copy of Valerie Solanos's *S.C.U.M. (Society for Cutting Up Men) Manifesto*. There was one passage my mother pointed out as peculiarly apt. 'Men will wade through miles of vomit if there is pussy at the other side.' Greta, Dolly and I had a lovely time, thank you very much, with no demanding, unreasonable men in our lives. Twice a week my mother treated us to hand-made truffles which we sucked and sighed over while watching our favourite programmes. We joked and roared at Stanley Baxter. We made an exhaustive study of men's vile habits, drug addiction and mental illness. I was becoming an expert.

My father had to go because Greta and Charlie were strength in opposition, and no man could come between them. He saw to that. When she married the up-and-coming croupier who stayed out all night playing poker and chasing women, Charlie knew she had married a version of himself. He could see it in Pino's fastidious attention to detail; in the self-satisfied glow he emitted when dressed in his silken finery. He saw it in his innate disrespect of the system. It was as though Greta were reliving the nightmare of her childhood over and over again. But always in secret, and the secrecy was so efficient she never escaped the pattern it attempted to conceal.

.

The realization of a lifetime of lies comes rushing over me. The silence was manifest because there was so much that could not be said. Each child loves the thing that comes to kill them. To admit it would be the undoing of everything in which my mother believes, but her relationship with Charlie had history on its side. It was built on his covetousness of her, and her resistance to his presence. They each knew what the other wanted.

Her dismay and disappointment in me were dreadful. Though I did not know it, her stepfather was appearing at the Old Bailey and now her daughter had been arrested as a common thief. But she accepted it with the same weary resignation that had greeted my first show of menstrual blood. I was not her innocent child any more. I was the same as the rest.

On 12 May 1978 Alfred Taylor (the indignity of being stripped down to Alfred was terrible; some newspapers even called him 'Albert') claimed that he had been on holiday with a former Deputy Assistant Commissioner of Scotland Yard. While being questioned by his expensive barrister he told the jury how he had taken the Yard officer and his wife to Ireland in his own Rolls-Royce, which was driven by his own chauffeur.

'Is that the measure that this Court can take of your friendship and association with the man called Reg Davies?'

'Yes.'

The defendant also told of his dealings with Detective Chief Superintendent Etheridge at the Fraud Squad. Charlie aka Alfred elaborated: 'Etheridge said to me, "Is Ash a rich man?" and I said, "Yes, Ash is a very rich man." He then said something to the effect that he might be able to help Ash "if he comes across".'

Durand gave Charlie his cue: 'That is, in one word, bribery, is it not? That is what was in the offing?'

My grandfather, who could not, even now, display his trump card without prevarication, replied: 'It could be.'

Charlie went on to talk about the parties at Leigham Court. What fun they had been, and no expense spared – such a generous man, if a little naïve. He said that Deputy Assistant Commissioner Reg Davies and a famous viscount had attended the weekly gatherings. He tried to make proceedings lively for the jury – a few spicy details here and there and they'd be eating out of the palm of his hand. When asked how his relationship with the police had developed, he reeled off a sob story: 'I had to because of my sons. They have serious problems with drugs, and I needed the police to help them fifty if not a hundred times.'

He thought he would have the jury in tears, but he was kidding himself.

•

Mariella came back into the picture on 6 May 1978, when Leonard claimed he knew nothing about the dollar premium fraud. He said that he had been framed by the police because of information he passed on to Mariella, who worked for an intelligence department under the code name Henry. The court erupted. This was more like it – *cherchez la femme*! So he went on to say that he had been giving her information on a daily basis about police officers and their association with criminals.

'That has led to several Scotland Yard officers being suspended,' he declared. Lennie further alleged that an assistant commissioner had been transferred from Scotland Yard as a result of his information. All this was true but unsuitable fodder for public consumption. In the Seventies, no man 'fessed up to police corruption.

So Charlie should have known better. But on his sixty-second birthday, he reckoned he had one last card up his sleeve. He could not keep his police friends disciplined and he was no longer Charles, nor even Charlie, just plain old Alfred, but he managed to get Mariella's flat turned over. It was time to sing. He gave that nice man, the investigative journalist from *Time Out*, a plastic bag containing her diaries. He admitted in court to being defrauded by Reg of the Flying Squad and a man named Roberts of £30,000 of 'hard-earned money'. But with that telling phrase he overplayed his innocence for the last time. He had tried passing himself off as the victim of other men's wickedness before. He had tried pleading not guilty. But he did not look like a mug, and the judge refused to believe him.

■

Each night, when he got back from court, Charlie made James take a solemn oath.

'I want you to promise me two things. Carry on the betting scam when I die, and knock the undertakers. You must do it. Do you promise me?' Over and over again, James swore he would carry out his father's last instructions.

When he wasn't climbing the walls, he was on the telephone to his journalist. 'I want to talk to you before I die,' he told him. In daily instalments, he confessed his life story. He told of Stonebridge and Lincoln, a printing press and the hotel racket, lords, ladies, the Army & Navy and a dollar fraud.

Then his talk ran out. He was breathless, and there was only one thing on his mind: 'When I die when I die when I die . . .' Sometimes he fell asleep whilst talking on the telephone, and all the journalist could hear was shallow breathing. Malign, unwelcome, the contents of what crept into his recollections reclaimed him. That he was moving into madness was the only explanation he could offer himself. Death had to be better than this, though when he reached the breach he was terrified to be so out of his depth. Unlike the revolutionary Arthur Thistlewood, he would never be privy to the last grand secret.

All Charlie had to say for himself was, 'I'm on my way to the happy hunting ground in the sky.' For the record, he left us fond and foolish clichés inspired by nostalgia for a rank-Irish squaw born during Custer's last stand. I suppose it must have comforted him to think of all that empty space in which to manoeuvre.

So the last time Victor saw his father – on the morning of 24 May 1978 – he knew Charlie was going to die. He could see it in his eyes. They had in them a look of reproach. It was the same wordless reproof with which he met my defiant gaze.

Where I had looked for strength and security I found someone confused and helpless. Which makes me the winner of our confrontation – because his eyes betrayed the self-pity of the weak and the discontented, of one who has never struggled against himself. They said, it's not fair, it's not my fault, I can't help you, I can't help myself. He was just as his strapping great nephews had once said he was – a strutting, blustering coward.

His death was farcical. As he left the Mortlake house, he stumbled against some milk bottles that had been put there that morning. The last words Charlie spoke to his family were, 'Don't pay that bill.' After a doom-laden day in court, it was clear that prison was inevitable. Worse, his accomplices had found out that he had grassed on them. 'What must your wife think of me, luvvie?' he asked Tricky Dicky, who had given him a lift to Waterloo Station. That he was as bad as the rest of them I should think. My poor old grandfather died on the concourse where a year previously he had still been in the game of putting one over.

Larry Hawkins says, 'His death was a good thing for every copper. It wasn't suicide because Charlie was revelling in the notoriety of the court case. He would have enjoyed being centre stage in the biggest corruption trial in history. Nine of the highest-ranking cops in the country were in his pocket.'

'No,' he continues. 'He was given a pill at Waterloo Station.'

Perhaps Tricky Dicky gave it to him. Perhaps an old police friend suggested he fall on his sword. Whatever the case, if there is some nefarious conspiracy behind my grandfather's death let it stay in the gloom of London's underworld, where it belongs. Although he would have liked the talk around his death to be endlessly involved and mystifying, even providing another alternative – suicide – of which he was certainly capable, I refuse to take the bait. If my grandmother didn't care about the cause of death why should I? After a lifetime of thraldom to her husband, she simply said: 'At last I'll have the bed to myself.'

The truth behind Charlie's death is this: he was taking massive amounts of barbiturates. He had a heart condition. He was a heavy smoker. He drank tea with the cream of the milk and three sugars. His death was a release for us all.

·

The Gold Sovereign case was tried after Charlie's death. He and his co-defendants had always maintained they knew nothing about the evidence Bert Wickstead had so carefully assembled. Charlie, Tricky Dicky and Larry strongly denied his version of conversations they were alleged to have had whilst in police custody. Conversations that implicated them in the forgery.

During his closing speech Larry's defence barrister played on the idea of Aladdin's cave. This was a term my grandfather had used to describe the property room at Loughton police station after he had been taken there to look at the exhibits.

'You've heard of Aladdin's cave?' the lawyer asked the jury. 'Well, two floors up we had Commander Wickstead, the Old Grey Fox himself in the guise of Ebenezer. You remember Ebenezer? New lamps for old? Only this time it was new words for old, new words where old words never existed.' But Charlie missed his moment of vindication.

In his summing up Judge Grant explained the position to the jury.

'You've seen these officers coming into court; one of them is a clean-cut young man with a great future in the police force. Would these men jeopardize their careers by telling lies?'

The jury seemed to think they would. The defendants were acquitted on all major charges. Charlie got away with it *in absentia*.

Bert never did become head of the Flying Squad, but he did become head of security during the print disputes at Wapping. From being commander-in-chief of the Flying Squad, Jock Wilson was demoted to lowly Traffic. Reg Davies took early retirement. John Bland resigned in a hurry. Leonard Ash received a two-year prison sentence to be added to the five years he had already received for the Lincoln fraud. After eighteen months of painstaking inquiry the Pain Report, which has never been made public, resulted in several more police officers leaving the force. The others are dead. Those that live prefer to forget. Certainly, no one remembers Mariella Novotny, who died of an overdose of sleeping-pills in 1983. She was found face down in a bowl of jelly. Billy Hill died the same year, 'the richest man in the graveyard', according to Jack Spot. His death certificate recorded his life's occupation with one singularly appropriate word: 'Demolition'.

•

Given Charlie's abominable record with women – at least the ones in my family – it seems fitting to me that Mariella Novotny was the instrument of his downfall. At last, and on his own terms, a woman well and truly got one over him.

As for Lily, her fear of asylums became reality, and she was committed to a mental hospital. On her release my mother took her in. The last time I saw her I asked who had been her favourite child. A jaunty knitted hat bobbed up and down as she nodded in remembrance. It was Victor, she sighed, because he would run into her arms and tell his mother he loved her over and over again. Why couldn't she love my mother like that, I wanted to ask her.

Victor the blue-eyed boy sought refuge one last time at Tooting Bec. Ten years later he found his way out. James took care of Charlie's funeral arrangements. Lily and her boys were surprised at the number of plain-clothes policemen in attendance. They watched them over the salmon-paste sandwiches Dolly had made: there were more detective inspectors than genuine mourners. The undertakers' bill came to £1,060. James did not forget his father's last words to him. He left Mortlake without leaving a forwarding address. The undertakers never caught up with him. My wicked uncle did not, however, fulfil the second half of his promise to his father. He didn't go to the dogs.

•

My grandfather was featured on television twice. The second time was after his death. My mother turned over just as it got interesting. But this is what I heard.

His name was Charles, or Charlie, Taylor. He was sixty-two years old. He was on trial with others for plotting a £1 million fraud to swindle the Bank of England. But Charles Taylor never lived to hear the verdict in that case. That afternoon a friend and business associate drove him from the court to Waterloo Station. He was going to catch the train to Mortlake, where he lived. After eighteen months of police investigation Taylor was a sick and exhausted man. Before he could board the train that night he collapsed in agony on the station concourse. He had suffered a severe heart attack.

On the whole you could say he was a generous person, a family man. Most people who knew him would say he was very generous. People would go to him for money. He would lend them money. Anything his family wanted, they would get. A family man, he had a mistress, of course.

But I knew that already. What I have discovered was how seductive it was to be balanced so close to the edge; that the conventions of organized crime intensify the conventions and tensions of family life. You stick together, quite simply, because you have to. The violence, which is rare but horrific, the ruined lives that are rubble to be trampled underfoot, undermine every member of that family's ambition to exist outside it. It is a closed world – this thing of ours. And it is ruled by the hypnotic charm of a man on the make. His ruthless intelligence transformed everything. You see, for us, everything was somehow more so.

■

I am lucky. I came in at the end, and the worst and the best were over. I was too late to be the object of my grandfather's obsession. Too late to be his Miss World or his partner in crime.

All that is left for me to do is to rob the secrets of his grave. Except he has not got one. How typical of my elusive grandfather. However much I tramp the streets of London I will not find him. His last commission to Brother Will was that he should scatter his ashes at Gate Six of White City Stadium. But Stutterin' Bill did not carry out his dead brother's wishes. He was too far gone by then. We all were. You see, Charlie, ultimately, no one cared enough. We were tired of your depravity.

Acknowledgements

I owe a huge debt of thanks to James Morton for introducing me to London's underworld. His kindness and generosity in suggesting books and leads were indispensable to my researches. His own books, *Bent Coppers* (Warner Books, 1996) and *Gangland* (Warner Books, 1992) are essential reading for the student of true crime. Thank you, James. Thanks also to Steve Haywood, Terry Adams and Richard Sullivan for filling me in, and to Fergus Linnane for showing me his manuscript on the history of crime in London, to be published by Robson Books.

I have listed the books that I found useful below, citing the editions in which they were available to me. The books that are out of print can be found at the London Library, or failing that, the British Library.

The Heart of the Empire, C. F. G. Masterman et al, T. Fisher Unwin, 1901.

The Victoria History of the County of Middlesex, OUP, 1885.

Round About a Penny a Week, Maud Pember Reeves, Virago, 1999.

The Railway Navvies, Terry Coleman, Pimlico, 2000.

Harry Neal Ltd, M. Gaskell, Granta, 1989.

The Spiv's Progress, John Wilby, Allen & Unwin, 1937.

The Long Weekend, Robert Graves and Alan Hodge, Abacus, 1995.

Boss of Britain's Underworld, Billy Hill, Naldrett Press, 1955.

London at War, Philip Ziegler, Arrow, 1995.

The Avenue Goes to War, R. F. Delderfield, Hodder & Stoughton, 1958.

Crime in Wartime, Edward Smithies, Allen & Unwin, 1982.

A History of the Royal Sussex Regiment, G. D. Martineau, Moore & Tillyer Ltd, 1962.

The Willesden Survey, Corporation of Willesden, 1949.

'The Spivs' by David Hughes from *The Age of Austerity: 1945–51*, ed. Michael Sissons and Philip French, Hodder & Stoughton, 1963.

The Underworld, Duncan Campbell, BBC Books, 1994.

Alms for Oblivion, volume one, Simon Raven, Vintage, 2000.

Crime in London, Gilbert Kelland, Grafton, 1987.

Mad Frank and Friends, Frankie Fraser with James Morton, Warner Books, 1998.

The Profession of Violence: The Rise and Fall of the Kray Twins, John Pearson, HarperCollins, 1995.

London Psychogeography: Rachman Riots and Rillington Place, Tom Vague, Speed History, 1998.

Absolute Beginners, Colin MacInnes, MacGibbon & Kee, 1959.

Groupie, Jenny Fabian and Johnny Byrne, Omnibus Press, 1997.

The Truth at Last – My Story, Christine Keeler with Douglas Thompson, Sidgwick & Jackson, 2001.

Stoned, Andrew Loog Oldham, Secker & Warburg, 2000.

The Neophiliacs, Christopher Booker, Collins, 1969.

The Property Boom, Oliver Marriott, Hamish Hamilton, 1967.

Honeytrap, Anthony Summers and Stephen Dorril, Weidenfeld & Nicolson, 1987.

The Phantom Capitalists, Michael Levi, Heinemann, 1981.

A Bit of a Flutter, Mark Clapson, Manchester University Press, 1992.

The Complete Illustrated Guide to Gambling, Alan Wykes, Doubleday, 1964.

Inside the Underworld, Peta Fordham, Allen & Unwin, 1972.

London: The Biography, Peter Ackroyd, Chatto & Windus, 2000.
The London Encyclopaedia, edited by Ben Weinreb and
   Christopher Hibbert, Macmillan, 1995.

Thanks are also due to the British Film Institute which keeps
copies of:

Waterloo Road, 1945.
Dancing with Crime, 1947.
Good-time Girl, 1943.
The Blue Lamp, 1949.

And the British Library Newspaper Library which keeps copies of:

Time Out
Wembley News
Willesden Chronicle
The Times
Daily Express

I have reproduced the following lyrics:

'Music Maestro Please' words by Herb Magidson.
'The Rolling English Road' by G. K. Chesterton.
'The Navvy's Chorus' from *Songs of a Navvy* by Patrick MacGill,
   published by himself, printed by the *Derry Journal*, 1912.

I would like to thank my family for allowing me to tell their stories,
David Godwin for his unstinting encouragement and support,
Louise Harrison for being a sympathetic and wise Streatham girl,
and my steadfast and true David Milner. I couldn't have done it
without him. Finally, I must thank Duke, Nellie and Picador.

PERMISSIONS